121/6

PRIESTHOOD

PRIESTHOOD

A RE-EXAMINATION OF
THE ROMAN CATHOLIC THEOLOGY OF
THE PRESBYTERATE

*

PATRICK J. DUNN

ALBA · HOUSE alba house NEW · YORK

SOCIETY OF ST. PAUL, 2187 VICTORY BLVD., STATEN ISLAND, NEW YORK 10314

Library of Congress Cataloging-in-Publication Data

Dunn, Patrick J.
    Priesthood : a re-examination of the Roman Catholic theology
of the presbyterate / Patrick J. Dunn.
        p.   cm.
    Includes bibliographical references.
    ISBN 0-8189-0581-6
    1. Priesthood. 2. Catholic Church — Clergy. 3. Catholic Church
  — Doctrines I. Title.
    BX1912.D87   1990   90-37005
    262'.142 — dc20   CIP

Nihil Obstat:
Francis J. McAree, S.T.D.
Censor Librorum

Imprimatur:
Patrick Sheridan
Vicar General
Archdiocese of New York
May 9, 1990

The Nihil Obstat and Imprimatur are official
declarations that a book or pamphlet is free of
doctrinal or moral error. No implication is contained
therein that those who have granted the Nihil Obstat
and Imprimatur agree with the contents,
opinions or statements expressed.

Designed, printed and bound in the United States of
America by the Fathers and Brothers of the
Society of St. Paul, 2187 Victory Boulevard,
Staten Island, New York 10314, as part of their
communications apostolate.

Printing Information:

Current Printing - first digit   2 3 4 5 6 7 8 9 10 11 12

Year of Current Printing - first year shown
        1991   1992   1993   1994   1995   1996   1997

Contents

PRIESTHOOD

CHAPTER I

Introduction

1. The Plight of the Priesthood

The Roman Catholic Church currently finds itself in an increasingly perplexing situation with regard to ministry.

On the one hand, the Church is suffering from what is commonly called a "vocations crisis," and is facing a considerable diminution in the number of clergy available for parish and other work. The causes of this rather precipitous decline are complex. But on the other hand there has been a most encouraging growth of lay involvement in ministry, and much has been written in recent years to develop a sound theology for these expressions of the "common priesthood" of all the baptized.

These two developments are undoubtedly linked. With more varied opportunities now available for involvement in pastoral work, and with many tasks which were previously reserved to the clergy now seen as being more appropriately the responsibility of the laity, it is only natural that some blurring of the traditionally very precise distinction between clergy and laity should result. Although the Second Vatican Council emphasizes that the common priesthood and the ministerial priesthood "differ from one another in essence and not only in degree" (LG. 10),[1] the nature of this distinction has not always been clearly perceived.

4 PRIESTHOOD

English theologian Michael Evans writes that, as a result of this blurring, the 1984 U.K. National Assembly of Priests claimed that many priests were now working in "a theological vacuum" concerning their role in the Church.[2] Moreover much contemporary writing on ministry, usually in an attempt to encourage the growth of lay ministries, has often tended as a result to overlook the position of the ordained ministers.

2. The Intention of this Book

This book took shape during 1988-1989 in the course of a period of post-graduate studies at the Melbourne College of Divinity.

For some years prior to this I had been the Vocations Director in my own diocese of Auckland, New Zealand. During 1986-1987 I had also been the director of a "Pre-Seminary" House for our diocese, which had been set up as a preliminary stage for young men who felt called to the priesthood.

As a result of this work I had become acutely aware of the questions that are being addressed to the priesthood, especially those concerning the distinction between clergy and laity within the Church. It is in the light of these questions that I have tried to re-examine the identity of the ordained presbyter.

Because my concern has been to be practical rather than speculative I am presuming that there will be no change with regard to celibacy or the ordination of women.[3] My starting-point is the concrete situation in the average diocese — where there is a diminishing and aging group of presbyters, with a mere trickle of possible candidates to take their place.

The opening chapters try to give an over-all glimpse of the present situation. I examine the statistics which so dramatically remind us of the critical shortage of priests which seems to be confronting certain sections of the Church. I then glance at some of the explanations which have been attempted to account for this development, along with a cross-section of contemporary authors who are all in one way or another challenging the traditional position of the priest.

Then, having tried to isolate the questions, I begin the task of re-examining the scriptural foundations and the factors which, especially in the early formative centuries, have contributed to the shape of the presbyterate as we now know it. Special attention is paid to the sixteenth century because questions concerning ministry were so much a part of the Reformation controversies.

In the light of this historical over-view, and then of the indispensable teachings of the Second Vatican Council, I finally attempt to readdress some of the issues which are presently attracting so much attention — in the hope of clarifying in some small way the identity and the role of the presbyter in contemporary Roman Catholic theology.

3. *"What Do You Stand For?"*

As my writing progressed it seemed to evolve, almost accidentally, into a prolonged critique of many features of Dutch Dominican Edward Schillebeeckx's theology of ministry. One of Schillebeeckx's premises is that there are no such things as "hard facts" in social history — "there are only interpreted facts."[4] By this he means that one's own particular bias inevitably "colors" one's interpretation of source material. Schillebeeckx then tells us that the particular bias in his own study of ministry stems from his concern to make "a plea for humanity in the church."[5]

Schillebeeckx asks of us: "What interest do you seek to serve with a particular socio-historical investigation? . . . What do you stand for?"[6]

My own intention has been to try to ensure that, in the midst of so much stimulating reflection on the theology of ministry, the essential significance of the ordained priesthood is not further obscured. In modern literature even Graham Greene's famous "whisky priest" bears witness to something of the "wonder" and the "mystery" of this ministerial priesthood — as it has consistently been appreciated through history, and as it continues to be reaffirmed in all official Catholic teaching.

"He began the Consecration of the Host... Impatience abruptly died away: everything in time became routine but this — *'Who the day before he suffered took Bread into his holy and venerable hands...'* Whoever moved outside on the forest path, there was no movement here — *'Hoc est enim Corpus Meum.'* He could hear the sigh of breaths released: God was here in the body for the first time in six years. When he raised the Host he could imagine the faces lifted like famished dogs..."[7]

"A little group of Indians passed the gate, gnarled tiny creatures of the Stone Age.... 'The Indians have heard you are here,' Miss Lehr said. 'They've walked fifty miles — I shouldn't be surprised.' They stopped at the gate and watched him; when he looked at them they went down on their knees and crossed themselves — the strange elaborate mosaic touching the nose and ears and chin..."[8]

" 'But it doesn't matter so much my being a coward — and all the rest. I can put God into a man's mouth just the same — and I can give him God's pardon. It wouldn't make any difference to that if every priest in the Church was like me.' "[9]

CHAPTER II

The Priesthood In Crisis

1. The Statistics: A Crisis of Numbers

The ordained ministry in the Catholic Church, and to some extent in other Christian churches, is in a state of crisis. Pope John Paul II has called the situation "the fundamental problem of the Church," and sees it as "part of the spiritual crisis which exists in the whole of modern civilization."[1] The U.S. Bishops held a special assembly in 1986 to consider the question.[2] The "crisis" presents itself most obviously in the dramatic fall-off in numbers of the who are offering themselves as candidates for ordination.

The Dutch Catholic Church is the one in which the trends are most marked.[3] The pattern there has been one of a dramatic reduction in numbers of those being ordained, reaching its lowest point (15 ordinands) in 1978; this was paired with a burst of resignations which peaked with 244 priests in 1969, and 243 in 1970. Since then both figures seem to have stabilized, but while the level of resignations has diminished to what it was previously, the number of ordinations remains at only a fraction of the earlier pattern.

Throughout Europe in 1975 the number of ordinations to

8

the diocesan priesthood surpassed the numbers of deaths and resignations only in two countries: Poland (175.5%) and Yugoslavia (160.2%). The replacement level (i.e. ratio of ordinations to the diocesan priesthood over deaths and resignations) in Holland by contrast was only 7.7%. The percentages for other European countries were: France (17.9%), Hungary (32.1%), West Germany (34.0%), Italy (50.2%), Great Britain (73.4%), and Ireland (45.3%).[4]

Religious orders report a similar drastic reduction in numbers of candidates. French Dominican Jacques Pohier reports that when he entered the Order in 1950 there were in his province about 100 men aged 20-30 who were involved in the seven-year study program; when the program was finally closed down in 1975, there were only 15 students: an 85% decrease in a quarter of a century.[5]

Yet the French Dominicans had had remarkable successes in their active lives. They were in the forefront of the worker-priest experiment; they contributed notably to the progress of biblical scholarship and helped produce the Jerusalem Bible. In all areas of Church renewal, and then in the Second Vatican Council, the Dominicans were prominent. But now, fifteen years on, Pohier sees his congregation as merely surviving, in a state of advanced coma: some organs still functioning, but the organism itself now close to death.

In the dioceses of Australia and New Zealand the numbers of ordinations have reduced to a trickle and fairly accurately reflect the European trend. In 1988 in Auckland, New Zealand, it was almost twenty years since a European New Zealander (a "Pakeha") had left secondary school and gone on to be ordained a diocesan priest. Any Pakeha ordinations in recent years had all involved older men who had left secondary school more than twenty years previously.[6] In February 1981, 64 (67%) of Auckland's 96 diocesan priests had been ordained for over twenty years. Seven years on, in February 1988, 63 (79%) of Auckland's 80 priests were in that category.[7] In Melbourne, Australia, the average age of priests in 1977 was 45; in 1988 it was 54.[8]

The situation in the United States of America is similar. In the thirty years 1955-1985, the U.S. Catholic population increased by 19 million. In 1955 there were 48,000 priests; in 1975 there were 58,000 priests; and in 1985 there were about 56,000 priests. The ratio of priests to Catholics had diminished from 1:700 (1955), to 1:800 (1975) and 1:900 (1985). While these figures do not seem to be too bleak, the number of seminarians has plummeted from 48,992 in 1965 to 10,800 in 1985. The median age for priests in the U.S.A. in 1981 was 56 years.[9]

By contrast, the Episcopalian Church in the U.S. had 13,000 priests in 1978 compared with 11,000 in 1970.[10] Terence Card in the U.K., however, argues that the crisis in numbers is just as real in the Church of England and in the Free Churches. The 1976 General Synod endorsed a proposal from the bishops for an annual target of 400 to 500 recommendations for full-time ministry. In fact ordinations themselves remained virtually static between 1977 and 1982, varying only from 301 to 313.

Furthermore, since 1963 the U.K. population had increased by approximately four million, while the number of full-time clergy has declined from 15,488 in 1962 to 10,789 in 1982, and a large proportion of these are near retirement. A minimum number of 11,600 full-time clergy was recognized as necessary in 1986 if traditional parochial structures were to continue to be viable. There is now little possibility that this number can be achieved.[11]

So the "crisis" afflicting priesthood and ministry is most apparently a crisis in numbers. At some stage over the last couple of decades, in countries sometimes thousands of miles distant from one another, large numbers of full-time clergy began abandoning their careers, and the source of their replacements seemed to dry up just as abruptly.

2. *The Sociological Explanations*

A great variety of "semi-sociological" explanations have been proposed to try to explain this phenomenal decline in vocations to the priesthood.

(i) "Someone's To Blame"?

One simple solution is to search for a scapegoat — be it the priests of the last few decades, or the bishops, or those responsible for religious education. Undoubtedly each of these would admit that mistakes have been made — but French Dominican Jacques Pohier notes that it is difficult to maintain that priests or bishops today are markedly worse than they were earlier this century when seminaries were blessed with an abundance of vocations.[12] And many parents find the religious education their children are now receiving, for all its limitations, still an improvement on the way in which they were taught. It is tempting to blame the selfishness of the youth of today — but every generation tends to fear that the next one is "going to the dogs."

(ii) A General Decline in Church Observance?

English sociologists Robert Towler and A.P.M. Coxon see the decline in clergy numbers in the Church of England as a consequence of a general decline in church observance. They claim that from the years immediately prior to the First World War until the 1960s the proportion of the population being baptized, confirmed and making their Easter communions remained stable. Then substantial changes began to occur, "for which no immediately obvious reasons suggest themselves."[13] At the turn of the century, 60% of the population was being baptized. This rate was maintained until 1958; it fell below 50% in 1968, and still further in 1970.

(iii) The Anomalous Position of the Clergy?

Towler and Coxon also argue that the clergy occupy an anomalous position in society. We live in an age which evaluates people by what they "do" — and we esteem and reward financially those who possess some technical skill: we are impressed when we meet a brain surgeon or an airline pilot. But through most of human history (and still in many non-European societies) persons tended to be recognized more for who they were rather than for what they did: so a medieval earl or cleric may have done any number of things, but these were very peripheral to the status the individual held in society. Towler argues that the status which traditionally attaches to the priestly office is felt to be slightly incongruous in the contemporary world. Some clergymen try to escape from this uncomfortable marginality (which has also undermined the attraction of motherhood!) by developing teaching, counselling or management skills.[14]

(iv) The Collapse of the Ghetto?

A number of sociologists have also pointed out the tendency of Christian denominations to live within their own boundaries, and to create technical "ghettos." Dutch church historian L.J. Rogier has spoken of the curious situation which had existed in the Netherlands: It was

> "... an almost self-sufficient Catholic community, within
> whose limits one not only votes, subscribes to Catholic
> newspapers and magazines, and educates one's children,
> but also listens to the radio, travels, takes out insurance
> policies, and participates in cultural and sports
> activities."[15]

In Holland one could begin one's education at a church kindergarten, and finish it at the Roman Catholic University of Nijmegen (established in 1923).

U.S. psychologist Eugene Kennedy writes similarly that the Catholic Church in the U.S.A. had tended to be essentially an "Immigrant" Church.[16] The dominant culture was White, Anglo-Saxon, and Protestant. Like all immigrants, Catholics responded by keeping to their own churches, sending their children to Catholic schools, playing for Catholic sports clubs, attending

Catholic socials, and urging their children to marry fellow-Catholics.

In the South Pacific, New Zealand theologian Neil Darragh has argued that most New Zealand Catholic parishes were established as ethnic chaplaincies to Irish immigrants.[17] The Church tended to identify itself with this vulnerable and economically depressed minority whose principal goal was to secure a better standard of living for their children. Darragh claims these parishes maintained this role, ministering to the descendants of Irish migrants, for a century.

But what is very interesting about this "Ghetto" theory is that everyone agrees that it became unworkable by around the 1960s/1970s.

Darragh states that the hegemony of the Irish-Catholic counter-culture fell before the influences of an increasingly multi-cultural society, the impact of Vatican II, and the emergence of New Zealand (and Australian) nationalism during the 1970s. The fate for any church which ceases in some sense to be counter-cultural is that it become "invisible" and somehow "indistinguishable" from the rest of the population.

Commentators on the Dutch situation observe that between 1930 and 1947, when Catholicism was apparently flourishing, an estimated 10,000 Catholics each year quietly left the Church, but that this considerable loss of adherents was hidden by the high Catholic birthrate.[18] But by the 1960s, the Netherlands had become one of the ten richest countries in the world. The Old Age Pension Plan (1957) relieved enormous pressure from people, but also loosened the ties between generations and made the young more independent of tradition. A wave of new ideas was channeled through the highly structured Catholic communications network which had so successfully nourished a more traditional faith in the preceding decades.

The Dutch Catholic community was subjected to a flood of criticism and self-questioning. Private confession was virtually abandoned, Christian marriage practices criticized, and priestly celibacy held to be intolerable. Sunday Mass attendance dropped from 70-75% in 1961, to 19.8% in 1984; 1,732 priests resigned within ten years (1965-1975); and ordinations dwindled from 318 in 1960 to 16 in 1977.[19]

In the U.S.A., Eugene Kennedy sees the election of Catholic President John F. Kennedy in 1960 as an important landmark. Prior to his election American Protestants were being urged to oppose ceding their rightful White House franchise to a Catholic[20] — and American Catholics appropriately rejoiced at his triumph. But with the passing of time Protestant fears proved to be groundless. Eugene Kennedy argues that the "Immigrant" Church has died, and with it have gone many of its staples: Catholic newspapers, Catholic periodicals, Catholic stores, Catholic sodalities — and also that abundance of priestly and religious vocations which depended on the stability of the culture of the Church. The present American bishops may be the finest achievement of the great vocational harvests of the mid-century — but the challenge facing them is that, because the Church from which they came exists no more, there is no rich supply from which to draw their successors.[21]

(v) The Cultural Revolution of the 1960s?

Cultural anthropologist Gerald Arbuckle agrees that "the old Catholic ghetto culture has been topsy-turvied."[22] Vatican II had sought to counter the inward-looking Catholic ghetto mentality which had hampered the missionary thrust of the Church for centuries. But the world to which Catholics had to turn was itself in extraordinary turmoil.

Arbuckle writes that during the 1960s and early 1970s the entire western world underwent a transformation in the assumptions and accepted practices which form the cultural foundations of the daily lives of ordinary people. This transformation was one of the swiftest and most dramatic in recorded history. What was considered shocking to the public in 1967 is so commonplace today as not to be noticed.

Arbuckle argues that by the early 1970s this cultural revolution was drawing to a close. "People can tolerate disorder only for limited periods of time."[23] But the combined effects of the theological changes of Vatican II, and the cultural revolution, left Catholics breathless, confused, and never quite sure what was going to happen next within a Church that for centuries had seemed to be unchanging. The mass of intricate cultural supports that had protected the ghetto Church for over a hundred years were suddenly removed. In the midst of the confusion and disarray the Church seemed, for the first time in centuries, to be sounding an uncertain trumpet.[24]

The "Revolution of Expressive Disorder," as Arbuckle describes it,[25] has left the Catholic Church with many questions to address concerning the nature of the priesthood, and of ministry in general. The statistical evidence which we have already examined indicates that the time for serious reflection is far from over.

3. A Theological Factor: The "Priestly" Laity

While it is certainly interesting to be aware of the sociological factors contributing to the current downturn in candidates for the ordained priesthood, there can be little doubt that theological issues are also involved. Few aspects of the documents from Vatican II received more attention than the emphasis on the dignity and role of lay people in the Church. Going explicitly beyond the early twentieth-century position that lay activity in the Church was essentially one of aiding the bishops in their apostolic task, the Council's key "Dogmatic Constitution on the Church" speaks about the initiative and responsibility that lay men and women should exercise by virtue of their baptism (LG 30-38).[26]

The Council taught that the whole people of God are called by baptism to share in the kingship, the priesthood and the prophetic office of Christ. But while "kingship" was mentioned rather briefly, the notion of "priesthood" was developed extensively. Some of the Fathers, especially the Orientals, feared that the special status of the consecrated priesthood might be lost as a result of this emphasis.[27] However, the scriptural foundations of the common priesthood were felt to be sufficiently solid to permit a stronger development of this notion — which had already been launched in the encyclical *"Mediator Dei"* (1947), and in the "Constitution on the Liturgy" (SC 14).[28]

To avoid any false interpretations, the Council insisted from the very beginning that the common priesthood and the hierarchical priesthood differ from each other "in essence and not only in degree" (LG 10).[29] This "essential" difference was maintained to show that the special priesthood is not simply a gradation or intensification of the common priesthood. Walter Kasper has observed that if this were so, the clergy would have to be acknowledged as being somehow "better" or "more complete" Christians — which is not what is being stated.[30] The common and special priesthood are not different on the level of being Christian: the distinction has to do with calls and missions.

But the Oriental bishops were not alone in their concern about a blurring of the relationship between clergy and laity. Cardinals Suenens, Heenan, Cardijn and others wanted more emphasis placed on the leadership function of the priest. And eighty French bishops complained that

"the true evaluation of the function of the laity had sparked off a chain reaction: a confused idea of vocation, a depreciation of the special priesthood, and a lack of interest concerning this priesthood among the young."[31]

However, most of these issues were still academic in the 1960s. In the aftermath of the Council, clergy and laity alike generally welcomed its teachings that *"the laity have an active part to play* in the life and activity of the Church" (AA 10).[32] The Council had even encouraged the laity to study theology.[33] The response was gradual, but over the years as lay-people have begun to step into the gaps left by the deaths or resignations of religious and clergy, the former clear lines which had existed between "ministers" and "non-ministers" have become blurred.

Thomas O'Meara reports that the German bishops have set up three new ministries. The "pastoral assistant" works in areas of teaching and personal counselling; the "community assistant" helps in parish and liturgical activities; and the "administrative assistant" shoulders the burdens of administration. The German Church has also established a training program for non-ordained "preaching ministers."[34]

The Archdiocese of Baltimore is beginning to experiment with a new role, that of the non-ordained "pastoral leader," who will care for a parish when no priest is available.[35] Similar experiments are being repeated in dioceses around the world — with the lay pastor being responsible to some nearby "priest moderator" (the expression used in Portland, Oregon)[36] who visits the parish at regular intervals to celebrate the Eucharist and other sacraments.

In a 1985 Chicago study of lay pastors, Peter Gilmour delineated three problems which emerge.

The first was the difficulty of separating liturgical leadership from community leadership: people would be prepared for marriages or baptisms by the lay pastor, and then would have to celebrate the sacraments with a priest they may never have previously met. The situations were felt to be spiritually jarring.

The second problem is that canonically the lay pastor is regarded as an "assistant" to the visiting priest — whereas realistically the situation would seem to be the opposite.

The third difficulty was that experienced by some of the "circuit-riding" priests, who at times felt like permanent outsiders.[37]

This developing situation has encouraged contemporary theologians to look more closely at the theology of ministry, and more specifically at the clergy-laity distinction. Much of this writing raises legitimate questions concerning the nature of the Catholic priesthood, but sometimes at the cost of obscuring what have been regarded as crucial elements in Scripture and tradition. O'Meara is correct in noting that we must "interpret the teachings at an ecumenical council through its historical context and theological language"[38] — but we should also be a little wary of too lightly ignoring the Vatican II teaching on the difference "in essence and not only in degree" between clergy and laity.

My proposal, therefore, is to examine a cross-section of contemporary writing on ministry — but focusing specifically on the questions they seem to be raising concerning the identity of the ordained priest. I will then look more closely at the work of Edward Schillebeeckx, before glancing at the bases of presbyteral ministry in Scripture and tradition in order to try to clarify the teachings of Vatican II — all as a necessary prelude to any serious consideration of possible future directions.

CHAPTER III

Contemporary Questions About Ordained Priesthood

1. Joseph Martos: Ministry No Longer Identical With Priesthood

Joseph Martos, in his historical introduction to the sacraments, maintains that it was initially as a result of historical studies that the modern Catholic theology of the priesthood has come under scrutiny. Scholars have reminded us that the Apostles in the New Testament would not have seen themselves as "priests," and that prior to the fourth century it was only bishops who had been called "*sacerdotes.*"[1] The place of clerical celibacy has been questioned anew with the realization that, prior to the twelfth century, many priests and a good number of bishops had in fact been married.[2]

Further questions were raised during the 1960s and 1970s. Biblical research led Catholics to question the hierarchy's competence to make authoritative pronouncements concerning what is written in the Scriptures. Philosophical developments led to the abandonment of the scholastic conception of priesthood being defined in terms of power and authority; instead there was a switch to more personalist notions of community and service. Ecumenical contacts have forced Catholics to see the Protestant Reformation more in terms of an honest revolt against the abuses of the Medieval Church, and to admit that the new forms of ministry which had developed are not totally without merit. The experience of democracy has made lay-Catholics wonder if perhaps they should have a greater say in Church affairs.

Liturgical renewal, with its greater lay participation, has further obscured the traditional understanding of the priest's uniqueness. And changing morality, most publicly and controversially in the area of birth control, has led many Catholics to wonder about the clergy's expertise in areas of moral guidance and has probably contributed towards the dramatic decline in the use of the sacrament of Penance, with all its particular ramifications for the priest's own sense of identity.[3]

The result, observes Martos, is that the position of the priest as "the" authority in religious matters, and as the virtual center of Catholic religious life, is all now in question — despite the assurances of the Vatican II documents. By the mid-1970s, the easy identification of priesthood with ministry had to be abandoned in theory — because it had already been abandoned in practice.[4] At present the only functions exclusively reserved to priests are some liturgical, and most sacramental duties. The present proliferation of ministers within the Church can make priestly ordination seem somewhat anomalous because so many ministers who are not ordained are now also involved in the liturgy. And increasingly today pastoral ministers are being installed in public ceremonies very analogous to ordination. In the midst of all this, the position of the traditional priest is being queried more and more.

2. Leonard Doohan: The "Lay-Centered" Church

Leonard Doohan for example argues that, in view of the teachings of Vatican II, the term "laity" is now theologically dead.[5] It has been used too often through history to denote the "passive" side of the Church — in contrast to the "hierarchy" who played the "active" role. The laity used to be taught that they were a "bridge" between the Church and the World — but as Doohan notes, the laity "are" the Church.[6] Any superficial distinctions between priest/sacred and lay/temporal are now no longer tenable. Vatican II called the laity to active participation in the "sacred" liturgy; and priests, by their vowed lives "in the world" powerfully challenge the misuse of wealth, sex and power.

Doohan observes that the deep-seated attitude equating the laity with the purely secular has often limited lay ministry to areas of finance and management. He argues that those "sacred traditions" which restrict to the hierarchy the rights to teach, preach and govern, must not be preserved at the cost of such values as baptismal equality.[7] Doohan maintains that the total absence of laity from leadership roles is extremely unhealthy. Lay ministers generally have little security of tenure if a priest decides he no longer needs their services. He talks of the present "chasm" between clergy and laity as the fundamental problem in the Church.[8]

Doohan blames the development of monasticism and the emergence of "a clerical group" for the neglect of a fitting baptismal spirituality. The early esteem in which martyrs, ascetics and monks were held introduced a tiered approach to Christian spirituality and a "second-class citizen" attitude towards the general body of the baptized. Similarly the presence of strong bishops like Ignatius of Antioch or Clement of Rome created a sharp distinction between "leaders" and "followers." By the time of Gregory the Great (d. 604) the laity were mere "children of the Church," while the clergy were "shepherds, preachers, teachers, rulers, and prelates."[9] Little wonder, he observes, that baptism alone no longer seemed sufficient for those who wished to follow Christ seriously.

3. Richard McBrien: How Authentic Is Clergy-Laity Distinction?

U.S. theologian Richard McBrien objects to the very notion of a "theology of the laity" — because the expression betrays an allegedly untenable presupposition that the mission of the non-ordained comprises merely a "limited" aspect of the total mission of the Church.[10] The traditional spirituality of "Catholic Action" (1930s+) saw the laity as called to share in the apostolate of the Church's hierarchy — but the underlying assumption was that it was to the hierarchy alone that Jesus entrusted the mission of the Church. McBrien continues:

> "There is no mention in Vatican II that the laity shares in the mission of the Church only to the extent that the hierarchy allows. The mission comes from Christ through the sacraments, and not through the leadership personnel of the Church."[11]

While one can agree that Vatican II never intends the hierarchy to play an obstructive role in the mission of the Church, it is misleading to give the impression that they are to exercise no authority. In fact the Council teaches the exact opposite:

> "The ministerial priest, by the sacred power he enjoys, *moulds and rules* the priestly people" (LG 10).[12]

In his recent booklet on *Ministry*, McBrien argues that right from the beginning there were

> "two diverging patterns of ministry: (a) 'charismatic,' as in the original Jerusalem community and later in Corinth; and (b) 'structured,' based on the synagogue model."[13]

The implication is that both patterns are equally legitimate, but that eventually the more institutional model prevailed — largely because it is claimed that the early Christians copied the patterns of contemporary municipal and political organization.[14] We will examine this "structured — charismatic" polarity in greater detail when considering the ideas of Edward Schillebeeckx. However we should note that there was something "structured" present right from the beginning — as seen in Jesus's own choice of the Twelve and in his empowerment of them for a special mission (Mk 3:14-15).

McBrien writes that "in the early Church there was no hard-and-fast distinction between clergy and laity." He claims that it only began to develop "with the establishment of Christianity as the state religion in the fourth century."[15] He accuses Vatican II of "ambiguity" with its talk of two priesthoods which differ "in essence," and is himself non-committal about the "sacred power" which the ordained are said to possess.[16]

McBrien is obviously trying to encourage the much-needed development of ministries within the Church — but in the process he makes the ordained priesthood appear to be a fourth-century innovation of rather dubious parentage. In doing this he is overlooking the authority so confidently exercised in preceding centuries by the Twelve, by Apostles such as Paul, Timothy and Titus, and by bishops such as Clement of Rome (d. 100) or Ignatius of Antioch (d. 107).

4. Thomas O'Meara: The Clergy-Laity Framework "Cannot Survive"

Thomas O'Meara argues that the distinction between clergy and laity is, in its historico-social form, a product of culture. He traces the initial separation of a Christian "clergy" from "the people" to the influence of surrounding pagan cultic life, and to an a-historical re-appropriation of Old Testament attitudes. Thus Hippolytus' liturgy of ordination and Cyprian's arguments for the purity of the *sacerdotes* both cite Old Testament texts. And Origen presents the clergy playing a role similar to that of their pagan counterparts: they are the maintainers of the Church's organization, and as such are contrasted with "the people."[17]

Thus, as the clergy became an elevated and sacred group, the term "laity" came to be applied to the passive mass of believers who were not members of this elite. Since pre-industrial societies tend to prize stability, there was a tendency to look at "church office" much as one would look at marriage: it was a "state" which had its own legal rights, and which contributed in its own way to the maintenance of a stable society.

The "being" of ministry was what was paramount — whereas O'Meara's argument is that ministry is primarily a "doing" thing. He defines Christian ministry as "the public *activity* of a baptized follower of Jesus Christ. . ."[18] and points out that the earliest Christians used "ordinary," rather than "sacral," words to describe Church ministries. Thus there was the missionary "apostle," the "teacher," the "prophet," and the "overseer" — but "over the centuries these Greek action words became sacred offices."[19]

O'Meara argues that the "doing" orientation of ministry needs to be rediscovered especially urgently in our own day because we live in a society which prizes freedom, individuality and action. We have already noted how the English sociologists Towler and Coxon would agree that the modern propensity is to assess people by what they do rather than by who they are, and that in this context the clergy as traditionally perceived certainly appear to be in something of an anomalous position.[20]

O'Meara's solution is to suggest that the traditional clergy-laity distinction must be broken down. It places the laity in too passive a role: he quotes Yves Congar to stress that, in the Scriptures, "there is no mention of laity."[21] The *laos* in the Scriptures refers to the whole "people of God," and is contrasted with the *goyim*, the nations of the world: "you, of all the nations, shall be my very own people" (Ex 19:5). It is in this sense that Congar, in his *Lay People in the Church*, makes the point that the Pope, the bishops, and the other clergy, are actually "laity" before they are anything else.[22]

O'Meara stresses that retaining the clergy-laity distinction leads to paradoxical situations where one has to maintain, for example, that the ordained secretary of the chancery is "in" the ministry, whereas a baptized Christian working as a full-time, professionally-trained hospital chaplain is still in the "lay" state. He agrees, with Congar, that any ecclesiology which is not founded upon a sound theology of the laity only ends up producing a clericalized Church confronting a laicized world. The New Testament actually presents a far richer model — where the Church is constituted not primarily by the acts of an official ministry, but by many kinds of services performed in various degrees by all the baptized:

> "the decisive pair is not 'priesthood-laity' as I used in my book on the laity but much more that of ministries . . . some freely raised up by the Spirit, others ordained by the imposition of hands."[23]

O'Meara fears that the clergy-laity distinction "suppresses diversity and standards of competency in the ministry." He dismisses the fear that the dissolution of the clergy-laity distinction may lead to a "pietist universalism" where any person can perform any ministry — on the grounds that the clear New Testament distinction between ministries will become more apparent "as the general Christian population grows in education."[24]

O'Meara claims that traditional religious life highlights in a particularly striking fashion the paradoxical nature of the clergy-laity distinction. He estimates that in the U.S. perhaps 70% of the ministry has been performed by religious women — yet these are still canonically regarded as "laity":

> "religious women present the most dramatic phenomenological 'non-compute' in the world of clerical and lay states."[25]

Religious orders of ordained men raise further questions, when one is confronted by the new emphasis on the ministry of the presbyter, as a community leader and liturgical president. Although they may well function as preachers and as liturgical celebrants, Jesuit or Dominican priests are not leaders of local Church communities.

In the face of all these contemporary influences, O'Meara concludes that "the social framework given by the clergy-laity distinction cannot survive."[26] We must adopt some other framework which allows for the far greater diversity which is actually apparent in the life of the Church.

5. Hans Küng: "Why Priests?"

Hans Küng wonders about the relevance of holding any distinction between "Ministers" and "People" in a pluralistic and democratic society.[27] He maintains that if the Church is to be relevant in western "democratic" societies, it must be seen to be compatible in its structures with the values of liberty, equality and fraternity so clearly proclaimed in the French Revolution.

Küng states that there is no room for the "paternalism" of a clerical system.[28] He admits that there "is" authority in the Church, but it is better seen in terms of "service" rather than "office." The notion of a "hierarchy," understood as a "holy rule," is as irrelevant now as the idea of a "prince-bishop."[29] In the New Testament all believers are "priests," so Küng concludes that "in principle all Christians are empowered to administer baptism and Eucharist."[30] The leader of the community simply has the responsibility to ensure that these sacraments are being celebrated.

In order that ordination may not "fall into even deeper discredit" Küng insists that it must no longer be seen as a "sacral investiture." Küng sees no point in talking of a "character" which distinguishes the ordained person from the laity — nor of his possessing a sacral "power" (potestas) which enables and authorizes him alone to consecrate the Eucharist and to administer the other sacraments.[31]

Somewhat surprisingly, Küng states that Paul never mentions ordination or presbyters.[32] One might wonder what Paul was referring to when he urged Timothy to "fan into a flame the gift that God gave you when I laid my hands on you" (2 Tm 1:6).

But for Küng it is the praxis of the "Primitive" Church rather than the Scriptures themselves which seems to be of primary importance: the Acts of the Apostles and the Pastoral Epistles have only a secondary interest, because they reflect developments which followed one or two generations after this all-important era.[33] This particular premise allows Küng to conclude that the New Testament era closes with a considerable and irreconcilable diversity of leadership models — which of course now gives us great freedom to get "in step" with the times and to remould ecclesial ministry where necessary for the good of the community.[34]

A basic principle for Küng is that the "service of leadership" is a *service to the community* — so the wishes of "the community" (however they are to be discerned) are of crucial importance.[35] Raymond Brown, however, has observed (I believe correctly) that "while Paul certainly thinks of himself as a servant, his primary emphasis in apostleship is not service to others but *service to Jesus Christ*" (2 Cor 4:5).[36] One could also ask, in reflecting on Küng's views, whether the "democratic" values proposed in the French Revolution really are an adequate expression of Gospel truths? Contemporary society certainly does exalt the notion of personal autonomy, but the ideal for a Christian — by contrast — is to submit finally to the Lord, and to be moulded and formed by Him.

6. Anton Houtepen: A Diversity of Ministerial Paradigms?

The accelerating shortage of priests is leading some theologians to argue that what is ultimately at stake is nothing less than the continued existence of the Roman Catholic Church as a hierarchical institution.[37] "The status of pastoral workers remains uncertain,"[38] but without priests anyway there is still no one authorized to preside at the Eucharist, "the source and the apex of the whole work of preaching the Gospel" (PO 5).[39]

Dutch theologian Anton Houtepen believes the first issue that must be faced is the inadequacy of the dogmatic distinction

between "laity" and "clergy" — highlighted by what he believes to
be the absurd situation where we have "pastoral workers who are
called 'laymen' but in practice do the same work as their ordained
colleagues."[40] Houtepen believes we must return to the
revolutionary New Testament insight, that the people of God, the
royal priesthood (1 P 2:5-9; Rv 5:10) does not derive its access to
God from mediators other than Jesus Christ, and that the whole
community, with all its gifts, ministries and functions, is responsible for continuing the mission Jesus has entrusted to his
Church.[41]

Houtepen argues that the root of present-day problems for
Roman Catholics has been the unbalanced focus on the "sacerdotal" character of ministry — which in turn led to an unnecessar-
ily restrictive selection of candidates from celibate males. The
contemporary proliferation of ministries is a reminder that

"cultic priesthood has only relative value in the building
up of the church, and that worship in a Christian sense is
somewhat different from that which is guaranteed by a
priestly ministry."[42]

The Reformers rejected the sacerdotal paradigm; but they simply
overemphasized another one, that of preaching and teaching.

Houtepen claims that "no norms can be derived from the
New Testament for any model or organization of the ministry."[43]
But he believes that the key to the full development of all Christian ministries lies in the "rediscovery of the abiding force of a
number of New Testament paradigms of the ministry," which
"correspond with titles which were given to Jesus himself."[44]
Thus, as Jesus was called "apostle," "evangelist," "prophet,"
"teacher," "shepherd," and eventually "priest" — so too were the
servants of the Church. Houtepen sees great ecumenical possibilities with resuscitating these scriptural paradigms because
they transcend the later, and now divisive, episcopal-sacerdotal
and presbyteral-synod forms.[45]

Houtepen argues for a new view of the apostolicity of the
Church. The "whole Church" is apostolic, "because it continues

the mission of the apostles."⁴⁶ Within this apostolic Church those who feel called to be servants and apostles, prophets and teachers, shepherds, and guides must be accorded some ordered recognition. Within this "enlarged" perspective of the ministry Houtepen evidently sees the "priestly" paradigms as being very secondary, and in fact totally dispensable.

> "There is no mention of the 'priest' in the title of this book (*Minister? Pastor? Prophet?*), and he is vanishing from the world. There is no need for him to return."⁴⁷

7. *Conclusion*

In order to try to evaluate this fleeting cross-section of contemporary views of ministry, all of which are raising searching questions about the identity of the traditional priest, it is obviously necessary to re-examine the foundations. What exactly are the ministerial structures we find in the New Testament? And how did these evolve during subsequent years, especially in the critical period before the conversion of Constantine (312 AD) when Christianity became enmeshed in the structures of the Empire? Once we have examined these formative centuries we may be in a better position to address some of the issues being raised today.

By way of transition towards a more methodical overview of these sources, it will be helpful to examine in greater detail the method and the approach of the major Roman Catholic theologian, Edward Schillebeeckx, in his writings on ministry.

CHAPTER IV

The Writings of Edward Schillebeeckx

The Dominican scholars. Edward Schillebeeckx has during this past decade written two books on ministry and priesthood, the second being an amplification and a revision of the first.[1]

1. Schillebeeckx's Concern

Schillebeeckx's concern, as with the writers we have already considered, is to try to make some sense of the contemporary "praxis" of ministry, especially as it is developing in response to the diminishing number of ordained priests. A particular concern he mentions is the trivializing of the Sunday Eucharist — where lay leaders preside over some sort of pseudo-eucharist, with consecrated hosts being brought in from elsewhere.[2] In response to a charge that he is trying to promote illegal practices, Schillebeeckx insists that canonically irregular practices are already a feature of Catholic liturgical life, and that the theologian's responsibility is to try to determine whether or not they are justifiable according to Scripture and tradition.

"Thus the theologian turns into theory, in a critical way, what is presented in the effective practice of Christian communities and their leaders today as a concrete solution to urgent pastoral needs."[3]

Once again the critical question is to somehow accommodate theologically the recent appearance of the non-ordained "pastoral worker." Schillebeeckx talks of a "blockage" — where pastoral care and community leadership are entrusted to professionally-trained and theologically-expert "lay" pastors, but sacraments are celebrated by visiting priests summoned from elsewhere.[4] Schillebeeckx does not see the permanent diaconate providing much of a solution unless it is given a "completely new content" — to help it to correspond more closely to what pastoral workers now in fact do.[5] A second alternative would be for the Church to inaugurate a "fourth ministry" — to complement that of episcopate, presbyterate and diaconate — by which pastoral workers would also receive ordination by the laying on of hands with an accompanying epiclesis.[6]

Schillebeeckx wonders if the present problems would be solved more simply by just ordaining married as well as celibate believers — but feels that there is instead a more fundamental need to acknowledge "more differentiated ministerial tasks" as a way of responding to the complex demands of contemporary life.[7] The traditional tripartite division of ordained ministry is, in his opinion, too limited; for this reason too he regards as inadequate and disappointing the recommendation of the World Council of Churches' "Lima Report" (Ministry, para. 25)[8] that churches which do not presently know the traditional threefold ministry should give thought to accepting it in some form.[9]

Schillebeeckx is particularly insistent that when one ventures into social history there are no such things as "hard" facts: "there are only interpreted facts."[10] This means that one's own premises will inevitably influence the interpretation one makes of sources. Schillebeeckx thus tells us that in his own consideration of ministry his particular bias will be to make "a plea for humanity in the church" — because, as he sees it, this was "Jesus's own choice."[11]

2. The Development of Ministry

Schillebeeckx's premise is that the earliest pre-Pauline Christian communities were totally egalitarian. He sees this ideal crystallized in a pre-Pauline baptismal catechesis quoted by Paul:

"For you are all children of God,
for all of you who are baptized in Christ
are clothed with Christ.
There is no longer Jew nor Gentile,
There is no longer slave nor freeman,
there is no longer man nor woman,
but you are all one in Christ Jesus" (Gal 3:26-28).[12]

Schillebeeckx acknowledges that the more the Church spread, the tighter its institutional forms became. But these institutional forms can always be criticized in the light of the prior New Testament emphasis on fundamental baptismal equality.[13]

The earliest churches comprised "free-fellowships"[14] which gathered in house communities. Thus we read of "the church which meets in the house of" — Aquila and Priscilla in Ephesus (1 Cor 16:19); Prisca and Aquila in Rome (Rm 16:5); Philemon in Colossae (Ph 2); or Nympha in Laodicea (Col 4:15). While the traditional Roman Hellenistic household may have been both hierarchical and patriarchal, Schillebeeckx alleges that these earliest Christian households were radically different: "a brotherhood and sisterhood of equal partners."[15] Rather paradoxically, however, Schillebeeckx believes that while these early "house churches" broke with the hierarchical pattern of contemporary family life, they conformed with the civil and religious "free associations" of the time — which were "democratic" in their form of government.[16]

From his analysis of the debate over the admission of non-circumcised Gentiles into the Christian community, Schillebeeckx claims that in the beginning "conflicts are resolved by particular Christians coming together, talking, and sorting them out."[17] He maintains that Luke and Paul give conflicting reports of the process by which the decision was made.[18] Luke makes it sound like an official synodal agreement by "the apostles and elders," with the whole Church concurring (Ac 15:22). Schillebeeckx believes that Paul sees the decision as one between two equal parties (James, Cephas and John from Jerusalem; and Barnabas and himself from Antioch) which they seal with a handshake "as a sign of partnership" (Gal 2:9). Schillebeeckx fails to mention that Paul himself, a few verses earlier, gives the impression that he went to Jerusalem not so much for a discussion between equals but to seek approval for his work from those with some higher authority — "for fear that the course I was adopting . . . would not be allowed" (Gal 2:2). The scriptural evidence does not warrant Schillebeeckx's conclusion that "Paul and Luke have clearly different views of church structures."[19]

Schillebeeckx never wavers from his hypothesis concerning the egalitarian nature of the primal Christian communities — although Paul urges even his earliest congregations "to be considerate to those who are working amongst you *and are above you in the Lord* as your teachers" (1 Th 5:12-13). On this passage, Schillebeeckx comments:

> "That Paul has to ask the community to show these people special respect indicates at least a degree of latent opposition towards non-egalitarian attitudes from a brotherhood and sisterhood in the church which was originally egalitarian."[20]

The question of who exercised final authority within the community was settled towards the end of the first century — "in favor of believers who took the title of '*episkopos*' (presbyter) and deacon."[21] Thus the power of the original "leaders of house churches," of both sexes, was neutralized and the earlier authority of the "prophet" was now appropriated by these later title-holders. "From now on women have to keep silent in services."[22]

Schillebeeckx sees this evolution as a surrender to "the non-Christian, pagan, patriarchal household code of the Graeco-Roman family. . . . Christians took over hierarchy."[23] The emphasis now is on obedience — of wife to husband, of slave to owner, and of the baptized towards their elders. Schillebeeckx believes that the primary motive for this radical dilution of the original gospel was "pastoral": it was a deliberate step taken to try to make the Church more acceptable to contemporary society. The tendency is already clearly emerging by the time of the Pastoral Epistles and 1 Peter.[24] After another few decades, as seen in the writings of people like Clement of Rome and Ignatius of Antioch

> "this system of authority and subjection — hierarchy —
> receives a theological and christological, ideological
> substructure."[25]

One might comment here that the tendency by Schillebeeckx and others to contrast "Christian" and "pagan" patterns of Church order is somewhat perplexing, given that both are to be found in the Scriptures. Hans Küng shows a similar "Pauline primitivism" — constantly preferring the testimony of the earlier over the later Pauline epistles, and often paying little attention to material to be found in allegedly later works such as the Acts of the Apostles or the Pastorals.[26] Such an approach raises its own theological problems, given the Vatican II teaching that,

> "the books of both the Old and New Testament in their
> entirety, with all their parts, are sacred and canonical
> because . . . written under the inspiration of the Holy
> Spirit" (DV 11).[27]

3. Minimizing of the Role of "The Twelve"?

The most extraordinary feature of Schillebeeckx's explanation of the scriptural background of ministry is his apparent neglect of the role of the Twelve.

In both his books he claims, as a "primary, fundamental datum of the New Testament," that "apart from apostleship or the 'apostolate', the Christian communities did not receive any kind of church order from the hands of Jesus." He sees "the Twelve" simply as "the symbol of the approaching eschatological community of God."[28] Thus the claim is that Jesus did not organize anything, and that the institution of "the Twelve" — to a merely "symbolic" role — was an insignificant departure from this "primary, fundamental datum." This leaves Schillebeeckx free to argue that all ministries grew from "what developed spontaneously from below . . . in accordance with the sociological laws of group formation."[29]

Scripture scholar Albert Vanhoye argues however that the Gospels, by contrast, are unanimous in stressing the crucial importance of "the Twelve," very deliberately chosen by Jesus to continue his mission.[30] Mark tells us that Jesus "summoned those he wanted . . . they were to be his companions and to be sent out to preach, with power to cast out devils" (Mk 3:13-14). Luke highlights their importance by telling us that Jesus spent the preceding night in prayer (Lk 6:12). Matthew insists on their link with Jesus by using the expression, "his twelve disciples" (Mt 10:1, 11:1). In John, the words of Jesus himself twice emphasize the initiative he had taken: " 'Have I not chosen you, you Twelve?' " (Jn 6:70, 15:16).

This foundational ministry of "the Twelve" did not develop "spontaneously from below," but instead was deliberately established on the Lord's own personal initiative. Contrary to Schillebeeckx's proposed pattern for the primitive Church, Jesus did not leave his disciples to fend for themselves until "obvious and spontaneous leaders"[31] emerged to guide them.

Moreover "the Twelve" do seem to have played more than a purely "symbolic" function. Because of his concern for the crowds, who were "harrassed and dejected, like sheep without a shepherd" (Mt 9:36), Jesus sent out the Twelve on mission, invested with his own authority (Mt 10:1, 10:40). They assumed this responsibility already during his public life, and continued it to a greater extent after his resurrection (Mt 28:16-20; Mk 16:14-15; Lk 24:48; Ac 1:8).

Schillebeeckx, however, makes no reference to Jesus's personal choice of the Twelve, nor to the place they so obviously hold in the Gospels. He calls them merely "a category which more than probably goes back to the earthly Jesus himself."[32] A text in which we are told that "the Twelve called a full meeting of the disciples" (*proskalesamenoi de oi dōdeka to plēthos tōn mathētōn*) (Ac 6:2) is misquoted by Schillebeeckx, in both of his books, as saying instead " ' the apostles, together with all the community' "[33] — which radically obscures the authority the Twelve in fact were exercising.

4. Notion of "Apostleship" Diluted?

Schillebeeckx also seems to dilute the notion of apostleship, instead of taking as a norm the strong sense of the word as seen in Paul's respect for the apostles in Jerusalem (Gal 1:17-19), or his own sense of special apostolic authority (Gal 1:1; 1 Cor 9:1). Schillebeeckx, however, sees apostleship as including "many of the first Christians who had come forward before the founding of the first communities or before the building up of newly-founded communities."[34] This vaguer definition means that he can overlook the special personal authority transmitted by Christ to the apostles which is so frequently mentioned in the New Testament. In *Ministry* Schillebeeckx eventually gives eight criteria for apostolicity, and none mentions the role of the original apostles as individuals personally commissioned by Christ.[35] He corrects this oversight to some extent, however, in the "four dimensions of apostolicity" in his later book.[36]

5. The Importance of the "Official" Church in the New Testament

Schillebeeckx tends to depict the relationship between "the local community" and "the official church" as being one of opposition. Thus, talking of what he sees as the local community's "right" to the celebration of the Eucharist, he writes that "the apostolic right of Christian communities may not be made null and void by the official church."[37]

The New Testament, however, sees the unity of the particular churches with one another as something that is achieved not "in spite of," but "as a result of," the interventions of "the official church." "The apostles in Jerusalem" send Peter and John to guide developments in Samaria (Ac 8:14); Peter "visited one place after another" (Ac 9:32); Barnabas is sent as an envoy to Antioch (Ac 11:21). Similarly, when a dispute occurred at Antioch it was agreed that a delegation "should go up to Jerusalem and discuss the problem with the apostles and elders" (Ac 15:2).

Paul's Letters reveal that none of his communities was permitted to go its own way. He insists that they remain faithful to what was done "everywhere in all the churches" (1 Cor 4:17, 7:17). Although so conscious of his own apostolic authority, we have earlier seen how Paul was still prepared to submit his version of the Gospel to "the leading men" in Jerusalem to be sure of their approval (Gal 2:2). Paul feared that without this recognition from "the official church" his own work would lose its validity.

On several occasions in the New Testament, what develops "spontaneously, from below" only serves to demonstrate just how necessary the apostolic authority actually is. In Jerusalem there is discord between the "Hellenists" and the "Hebrews" — which is solved on the initiative of the Twelve (Ac 6:1-6). In Galatia the local communities think they have acted sensibly by adding to their Christian faith the practice of circumcision and the prescripts of the Jewish Law — until bluntly reprimanded by Paul (Gal 1:6, 3:1, 5:4). And the Corinthians, who were so renowned for their charismatic gifts (1 Cor 1:17), became so devoted to one or other preacher that they broke into factions (1 Cor 1:11-12);

they were so broad-minded that even a case of incest in their midst caused them no shame (5:1-6); and they thought nothing of seeking solutions to conflicts before pagan tribunals (6:1-6). Schillebeeckx depicts Paul as the defender of charismatic spontaneity within his communities — and therefore contrasts him with whoever wrote the Pastorals, with their concern for church order. But "Paul's trust in the Spirit which dwells in the whole of the Christian community"[38] did not deter him from monitoring very strictly the expression of these gifts (I Cor 12-14):

> "If there are people present with the gift of tongues, let only two or three, at the most, be allowed to use it, and only one at a time, and there must be someone to interpret.... Anyone who claims to be a prophet or inspired ought to recognize that what I am writing to you is a command from the Lord. Unless he recognizes this, you should not recognize him" (1 Cor 14:27, 37f).

6. The Selection of Leaders in Early Church Communities

In his earlier book Schillebeeckx argues for a three-stage foundational pattern for early Church communities: (i) establishment of a community; (ii) departure of the founding apostle; (iii) spontaneous evolution of leaders.

> "It was natural that when these missionary apostles moved on, their function of leadership and co-ordination should be taken over by obvious and spontaneous leaders in the various communities."[39]

This apparent "spontaneity," we have already been told, was really "in accordance with the sociological laws of group formation."[40]

Vanhoye observes, however, that even according to "sociological laws" it does seem strange to think that the founder of a group would move on without concerning himself about its future ˙leadership.[41] Schillebeeckx himself notes that Paul "evidently chose carefully and tested"[42] those who were to be his "fellow workers." But he seems to presume that Paul allowed a far more spontaneous process to occur within his communities. As "historical evidence" for this, Schillebeeckx quotes Paul's appeal to the Thessalonians to respect those "who are above you in the Lord as your teachers" (1 Th 5:12).[43] In reality, however, this quotation tells us nothing of how these leaders were established: it only tells us that they were already in place.

The most detailed information we have on how early Church leaders were appointed comes from the account of the institution of "the Seven" (Ac 6:1-6). The initiative is taken by "the official Church," in this case "the Twelve," who call a full meeting of "the disciples," and suggest to them what should be done to settle the differences between the "Hellenists" and the "Hebrews." "The whole assembly approved of this proposal," held an election, and "presented these to the apostles": it is these "official leaders" who then, through prayer and the laying on of hands, confirm "the Seven" in office.

Other New Testament texts which refer to the instituting of ministers make no mention of any community role in the process — so, whatever form it may have taken, it certainly does not seem to have been the most decisive element. It is said of Paul and Barnabas, concerning the communities they had founded: "In each of these churches *they* appointed elders" (Ac 14:23). Timothy is reminded that "you have in you a spiritual gift which was given to you *when the prophets spoke and the body of elders laid their hands on you*" (1 Tm 4:14). Titus was left behind in Crete "to get everything organized there and *appoint elders in every town*, in the way that I told you" (Tt 1:5).

Schillebeeckx, of course, rejects the Pauline authorship of the Pastorals.[44] But the fact remains that, whenever the New Testament expresses itself clearly on the subject, it contradicts Schillebeeckx's theory of "spontaneous" growth "from below," and consistently presents ministry in the Church as being constituted by appointments "from above" — from the case of "the Twelve" onwards.

7. *What is Normative for Schillebeeckx?*

The difficulty for anyone reading Schillebeeckx is trying to find if there is anything at all which is normative in history. He himself warns that

> "one can never give an absolute cut-and-dried formulation of what is specifically normative for Christians, since this can only be found in changing historical forms."[45]

Thus there are no unchanging forms, no unchanging facts (since these are always "interpreted"), and of course no unchanging theories, but only "changeable theories which we make ourselves."[46]

The ultimate criterion for Schillebeeckx often seems to be sociology, according to which, for example, he criticizes the Church for having failed to recognize the historically-conditioned and changing nature of her own existence: "This is true, even sociologically, of any system in society. . ."[47] He is careful, however, not to reduce theology simply to a branch of sociology — thus he stresses that what is given us "from below" (i.e. from historically conditioned circumstances) is also experienced as "from above" (i.e. as a product of grace).[48]

8. *Relationship Between Theory and Practice*

Schillebeeckx claims that there are no "pure" facts — only our own "interpretations" of them, which are therefore simply "theories." But what are these theories based on — if factual reality is itself inaccessible? Joyce A. Little, in reviewing *The Church With A Human Face*, concludes that

"the ultimate criterion of Schillebeeckx's theory is his own
constructed theory as to what constitutes an authentic
Christian community (and, by extension, ministry)."[49]

Thus Schillebeeckx himself says

"only theological theory can demonstrate whether the direction of the practice is *orthos*, right, in the light of the
inspiration and orientation of the great Christian tradition, even if this practice should be completely new."[50]

Little finds this statement amazing:

"To place the concrete, material and historical order at the
mercy of such non-material and non-historical realities as
changing, fabricated theories goes far beyond anything
Plato himself ever dreamed of by way of relativizing the
world we live in."[51]

Even Plato believed our fragile material forms participated in
reality by somehow reflecting real immaterial entities.

9. *"There Are Only Interpreted Facts"*

Schillebeeckx insists: "There are no such things as 'facts'. . . .
There are only interpreted facts. We can only arrive at facts within
changeable theories which we make ourselves."[52] Little observes
drily that it is irrational to assert as "fact" that there are no facts —
and the assertion itself is only a theory anyway![53] It also means
that the reader must place Schillebeeckx's theories above traditional practice in order to agree with Schillebeeckx's conclusions.
And it makes criticizing his historical analysis of ministry impossible, since the "interpreted facts" he offers are, by his own account-
ing, not real in themselves but only products of his theory.
    Schillebeeckx, for example, says of Jesus: "He was probably
born in Nazareth."[54] This "probable fact" is, of course, an

"interpreted fact," which arises from and conforms to Schillebeeckx's theological theories. Christ's birth at Bethlehem, as in the infancy narratives of the Gospels, is similarly an "interpreted fact" which arises from and conforms to the theological theories of Matthew and Luke. To seek to find where Christ "actually" was born is probably a futile exercise in Schillebeeckx's thinking because it involves pursuing an "uninterpreted" fact — and no such things exist!

Schillebeeckx's interpretation of Galatians 3:28 ("there is neither male nor female") is instructive. He says that it refers back to Genesis 1:27 ("male and female he created them") and indicates an eschatological restoration of an equality "which was destroyed historically and in society."[55] The Genesis passage, however, is linked to our being created in the image of God, and is part of the pre-fallen creation (the Fall does not occur until Genesis 3) which the Church, like God, has always understood to be "very good" (Gn 1:31).

It hardly seems likely that the "new" creation should annihilate that sexual differentiation which was intrinsic to the original "good" creation. Yet that is precisely what Schillebeeckx intends us to understand as having happened "in Christ." Because, for him, facts arise out of theories, and part of his "theory" regarding the Church includes the notion of an "egalitarian" community,[56] he has to ensure that Galatians and Genesis be interpreted accordingly. Thus the danger is that one ends up not with theology serving revelation, but with revelation serving a particular theology.

10. Practice "Must Be Justified In Theory"?

Schillebeeckx tells us that the actual practice of Christian communities "must be justified in theory."[57] One consequence of this position is that it gives the theologian the authority to determine whether or not any given practice is authentically Catholic — but always of course according to his or her own "theory." However, if the theologian's "theory" differs with that of the Magisterium, it can distance him from "official" Catholic practice and therefore from theological realism. Scientific experimentation works in the opposite direction. Theories are not used to justify practical experiments; rather, practical experimentation is used to test theories. If hypotheses are maintained, even in the face of experimentation which proves the opposite, then the scientist has lost touch with reality.

Joyce Little concludes her review of *The Church With A Human Face* by observing that the book cannot fail, because the facts which Schillebeeckx presents for the reader's judgment

"arise out of the theory with which he begins, and necessarily point to the conclusion which his theory already presupposes. This is a fail-safe method for getting to where one wants to go. Unfortunately, it gets there by way of an enormous detour around the facticity of Catholic faith and practice."[58]

Little's observation is certainly corroborated by my own investigations. Schillebeeckx's use of Scripture and of tradition is narrowly selective, highlighting only material which supports his own hypotheses. It is always helpful to have creative and imaginative thinkers, but one cannot simply dismiss the often very substantial testimony of centuries of Catholic faith and practice. If we are to address contemporary challenges in the area of ministry and priesthood in a realistic way, we cannot do so by jettisoning principles and practices which Scripture and tradition have unanimously regarded as normative.

CHAPTER V

Ministry and "Priestly" Language in the New Testament

1. Introduction

Bearing in mind the "crisis" which the priesthood is now facing, the point is often made that there are no New Testament references to any ministerial "priesthood."[1] Hans Küng, along with a number of other contemporary writers, would argue from this that words such as "priest" or "cleric" should be dispensed with, because the New Testament insists that all believers are "priests."[2]

Raymond Brown, however, makes the point that the earliest Christians acknowledged the Jewish priesthood as valid and therefore never thought of needing a priesthood of their own. For the emergence of a special Christian priesthood some major changes had to occur. In the first place, Christians had to see themselves as constituting a new religion distinct from Judaism. And secondly, they had to have a sacrifice at which a priesthood could preside.[3]

But before we turn our attention too exclusively to the idea of "priesthood" it will be helpful to survey the variety of ministers we do find in the New Testament.

2. A Variety of Ministries

(i) "The Twelve"

After his baptism Jesus preached to the crowds about the coming of the Kingdom of God, and the conversion necessary for its acceptance. His message was addressed to every Israelite, but gradually a more restricted group of "disciples" was formed. Jesus called these to leave their work and to follow him (Mk 1:16-20). The calling of "the Twelve" occurred within the membership of this inner group.

The formula "one of the Twelve" is applied to Judas in the Passion Narratives (Mk 14:43) and so belongs to the oldest sources of the gospels.[4] Despite scriptural references to "the twelve apostles" (Lk 6:13; Mt 10:2), the Twelve at this early stage were not "apostles."[5] But the prominent manner in which their appointment has been handed down in the Gospels highlights their importance in Jesus's public life.

The Twelve were called "to be his companions, and to be sent out to preach, with power to cast out devils" (Mk 3:14-15). The mission of the Twelve is in this way modelled on that of Jesus himself: "As the Father sent me, so am I sending you" (Jn 20:21). The purpose of the mission is also similar, since preaching and the expelling of devils are stressed in Mark's description of the beginning of Jesus's public ministry (Mk 1:21-28, 39). The "secret of the kingdom of God" (Mk 4:11), the whole project entrusted to Jesus, is also shared with them.[6]

Jesus's intentions were that the Twelve would be leaders who would "judge" the Twelve Tribes of Israel (Mt 19:28; Lk 22:28-30). When Jesus was recognized as Messianic King, the Twelve would be his Ministers. Luke's account makes even more explicit the power being entrusted to the Twelve: "You are the men who have stood by me faithfully in my trials; and now I confer a kingdom on you, just as my Father conferred one on me" (Lk 22:28-29). It seems fair to presume, with Jean Galot,[7] that Luke sees some link here between this apostolic authority and the power to celebrate the Eucharist, since he has just previously recorded the institution of the Eucharist, with Jesus's instruction to "do this as a memorial of me" (Lk 22:19). The Gospels further refer to this authorization to rule in the parable of the steward who is told by his master to supervise his servants and is called upon to give an account of his fidelity. Luke tells us that this parable was meant for the benefit of Peter and his companions (Lk 12:42-46).

The Gospels bear witness to a position of leadership involving a responsibility to preach, a power to celebrate the Eucharist, a commission to baptize all nations (Mk 16:16-18), and even the power to remit sins (Jn 20:20-22). All these indications show an intention by Jesus to impart to the Twelve the full extent of his own pastoral authority. Peter is their leader.

(ii) The Position of Peter

The position of Peter is intriguing. It appears that right until the end of Jesus's ministry, the Twelve argued among themselves as to who should take first place in the kingdom (Lk 22:24-27; Mt 20:25-27). Peter did not become their leader on the strength of his personal prestige. The decisive factor was that Christ willed it:

"So I now say to you: you are Peter and on this rock I will build my Church. . . . I will give you the keys of the kingdom of heaven: whatever you bind on earth shall be considered bound in heaven; whatever you loose on earth shall be considered loosed in heaven" (Mt 16:18-19).

Contemporary research now recognizes the Semitic idioms and the genuine historicity of this passage. In archaic language, deeply rooted in Jewish tradition, Peter is entrusted with a responsibility which was never envisioned by the Old Testament prophets.[8] While Matthew is the only one of the synoptics to record Jesus's words to Peter, all three agree on the striking fact of Simon's change of name (Mk 3:16; Lk 6:14). Jesus intends to

share with the man now named Peter the position he himself
occupied: the stone that has become the keystone (Mt 21:42).
Jesus corroborates his intentions; as the one to whom "all power in
heaven and on earth" has been given (Mt 28:18), he explicitly
entrusts to Peter "the keys of the kingdom of heaven."
     Galot argues that it would be arbitrary to dismiss the con-
siderable importance of the words addressed by Jesus to Simon.[9]
It was an extraordinarily original initiative on the part of Jesus to
choose one of his own disciples and to appoint him as the universal shepherd (Jn 21:15-17) in the image of himself (Jn 10:11) —
while entrusting to him as particularly his own the mission of
strengthening his brothers in their faith (Lk 22:32). The early
Church understood what Christ had willed: Peter assumes the
role of uncontested leader certainly from the Day of Pentecost
onwards (Ac 2:14ff.).

(iii) The Co-Workers With The Twelve

     Jesus was surrounded by many disciples. It would therefore
be a mistake to think, as David Power implies, that the Twelve
were "the" original Christian community.[10] Luke tells us of
several women who accompanied Jesus (Lk 8:1-3); John tells us
that after Jesus's discourse on the "bread of life," "many of his
disciples left him and stopped going with him" (Jn 6:66). Galot
maintains that many of the "disciples" in the Gospels are more
than simply "believers": they were persons who had responded to
a call, who had begun to follow Jesus, and who were prepared to
devote their energy to the work he had begun.[11]
     It is interesting on this score to note that the invitation to the
rich man to "go and sell everything that you own . . . then come,
follow me" (Mk 10:21) is recorded in all three synoptics well after
the original call of the Twelve. Similarly Matthias is elected to
replace Judas from a larger pool of disciples who had been "with
us the whole time that the Lord Jesus was travelling around . . .
right from the time when John was baptizing" (Ac 1:21-22).
     After the Twelve had been sent out on their mission (Lk

9:1-10) Luke reports that others were also entrusted with the mission of proclaiming the kingdom of God:

> "After this the Lord appointed seventy-two others and sent them out ahead of him, in pairs, to all the towns and places he himself was to visit" (Lk 10:1).

It is interesting to note that there are no significant differences in the instructions issued to each group. Both are to proclaim the good news, and both groups are endowed with Christ's authority to teach: "anyone who listens to you listens to me" (Lk 10:16). The power to cast out devils, specifically accorded to the Twelve (Mk 3:15) is exercised also by the Seventy-two (Lk 10:17).

It seems clear that Jesus willed to share with the Seventy-two, as well as with the Twelve, his own mission to proclaim the Gospel and his power over the forces of evil. The Twelve, although with their own particular authority, are thus accompanied by a larger number of disciples who share the same mission. Jean Galot admits that Jesus nowhere speaks explicitly of successors, yet warns that we must be wary of concluding that he therefore had no intention of any continuing ministerial structure among his followers.[12] In his eschatological discourses Jesus emphasizes that no one but the Father knows when the world will end (Mt 13:32). The Eleven are entrusted with a mission to teach all nations (Mt 28:19-20) — a task so immense in its scope that it would seem Jesus must have been aware that he was assigning a responsibility which would be passed on to many successors.

Galot argues fairly persuasively that these "co-workers with the Twelve" constituted the original "presbyteral college" — to use the language of later theology! It was the group from which the Twelve were chosen; it was the group the rich man was invited to join; it was from this group that the Seventy-two were sent out on their mission; it was this group, now comprising "about a hundred and twenty persons" (Ac 1:15), which gathered after the resurrection to elect a successor to Judas; and it was this group which comprised the "elders" when "the apostles and elders" gathered for the Council of Jerusalem (Ac 15:23).[13]

(iv) "The Seven"

"The Seven" were chosen in response to complaints by Greek-speaking "Hellenist" Christians in Jerusalem that their widows were being overlooked "in the daily distribution" (Ac 6:1-6). Although they are called to "service" (*diakonia* in 6:1, 4), Luke does not call the chosen seven "deacons" — although a long tradition has seen in their ordination the beginning of the diaconate as an institution. In later centuries the number of deacons in a diocese was often restricted to seven. The fact that they were such a small group often meant that they exercised considerable power and influence.[14]

However an equally venerable line of interpretation, stretching back as far as John Chrysostom, has resisted this tendency to identify the Seven with the first deacons.[15] The Seven were named to help with "the daily distribution" — because the Twelve did not feel it would be right for them to neglect the word of God "so as to give out food" (Ac 6:1-2). The presumption was that they were being entrusted with the care of the poor, especially since it was "widows" who were being overlooked. But there are significant counter-indications to this interpretation.

In the first place the number seven seems disproportionately large to oversee relief for what must have been a relatively small number of needy Hellenistic widows in Jerusalem. It also hardly seems likely that the improvement of inadequacies in a relief program should have required the calling of a full meeting of the community — nor that such an appointment should conclude with the liturgical imposition of hands. Nor would such a task necessarily demand men "filled with the Spirit, and with wisdom" (Ac 6:3). It is also curious that there are no further New Testament references to men being ordained for such a task — although we may presume that the work of caring for the needy was always taken seriously.

As for the Seven, we know that Stephen devoted himself intensively to preaching (Ac 6:10), and Philip undertook missionary journeys (Ac 8:4-8). Stephen, moreover, was an accomplished Scripture scholar, and was renowned for the "miracles and signs" he worked among the people (Ac 6:8). The fact that there is no explicit reference to either of them being involved in relief programs should encourage us to explore other possibilities as to the role of the Seven.

It may be important to remember that the term "widow" in the New Testament refers not just to those who are needy, but also to women who lived some form of consecrated life (1 Tm 5:3-16). The "daily distribution" of food can also be seen in another light when we recall Luke's earlier pen portrait of the life of the Jerusalem community: "They went as a body to the Temple *every day* but met in their houses *for the breaking of bread*" (Ac 2:46). The allusions are obviously Eucharistic — especially in the writings of Luke who records the resurrection appearance on the road to Emmaus when Cleopas and his companion finally recognize the Lord "at the breaking of bread" (Lk 24:35).

For all these reasons Jean Galot suggests that the problem being faced by the Hellenists was not some deficiency in a relief program, but a lack of Greek-speaking ministers who could preside at their daily Eucharistic celebration — the "daily distribution."[16] As the number of believers grew larger, this was bound to cause problems. The complaint comes especially from the devout women ("widows") in the community. The Twelve, knowing that their primary duty is evangelization ("the service of the word"), have already decided that they cannot be monopolized by the service of many Eucharistic meals in private houses. Thus they call a meeting of the whole community and propose the creation of new ministers to serve the Hellenistic community.

The candidates must be "filled with the Spirit and with wisdom" (Ac 6:3). They are empowered to preside at "the daily distribution," at the meal with which the Eucharist was brought to a close. Since part of their responsibility involves the "proclamation of the Good News" (Ac 5:42) Stephen and Philip are obviously nominated because they are known to be good preachers. Galot sees this as a "presbyteral" ordination: the Seven preside over the Eucharist, but are still under the supervision of the Twelve.[17] When Philip evangelizes Samaria, Peter and John are sent to confer the Holy Spirit on the newly baptized (Ac 8:14-17).

With the martyrdom of Stephen, the Hellenists are forced to flee from Jerusalem (Ac 8:1) and the Seven lose their particular identity — probably being absorbed into the more general grouping of the (presbyteral?) "co-workers with the Twelve."[18]

(v) Apostles, Prophets and Teachers

With the opening of the Church to the Gentiles, the great missionary epoch began; it would close with the deaths of the two great "apostles," Peter and Paul, in Rome around AD 64-67.[19] The organization of this missionary era of the "apostles" seems to have originated in Syrian Antioch — where the Gospel was first preached to the Greeks and where the disciples were first called "Christians" (Ac 11:20, 26).

The church at Antioch, led by "Prophets and Teachers," decided through the inspiration of the Holy Spirit to send two of its members, Barnabas and Saul, as "Apostles" to the island of Cyprus, and then on to the towns of southern Asia Minor (Ac 13:1-3). When Paul lists in his letters the organization of the ministry, he names the ministers he knew at Antioch: "God has given the first place to apostles, the second to prophets, and the third to teachers. . . ." (1 Cor 12:28). This structure is also mentioned in the *Didache*, XI-XIII, a contemporary missionary document also from the region of Antioch.[20]

The *Apostles* were missionaries sent out by important Christian communities. Their task was to found a community, and then to move on. They were sent out in pairs — Barnabas and Saul, or Judas and Silas (Ac 15:26) — and were expected to report back to the mother community. In order to avoid clashes, the apostolic responsibility was divided on "ethno-cultural," rather than mere geographical, grounds.[21] Some, like Peter (1 P 1:1), concentrated on the mission to the Jews, whereas others, notably Paul, were specialists in proclaiming the good news to the Gentiles (Rm 11:13). This division meant that in larger cities it was possible for each party to be at work, but dealing with different groups — as at

Antioch (Gal 2:11), Rome (Ac 28:30), and possibly Corinth (1 Cor 1:12?).

The *Prophets* were recognized by their speaking "in the spirit" (*Didache* XI; 1 Cor 14:29-32). They could give oracles as in the Old Testament. It was during the liturgy at Antioch that the community received the prophetic message that "I want Barnabas and Saul set apart for the work to which I have called them" (Ac 13:2). At Caesarea the prophet Agabus by a symbolic action warns Paul of his impending imprisonment (Ac 21:11). Because the New Testament links the Eucharistic "breaking of bread" with "proclaiming the death of the Lord until he comes" (1 Cor 11:26), it is no surprise to find that in the *Didache* (X)[22] celebrants of the Eucharist during these earliest decades are often called "prophets."[23]

The ministry of the *Teachers* was always linked with that of the Prophets, but they seem to have concentrated more on systematic catechesis — giving the sort of instruction that Saul received from the Rabbi Gamaliel (Ac 22:3).[24] Prominent teachers in the early Church were Apollos, "an eloquent man, with a sound knowledge of the Scriptures" who had been trained in the school of Alexandria — but also Priscilla and Aquila who completed his instruction "about the Way" (Ac 18:24-26).

These three specialized ministries, of Apostle, Prophet and Teacher, supervised the extraordinary expansion of the Church from Antioch in the first century. But in the meantime the ministry in other contemporary communities was developing according to different models — however, often under the direct supervision of such Antiochene Apostles as Paul and Barnabas.

(vi) *"Presbyteroi" — "Episkopoi" — "Diakonoi"*

After the persecution of the Hellenists (Ac 6:7), the church in Jerusalem organized itself along traditional Jewish lines:[24] they had a group of "presbyters" ("apostles and *elders*") presided over by James, "the brother of the Lord" (Ac 11:29-30; 15:2, 4, 22, 23; Gal 2:9).

The Jewish-Christian communities of Cilicia and southern Asia Minor seem to have been organized according to this presbyteral model: "In each of these churches they (Paul and Barnabas) appointed elders (*presbyteroi*)" (Ac 14:23). Around AD 50, Paul urges his Thessalonian converts to respect those who are "above you in the Lord *as your teachers*" (1 Th 5:12). Not far from Thessalonica, the church in Philippi is led by "overseers and ministers" (*episkopois kai diakonois* — Ph 1:1). The *Didache*, in addressing these communities, advises: "You must elect overseers and assistants (*episkopoi kai diakonoi*). . . . Their ministry is identical with that of the prophets and teachers" (*Did.* XV).[25]

Alongside the "elders-overseers" (*presbyteroi-episkopoi*), Ephesus also had "ministers" (*diakonoi*). We are given few details as to what deacons actually did (1 Tm 3:8-13); it seems that women, such as Phoebe at Cenchreae (Rm 16:1), may also have exercised this ministry (1 Tm 3:11) — although André Lemaire cautions that at this stage *diakonos* may not have attained its technical meaning of "deacon" and may simply mean "minister."[26]

By the end of the first century, with the Pastoral Epistles, the primitive Church has known several "structures" for her ministry. And it is still evolving: the "bishop" is not yet clearly distinct from the "presbyter" — and the threefold hierarchy which Ignatius of Antioch (d. 107?) took for granted is not found everywhere to be quite so clearly defined.[27]

3. "Priestly" Language in the New Testament

(i) Jesus, Our "High Priest"

There are no New Testament references to any ministerial "priesthood."[28]

"The New Testament never uses the term 'priesthood' or 'priest' (*hiereus*) to designate the ordained ministry or the ordained minister."[29]

The dominant "priestly" theme in the New Testament is that of the "High Priesthood" of Jesus — developed with considerable originality in the Letter to the Hebrews.

Seeing Jesus as a High Priest involves making several alterations to the Old Testament model of priesthood.[30] The Old Testament does not stress the fact that a High Priest must be chosen from "among men" — because that was self-evident! Its big emphasis is on "separating" the High Priest from others — by means of special vestments, anointing with chrism, and the observation of special purity laws (cf. Lv 21). Hebrews, in contrast, stresses with regard to Jesus that "he had to become in all things like his brothers": tempted, suffering, and finally dying. This "identity" with those whom he represents is what makes him a "merciful" High Priest (Heb 2:17). The Old Testament tended to stress the "severity" that was required for a High Priest: he needed to be able to stand up to sinners (cf. Ex 32:25-29). Christ's priesthood is radically different. He does not stand up "against" us; on the contrary, he threw in his lot "with" us (Heb 2:10).

Priesthood, in Hebrews, consists in making offerings to God:

". . . it is the duty of every high priest to offer gifts and sacrifices . . . every high priest has been taken out of mankind and is appointed to act for men in their relations with God, to offer gifts and sacrifices for sins" (8:3, 5:1).

The writer of Hebrews thinks along almost Platonic lines. The Old Testament priesthood was limited to the "earthly," as opposed to the "heavenly" plane.[31] The Jerusalem Temple was only a "model": the living God does not dwell within man-made buildings. Once each year the High Priest entered the Holy of Holies in order to make expiation (9:7); but then the sanctuary was closed for yet another year — so this type of high priesthood was not particularly effective in achieving open communication with God.

This "ritual of the flesh" was basically external and empty: "Bulls' blood and goats' blood are useless for taking away sins" (Heb 10:4). The ancient cult could not renew man deeply and interiorly, and so could not place him in a real and living relationship with God. Christ's sacrifice, however, was totally different: a supreme act of obedience and love. The Christian can now approach God, but he can do so only in union with Christ — "through the blood of Jesus" (Heb 10:19).

(ii) "Priestly" Aspects of the Ministry of Jesus

It has become commonplace to emphasize the fact that Jesus lived and died as a layman. Unlike his cousin, John the Baptist, Jesus was not born into a priestly family (Lk 1:5-38). He certainly never refers to himself explicitly as being a Priest; but nor does he refer to himself as being Messiah, Christ, or Lord. In fact, Jesus recoils from describing himself by means of titles — probably because, as Galot puts it, he does not want to "reduce the disclosure of his identity to a linguistic transaction."[32] As soon as Peter recognizes Jesus as "the Christ," we are told that Jesus "gave them strict orders not to tell anyone about him" (Mk 8:30). He is similarly evasive in making any clear admission of kingship — especially in the presence of Pilate when the potential for misunderstanding would have been at its greatest (Mk 15:2).

Yet, the dramatic struggle which forms the public ministry of Jesus, and which leads to his condemnation, indicates a fundamental difference between the faith Jesus preaches and that proclaimed by the hierarchy of Judaism. Jesus is consistently critical of the priestly establishment; in the parable of the Good Samaritan, the priest and the Levite pass by "on the other side" (Lk 10:31). Jesus's trial has a pronounced "priestly" flavor; Mark tells us that even Pilate realized that "it was out of jealousy that the chief priests had handed Jesus over" (Mk 15:10). Bernard Cooke writes that when the New Testament writers portray Jesus as the antithesis to the official priesthood, they are necessarily, even though implicitly, categorizing his own ministry as somehow priestly.[33]

Moreover, the infancy narrative of the Gospel of Luke sees a special significance in the Temple in Jerusalem, and in Jesus's relationship to it (Lk 1:13-17; 2:22-38, 49). Jesus's later cleansing of the Temple is really a blatant challenge to the leadership being offered by the priestly authorities (Lk 19:45-46). When Jesus talks about his own understanding of his ministry, his use of the "shepherd" image has distinctly "priestly" connotations. He is "the good shepherd" — who "lays down his life for his sheep" (Jn 10:11). The shepherd image, which has so many venerable Old Testament precedents, also calls to mind the Servant of God in Isaiah, who "offers his life in atonement" (Is 53:10). Because the good shepherd knows his sheep, and calls them by name (Jn 10:3, 14), Jean Galot notes that this image, with its allusion both to sacrifice and to pastoral care, evokes a far richer notion of priesthood — which is not as restricted to the domain of worship as Old Testament priesthood had tended to become.[34]

(iii) *The Priesthood of the Whole People of God*

While New Testament thought with regard to priesthood is dominated by the unique position of Jesus himself, the other "priestly" notion explicitly developed is that of a priesthood which is shared in common by the entire Christian people. Statements in 1 Peter (2:5, 9), and in Revelations (1:6, 5:10, 20:6), apply to all Christians the promise God made to the whole Jewish nation in Exodus (19:6): "I will count you a kingdom of priests, a consecrated nation." Whatever the precise interpretation of this text, it would be incorrect to presume that the cultic function attributed to priests is somehow being transferred to the whole nation: Jewish tradition never concluded from this passage that the particular responsibilities of the priestly tribe of Levi had been suppressed.[35]

Turning to the New Testament passages, what stands out most in Revelations is the "royal" quality of this priesthood. We are told that Jesus Christ has made all believers "a line of kings, priests to serve his God and Father" (Rv 1:6). They shall "rule the world" (Rv 5:10) and "reign with him for a thousand years" (Rv 20:6).

In 1 Peter, priesthood is still linked to kingship, but the emphasis is now on that more specifically "priestly" activity of offering sacrifices. Christians are urged to set themselves close to the Lord,

". . . so that you too, the holy priesthood that offers the spiritual sacrifices which Jesus Christ has made acceptable to God, may be living stones making a spiritual house . . . for you are a chosen race, a royal priesthood, a consecrated nation, a people set apart to sing the praises of God. . ."

This conception of a universal priesthood identifies the Church as the new Israel. She is heir to the promises made in Exodus (19:6) and Isaiah (61:6): ". . . you will be named 'priests of Yahweh,' they will call you 'ministers of our God,' " But the sacrifices now offered are the "spiritual sacrifices" of Christian lives offered to the Father in imitation of Christ's own gift of himself.

The Letters of Paul nowhere speak explicitly of a universal priesthood, but the Corinthians, for example, certainly knew that they were consecrated persons — thanks to Paul's use of the image of the temple: "Didn't you realize that you were *God's temple*, and that the Spirit of God was living in you?" (1 Cor 3:16-17). "Your body, you know, is *the temple of the Holy Spirit*. . ." (1 Cor 6:19-20). Similarly the Christians in Rome are urged to worship God "by offering your living bodies as *a holy sacrifice*, truly pleasing to God" (Rm 12:1). Writing to the Philippians, Paul refers to their faith as their "*sacrifice* and offering" — and later refers to their generosity in sending him financial help as "*a sacrifice* which God accepts and finds pleasing" (Ph 2:17; 4:18).

Hebrews emphasizes so strongly the absolute uniqueness of Christ's priestly act that there seems to be no room for what might be called cultic priestly activity on the part of Christians. But precisely because the priestly worship of Christ is a constant reality (Heb 10:12-14), and because he abides with his brethren whom he joins to himself in his Body (Jn 15:1-11), the entirety of Christian existence is caught up into a cultic context and is meant to be an act of worship.[36]

(iv) The Nature of Christian Worship in the New Testament

From the evidence we have already considered, it might seem that the initial decades of Christianity were devoid of any specifically Christian liturgical celebrations. Yet any such sweeping conclusion is challenged by the many allusions to the celebration of Baptism and Eucharist. The earliest Letters of Paul speak of Baptism as a practice already accepted unquestioningly (1 Cor 1:13-17).

With the Eucharist, as with Baptism, there is no clear New Testament indication about the ministry of liturgical leadership. What is clear is that no one, not even one of the Twelve, was looked upon as a cultic priest who offered sacrifice.[37] Hebrews 13:15 speaks of the Christian sacrifice as one of praise — and it is this only because it gives expression to the heavenly liturgy which the glorified Christ celebrates. The only priest who enters the picture is Christ himself.

What seemed to distinguish the Christian celebration of the Eucharist was the belief that the risen Lord was present in their midst, himself celebrating the all-sufficient heavenly liturgy. It was this heavenly liturgy which the Christian act of Eucharist reflected and expressed. Christians were a priestly people because they were the Body of him who is the one High Priest; in joining their lives to his sacrifice they were giving to the Father the worship that is his due.[38]

4. Conclusion

André Lemaire concludes his survey of ministry in the New Testament by observing that anarchy and disorder are nowhere seen as virtues: "God is not a God of confusion, but of peace" (1 Cor 14:33). Paul sees no opposition between "charismatic" and "institutional" because in his eyes every ministry is a gift of the Spirit.[39] The great Pauline image of the Body highlights the

necessity for order (1 Cor 12:12-30). The ideal for the Church is
not that it be a mass of individuals each directly attached to Christ,
but that it be a structured community infused with the Holy Spirit.
Albert Vanhoye agrees that the unambiguous testimony of
the New Testament is towards a hierarchical structure. The
choice of the Twelve and the pre-eminence of Peter are the first
and crucial indications of this pattern. He claims that to deny any
normative significance to these facts is to misunderstand the
catechetical intention of the Gospels as a particular literary
genre.[40]

The Letters of Paul can hardly be used to support Schillebeeckx's notion of a diaspora of autonomous churches which
somehow confer apostolicity on their respective leaders. [41] For
Paul, the apostle stands in the key position. In communion with
the other apostles (Gal 2:9), his responsibility extends to "all the
churches" (2 Cor 11:28). Then there are his fellow-workers, to
whom he entrusts missions to particular communities (1 Th 3:1-5;
Ph 2:19-23; 1 Cor 4:17; 2 Cor 12:18). Beneath them are the
leaders of the local communities, to whom the apostle gives his
support (1 Th 5:12; 1 Cor 16:16); and finally there are the
ordinary faithful.

The Acts of the Apostles presents a similar picture. "The
Seven" receive their ministry from "the Twelve" (Ac 6:1-6) but
remain under their authority: we have seen how the Apostles send
delegates to confirm Philip's ministry in Samaria (8:14-17). Similarly Paul also speaks with authority to elders of other local communities (20:17-35).

The Pastoral Epistles show a similarly hierarchical structure.
Over everyone stands the position of the apostle. Then come
individuals like Timothy or Titus, who receive from the apostle an
authority which is superior to that of the local leaders — whom
they are instructed to choose and to appoint (Tt 1:5; 2 Tm 2:2). A
"presiding elder" (*episkopos*) has "responsibility for the Church of
God" (1 Tm 3:5), whereas of leaders who are "deacons" it is said
simply that they "serve" (1 Tm 3:8-13).

Peter's apostolic authority extends over a huge area — "to all
those living among foreigners in the Dispersion of Pontus,

Galatia, Cappadocia, Asia and Bithynia, who have been chosen" (1 P 1:1). He is in a position to instruct both the ordinary faithful as well as their elders (5:1-11).

All of this ministry, as Schillebeeckx so correctly observes, is to be performed in a spirit of service and not of domination.[42] All hierarchical authority is intended to facilitate our unity in Christ (Ep 4:11-13). But, as Vanhoye observes, it can only work effectively for unity while it remains truly authoritative.[43]

However, as we come to the end of this brief glance at ministry during the New Testament period we find that there is certainly no trace of the notion that some designated minister has the function to "make Christ present." Rather, where two or more are gathered in his name, he is already present (Mt 18:20).[44]

In terms of "priestly" language, the priesthood of Christ is very clearly presented, especially in Hebrews, and so too is the priesthood of the Christian community, as in 1 Peter (2:9). But the scriptural evidence does seem to be lacking for any idea of a ministerial "priesthood" — as Küng and others have emphasized![45] This fact stimulated the Fathers of Vatican II to prefer the more scriptural term "presbyter" when referring to the "co-workers of the episcopal order" (PO 2).[46] But, for the moment let us fleetingly examine some key developments experienced by the priesthood during the intervening centuries.

CHAPTER VI

The Pre-Nicene Centuries

1. The Constantinian Turning-Point

When the Emperor Galerius died in AD 312, the young general Constantine (then aged twenty-seven) crossed the Alps in a daring gamble to capture Rome and install himself as the new Caesar. In a dream he saw a Cross in the sky and heard the message, "Conquer in this Sign." Constantine, a devotee of the sun-god Mithra, had always been a monotheist and his subsequent victory convinced him that Christianity was the purest form of monotheism. From this time onwards, until his death in AD 337, Constantine consistently declared his faith in Christianity and supported it in every way.[1]

The "Rescript of Milan" (AD 312) accorded to Christianity full equality with other religions of the Empire. By AD 380, under the Emperor Theodosius, Christianity became the state religion, and from 381 onwards, conversion to paganism became a punishable offense.[2] This institutionalization of Christianity as a state religion is an event with ramifications which are still being unravelled.

Richard McBrien has written that with this great turning-point "a division between clergy and laity began to develop"; he talks of "the transformation of the clergy into a kind of civil service."[3] There is obviously an element of truth in this observation, but it is not correct to think that the clergy-laity distinction is something that occurred only in the fourth century. Kenan Osborne sees the year AD 200, rather than the Constantinian period, as the crucial turning-point of this era. By AD 200 the "bishop" (*episkopos*) has already emerged as the major leader of the Christian community — assisted by his "council of presbyters" (*presbyterion*) and his deacons.[4] It is to this pre-Nicene development, and to the new tendency of talk of a ministerial "priesthood," that we must now turn our attention.

2. The Emergence of the Tripartite Pattern for Ministry

The most striking feature of this period is the universal, rapid and seemingly unchallenged emergence of the traditional tripartite ministerial structure of bishop, presbyter, and deacon. Even Schillebeeckx agrees that it argues for the "early Catholicizing" of the Church.[5]

Clement of Rome (d. 100?) rejects the Corinthians' claims that they were able to eject from office men who had been "commissioned by the Apostles (or by other reputable persons at a later date) with the full consent of the Church," and who had since been "serving Christ's flock in a humble, peaceable and disinterested way" (*1 Clem* 44).[6] The Church in Rome supported the Jewish practice, namely that "presbyters" held office for life, unless they committed some grave fault.

Ignatius of Antioch (d. 107?) emphasizes that there is "one" leader: the bishop. But the bishop finds his support in the council of the presbyters (*Smyrnaeans* 8:1; *Ephesians* 4:1). Deacons serve the bishop directly (*Philadelphians* 11:1). Women also held some office: Pliny the Younger in AD 112 writes from Bithynia that he tortured two *ministrae* (deaconesses?).[7]

The presbyterate seems to have been a prominent agency for directing and nurturing early communities founded by Jewish

Christians (Ac 11:29-30, 14:23). [8] Another pattern, which seems to have been more common in Hellenistic communities, derived from the practice of having a single designated person in charge (2 Cor 8:16-20; Ph 1:1).

As the convergence of these patterns began, Bernard Cooke writes that the presbyters seem to have acted as a corporate counselling body, while the executive role of directing the community rested with the "bishop" (*episkopos*), assisted by the deacons.[9] Cyprian of Carthage (d. 258) reveals the cooperative nature of ecclesiastical authority, as he understood it, when writing to his presbyters and deacons that "I am determined to do nothing on the basis of my own opinion alone, without your advice and the consent of the people."[10]

By the end of the second century this tripartite structure seems to have been firmly established throughout the Church.[11] The bishop has become

> "the center and pivot of the whole community. He holds the place of God in relation to his people; he is their father after God, their mediator with God, their high priest, their leader and king."[12]

This remarkable stabilizing of ministers was prompted by several factors.

(i) The Delay of the Parousia

The Church in its earliest stages consisted of relatively small and closely-knit communities which could depend on strongly personal and charismatic direction. But within a short time rapid growth set up new demands. And as the initial generations began to realize that the Second Coming of Christ might not be as imminent as was originally expected, they began to organize themselves on a more long-term basis.[13]

In a subtle manner the Church became more "settled."[14] It became more accepted as part of the social scene — even when such "recognition" took the form of persecution! It was natural that when non-Christians wanted to have any dealings with the community, or if they wanted to learn more about this new "Way," they would have wanted to find out who the "leaders" were. Christianity did not lose the notion of being a Spirit-filled community, but saw the Spirit as now providing for the needs of the Church by working increasingly through more structured agencies.

(ii) The Need to Preserve Orthodoxy

This attachment of the Spirit's workings to the role of the clergy helped the Church to face the increasingly urgent need to distinguish between true and false teaching, especially as raised by the popularity of Gnostic teachers and Montanist prophets. In the primitive Church the Spirit spoke to the community through prophets and teachers as well as through the presbyters and "bishops" (episkopoi). But now, in the face of widely varying interpretations, there was a pressing need for people to know precisely whom they should trust.

The bishops very soon emerge as the supreme teachers of the faith in their communities; even the Pastoral Epistles point in this direction (eg. 1 Tm 1:3-4), and Ignatius of Antioch (d. 107) clearly believes that he possesses prophetic inspiration as part of the Spirit's support to him in his pastoral function.[15] At the end of the second century Irenaeus (d. ca. 202) had spoken of the charism of truth attached to the bishop's teaching; and in the third century Cyprian (d. 258) was laying explicit claim to the kind of direct divine guidance usually associated with the gift of prophecy.[16] This no doubt explains the rather rapid disappearance of "prophets" within the Church at this time, and led to a fusion of episcopal and teaching offices. The great teacher, Origen of Alexandria (d. 254?), firmly believed that teaching in the Church belonged to the clergy, even though he himself was not ordained during a good part of his own career.[17]

One rather important weapon in the bishops' arsenal was their claim to be in the apostolic succession: it enabled them to counter Gnostic speculations with the objective reality of the Christ mystery. When Clement wrote to support the presbyters of Corinth (ca. 96), part of his argument had been the claim that the Apostles themselves had directed that bishops and presbyters should be appointed to succeed them in caring for the churches (*1 Clem* 42-44)[18] This notion was late stressed by Irenaeus of Lyons, and with some success since the Gnostics, especially, valued the idea of an uninterrupted succession from master to disciple.[19]

(iii) The Emergence of the Idea of the "Great Church"

The historical evidence seems to suggest that the emergence of a clerical "class" was primarily a response to the needs of an expanding Christianity.[20] As the Church grew in size, and the complexity of its community life developed, bishops with their deacons and presbyters became drawn into full-time ecclesiastical employment. By the end of the third century there is in the larger population centers an established pattern of clergy who are already seen as "official" Christians — in contrast to the remainder of the faithful. Canon 3 of the Council of Ancyra (314) and canon 27 of the Council of Elvira (ca. 305) both distinguish "clergy" from "laity."[21]

One consequence of this, especially as the role of the bishop becomes more central, is that the ties of bishops with one another became important. From a very early stage, there is a concerted effort by those in authority to preserve unity not just within each community, but also within "the great Church." The Letters of Paul himself (eg. 1 Cor 4:17, 7:17), Clement's First Letter to the Corinthians, and the Letters of Ignatius of Antioch, all bear ample witness to this concern. Thus, virtually from the beginning, the notion of a world-wide community, symbolized by this bond among all the bishops, came into common acceptance.

(iv) The Financial Factor

During the third century one very practical factor which added considerable weight to the bishop's authority was his financial oversight of the community's funds — which were used for helping widows and the poor, and for paying the ministers. The bishops of powerful cities like Rome or Alexandria became especially important — and also assumed a responsibility for other churches in the region.

André Lemaire notes that during this period the presbyter's role as counsellor to the bishop diminished: presbyters concelebrated with him less frequently because they had to preside at satellite centers. But the deacons, whose number was often still limited to seven, became more powerful. They distributed aid to the poor, made appointments for those who wished to see the bishop, and were paid the same salary as presbyters. Deaconesses, whose ministry was restricted to working with women, generally survive this period only in the East where the worlds of male and female were far more strictly separated than in the West.[22]

Eusebius of Caesarea (AD 265-340) writes that at the time of Pope Cornelius the Church in Rome was paying a stipend to 46 presbyters, 7 deacons, 7 sub-deacons, 42 acolytes, 52 exorcists-readers-janitors, and 1500 widows and poor people.[23] These figures give some idea of how complicated the ministerial structure had already become. Around AD 250 in Rome there were about 50,000 Christians out of a population of one million. The other great centers, such as Carthage, Alexandria, Antioch and Ephesus must have had equally large Christian populations.[24]

For these reasons alone, non-Christian civil officials were already dealing in the third century with the "officialdom" of the Christian Church. All the indications are that the dichotomy between clergy and laity, which would become far more evident in later centuries, was already well established long before the time of Constantine.[25]

3. *The Sacerdotalizing of Language*

(i) *The Notion of a Ministerial "Priesthood"*

As we move out of the apostolic period, there is still a striking absence of cultic language when referring to Christian worship or ministers. However, the early communities quickly developed a number of ritualized actions which were identifiably similar from one community to another. The most important of these were the Eucharist, baptism, the "laying on of hands" for ministerial ordination, and a little later the ceremonies of the exomologesis (the public reconciliation of penitents). By sometime in the second century there was universal recognition that presidency over such ritual acts was part of the function attached to those called "priests."[26]

Use of "priest" (*hiereus*) to designate the presbyter seems to be almost totally lacking during the entire ante-Nicene period, but one fairly significant exception is the statement in the early third century *Apostolic Tradition* (para. 9), which states that the deacon is ordained "not into the priesthood, but into the service of the bishop."[27] Passages in the *Didascalia* and in Cyprian also suggest that the presbyters share in the "priesthood" (*sacerdotium*) with the bishop, but the term "priest" is not explicitly applied to them.[28]

Thus bishops and presbyters eventually formed a sacral group within the Church. They had special functions reserved to them, at least from early in the second century, and they also had a position of dignity that had to do with special association with the divine.[29] What soon emerges is the understanding that if the bishop himself was not able to carry out some responsibility, the presbyter was the proper agent to be appointed in his stead. As the notion of *sacerdotium* gradually emerges it seems always assumed that presbyters were included in this term — yet not the deacons, despite their recognized function as liturgical assistants.[30]

(ii) The Significance of the Eucharist

By the end of the third century, both East and West possess a fully developed notion of Christian ministerial priesthood, shared in different levels of dignity by bishops and presbyters. This cultic dimenion will become more and more pronounced as the understanding of the Eucharist evolves in the post-Constantinian era and in subsequent anti-Arian reactions.[31]

Whereas in earlier times the term "overseer" (*episkopos*) described far better than "priest" (*hiereus*) the function of the leader of the community, the cultic aspects of his role now begin to take precedence. When Cyprian (ca. AD 250) writes giving the reasons why bishops should remain with their people despite the dangers of persecution, the reasons have to do almost exclusively with liturgical activity.[32]

Edward Schillebeeckx, trying to challenge the clerical monopoly on liturgical leadership, maintains that "in the ancient Church the whole of the believing community concelebrated, albeit under the leadership of the one who presided over the community."[33] David Power argues similarly that the Eucharist must be seen as

> "the worship of the Church gathered in faith and love, and not as an act of the ordained priest in virtue of a divine power proper to himself and of a public office that he holds by divine institution and transmission."[34]

Schillebeeckx goes on to explain that

> "the 'I' of the president never solely, or predominantly, indicated the subject of the celebrant of the Eucharist. . . . The people celebrates, and the priest presides simply as the servant of all."[35]

Patristic scholar Henri Crouzel rejects Schillebeeckx's suggestion (and Power's also, by implication). He quotes Tertullian (d. 220+) in *De Virginibus Velandis*: "A woman is not permitted to speak in Church, nor to teach, nor to baptize, *nor to offer the Eucharist.* . . ." If what Schillebeeckx states is correct, it would seem that Tertullian was excluding women from the Eucharistic assembly! In fact it is clear that, at least in Tertullian's view, it is only the ministers who "offer" the Eucharist.[36]

Similarly, canon 1 of the Council of Ancyra (314), talking of priests who had apostatized during persecution but had then made a sincere repentance, stated that they could be readmitted to the Eucharist, but "they are not able *to offer* (the Eucharist), nor to give the homily, nor to fill any sacerdotal role."[37] Thus once again, the work of "offering" is not being applied to the laity present but only to the president and his concelebrants. Crouzel observes that many other texts could be used to challenge Schillebeeckx's position.[38]

(iii) The Influence of Old Testament Thought

One the most potent forces in this "cultifying" of Christianity was the influence of Old Testament precedents. In New Testament times there had been a conscious struggle against the Judaizing tendency to impose the Jewish law, and a deliberate break with the official Jewish ritual and priesthood. Bernard Cooke suggests that this consciousness of the radical newness of the Gospel, which so marked the primitive communities, was lost at some very early stage in the historical evolution of Christianity.[39]

The sociological explanation for this development is very clear. Ordinary people saw the bishop doing very much what Old Testament priests did: namely, presiding over official prayers. This "sacerdotal current" becomes stronger all through the third century. Schillebeeckx claims that "Cyprian (d. 258) was one of the first to have a clear predilection for the Old Testament priestly sacrificial terminology." He says that this practice gradually grew, but "at first in an allegorical sense."[40]

Crouzel believes that the process was far more complex than either Cooke or Schillebeeckx suggest. Clement was already using

Old Testament imagery at the end of the first century (e.g. *1 Clem* 40).[41] And to talk of their use of Old Testament sources as being merely "allegorical" can be misleading. Allegory suggests a comparison between two disparate objects which may not be very closely connected in reality. But the New Testament writers and the earliest Christians lived within a "Platonic" world-view. For them, the Old Testament was the "type," or "shadow," whose full reality was then made manifest in the New Testament. The two are linked ontologically, and not just logically. The Eucharist was "foreshadowed" by the offerings made in the Old Testament, and what the Jewish "priesthood" was trying to achieve was perfected in the New Dispensation. Thus the earliest Christians tried to highlight both the similarities as well as the differences between the Old and the New — and for us to lose a sense of this very nuanced perspective is to misrepresent their position.[42]

(iv) The Practice of Celibacy

Another factor distinguishing clergy from laity was the practice of celibacy — although this would become far more widespread in later centuries. Edward Schillebeeckx has written that, prior to the law of celibacy promulgated at the Second Lateran Council in 1139, there was only "a long history in which there was simply a law of abstinence, applying to married priests."[43] In fact, however, laws concerning celibacy for clergy (and not simply abstinence) date from as early as the councils of Ancyra and Neocaesarea, both prior to Nicaea in AD 325.[44] Schillebeeckx also claims that "the dominant reason," and "the all-decisive and sole motive" for clerical celibacy was a "ritual purity," which in so many cultures demands that one abstain from sexual intercourse before approaching the divine mystery.[45] Henri Crouzel however objects that the motives proposed by the Fathers are far more diverse: some stress evangelical simplicity and the example of Christ himself; others ritual purity, as Schillebeeckx suggests; some will later link clerical celibacy with that of monks and religious whom the clergy are expected to support and inspire; others derive it from their own Platonic or Stoic world-views. But the point Crouzel emphasizes is that it is not historically correct to trace the celibacy of the clergy to any one "dominant reason."[46]

4. The "Source" of Authority within the Pre-Nicene Church

(i) Does Authority Reside in the "Office" or in the "Person"?

The story of Peter's denunciation of Ananias and Sapphira (Ac 5:1-11) reflects the belief of the early Church that judgment could be passed rather effectively (!) by at least some who held positions of authority. An interesting question to consider in passing, because of its later implications, is whether this ministerial authority was believed to come from the "office," or from some other source. That is, does an ordained minister possess an "authority" which comes with his office, and which thus distinguishes him from a non-ordained lay-person who may in fact be doing virtually identical pastoral work?

The earliest evidence would suggest that the authority came not from the office, but from the person himself. The usual practice was to look for those already endowed by the Spirit with the gifts necessary for episcopal, presbyteral or diaconal responsibility — and then to recognize these gifts by ordaining the man concerned.[47] The selection of Ambrose as bishop of Milan (AD 374) is an obvious example of this. But centuries prior to this Paul had already given Timothy and Titus very detailed instructions about the sorts of qualities they were to look for in men they chose to be leaders (*episkopoi/presbyteroi*) (1 Tm 3:1-13; Tt 1:5-9).

Hippolytus (d. ca. 236) had also stated in his *Apostolic Tradition* (10:1) that "if a confessor has been in chains in prison for the Name, hands are not laid on him for the diaconate or the presbyterate; for he has the dignity of the presbyterate by his confession."[48]

Such a recommendation suggests that ordination was seen as a recognition of the action of the Spirit already present, and therefore, perhaps, as somewhat superfluous. Schillebeeckx concludes, referring specifically to the Church in Africa in the middle of the third century, that

> "*the rite of ordination of a bishop consists in the election by the people....* This is followed by the laying on of hands by the neighboring bishops, which confirms the *ordinatio*."

He goes on to note that "only after this is the appointment legally complete (*ordinatio iure perfecta*)"[49] — but Schillebeeckx certainly gives the impression that he does not see such legal niceties as being of the essence of the ceremony. Schillebeeckx's line of thinking is obviously in marked contrast to the traditional view which would trust the Spirit at the time of ordination to inspire the candidates with the gifts needed for their particular ministry.[50]

(ii) The Necessity of Ordination

Bernard Cooke maintains, in contrast to Schillebeeckx, that the fact that the community selected their own bishop never implied that they thereby bestowed authority on him. Although they had discerned the gifts with which the Spirit had already endowed the candidate, this process of designation was not complete until the candidate had received "ordination" from at least one (and preferably more) of his fellow-bishops by the "laying on of hands." Of these two realities — election by the people, and consecration by episcopal colleagues — the latter, certainly by the end of the second century, was the essential.[51]

The situation concerning "confessors" — to which Hippolytus refers — is quite exceptional, and never applied in the case of candidates for the episcopate. Cooke notes that, while sanctity was always seen as necessary for sacerdotal effectiveness, it is interesting that no writer of the period ever "argued" that personal holiness alone could endow anyone with ministerial authority. On the contrary, the whole period bears witness to an enduring conviction that specialized ministry in the Church flows from some kind of ministerial charism that is distinct from grace and yet either recognized or granted in ordination.[52]

Those who had been ordained were believed to hold authority because God himself somehow acted through them (almost "vertically" as it were) on the occasion of their occupying the office. Ignatius, Irenaeus, and Clement of Alexandria all develop the idea that Christ himself still abides with his Church, working actively and authoritatively through his ministers — although this notion of a "real presence" of Christ in his ordained ministers became more nuanced during the next few centuries as the great trinitarian controversies led to a greater emphasis on the transcendence of Christ as the Son of God.[53]

5. Conclusion

However, the point we have been trying to make throughout this chapter is simply that the tripartite structure of ministry, and the use of sacerdotal terms to describe the episcopate and the presbyterate, had emerged long before the time of Constantine when the Church began her lengthy entanglement with the structures of Empire. How the priesthood evolved during these subsequent centuries is the issue we must now consider.

CHAPTER VII

Medieval Influences on Understanding of Priesthood

A s we continue to prepare the ground for some consideration of a contemporary theology of the presbyterate, it is important that we make mention of some of the more significant influences on the priesthood as it evolved through the medieval period.

1. The Clergy-Laity Distinction Accentuated

Although the distinction between clergy and laity had appeared very early, and certainly by the beginning of the second century — as in Clement of Rome and Ignatius — it was rapidly accentuated after Constantine. The Christian clergy, like their pagan predecessors, were granted exemption from civil and military service, from subjection to civil courts, and from taxation.[1] This grant was honored by Constantine's successors, and passed into the Theodosian and Justinian codes, and from them into the feudal legislation of the Merovingian and Carolingian periods. Quite effectively, a clerical society paralleling civil society came into being — with its own courts, its own laws and its own officials.[2]

Bernard Cooke also makes the point that bishops received an

entirely new source of authority with Constantine's decree that they could preside over courts. Many bishops could undoubtedly see the basic unrelatedness of such civil judgments to their episcopal responsibilities: Ambrose, Augustine and Basil all complain about the time involved! But it is still likely that being a "judge" became a prominent element in their own self-identity. From Leo I onwards (though anticipated by many of the Fathers) the basis for all episcopal claims to authority was attributed to the "power of the keys" that was given to Peter.[3]

Although the bishops become increasingly caught up in the work of administration, this period also sees a rapid crystallization of their ceremonial role in the liturgy. While the "priesthood" (*sacerdotium*) was now seen to include also the presbyters, the view of the bishop as "the" priest is so widespread that "priest" (*sacerdos*), when used without further qualification, always refers to the bishop.[4] It is probable that with the post-Constantinian shift of the liturgy into larger churches, the ceremonial role of the bishop simply became more observable.

Moreover, this was an era of outstanding bishops. At the great councils of Nicaea (325), Constantinople (381), Ephesus (431), and Chalcedon (451) all the outstanding theologians were bishops. Men like Ambrose of Milan wielded a personal influence far beyond that which flowed intrinsically from their episcopal office.

Yet the presbyterate was not completely eclipsed by the success with which the episcopacy tried to exploit the opportunities presented by the post-Nicene situation. Their most famous and influential spokesperson was Jerome, who argued that the bishop was merely a priest who had the additional power of being able to ordain other priests.[5] This debate had its theological repercussions in the Middle Ages when theologians refused to see the episcopacy as an order distinct from the presbyterate.[6]

Clerical celibacy became a critical symbol of the otherworldliness of the clergy, and of their independence of the affairs of ordinary life — although the councils of Nicaea (325) and Seleucia (486) reacted strongly against any attempt to make it compulsory.[7] Even in the East, where clerical celibacy was not imposed, the Justinian Code urges a celibate episcopacy:

"It cannot be that he, when occupied with life's cares (which children particularly provide for parents), should have his entire interest and good intentions about the divine liturgy and ecclesiastical affairs."[8]

From as early as Leo I (d. 461), one finds references to the distinction between a laity whose role was to "listen," and a hierarchy whose responsibility was to "teach": the *ecclesia discens* and the *ecclesia docens*. By the time of Gregory I (d. 604) this had become a commonplace assumption. Alcuin (d. 804), the theologian in the court of Charlemagne, writes that

"The priest's role is gently to advise the people of God as to what they should do; the people's role is humbly to listen to what the priest advises."[9]

2. The Growing Influence of Monasticism

The Constantinian recognition also meant that the Church was faced with the influx of thousands of new members who were anxious to be known as adherents of the "state religion." The consequence of so many "political" conversions was a tapering-off of spiritual vitality within the Church itself — and a resulting tendency for some to try to live the Gospel more seriously within the eremitical and later the monastic life.

Through the centuries, monasticism has wielded a profound influence on the way the clergy have lived. Many of the great bishops, whose thinking about their office helped to shape the Church's understanding of the episcopacy and the presbyterate, were drawn from the monasteries.

The fourth and fifth centuries do not give us the strong monastic influence that will come later with Gregory I (d. 604), with the Celtic missionaries of the seventh and eighth centuries, and with Gregory VII (d. 1085). But they do give us the great bishop Basil, the father of eastern monasticism; and Athanasius and Cyril of Alexandria, both deeply touched by Egyptian monasticism; and in the West bishops like Ambrose and Augustine, who tried to adapt monastic patterns of communal life to suit their "secular" clergy.

In the High Middle Ages, bishops and abbots were considered ecclesiastical peers. While some 400 bishops attended Lateran Council IV in 1215 — the greatest and most effective of the medieval councils — their number was dwarfed by the 800 or so abbots who were also present.[10] Thus it was natural to expect from both a similar level of "holiness" — with the result that the ideal of monastic life was transferred to the life of the clergy in general.[11]

Benedict was one of the great teachers of western Europe. Although many bishops ran excellent schools — and during the Carolingian era it was recommended that a school be attached to every "parish"! — it was the monasteries which had the wealth of manpower, the continuity of personnel, and in time the more valuable libraries.

It was from this monastic movement that there emerged the great medieval reforming drive which would strengthen the spiritual life of the Western Church, and especially that of its clergy. But the seeds of later difficulties were already present — in the pro-Roman alignment of the orders, in their eventual exemption from episcopal control, and in the deeper intellectual monopoly of Christian tradition by institutionalized religious life.[12]

3. The Sacraments Become Simplified and "Ritualized"

Almost all the sacraments underwent fairly dramatic changes in the wake of the Constantinian settlement, and this in turn certainly influenced the way in which the priesthood was perceived.

With *baptism*, for example, the adoption in AD 380 of Christianity as the "official" religion of the Roman Empire meant that the old practice of the catechumenate had to be drastically simplified to cope with the vast numbers of conversions. And because baptism was seen to be so important, it had already become the custom to baptize children while still babies. When Rome fell to the Germanic tribes in the fifth century, monks moved out to convert the new settlers. Huge numbers were baptized *en masse* — but with the simple rite of infant baptism which was now the only one the monks knew, because there had been only babies to baptize in the formerly Christian Empire![13]

The importation of the Irish custom of *penance* also had a bearing on the practice of the priestly ministry. In contrast with the classic discipline of the exomologesis, the Irish monks encouraged frequent confession of sins to be followed by absolution given by a priest. Despite strong opposition from official Church decrees, this practice had by the twelfth century become the norm — and naturally altered people's appreciation of what priests were supposed to do.[14]

But it was especially with regard to the *Eucharist* that people's understanding changed quite dramatically. Once Christianity became permitted within the Empire (AD 313) churches began to be built, and the clergy donned a distinctive dress. The sheer size of some of the new basilicas meant that the liturgy became more often something merely to watch: a divine spectacle rather than a commemorative meal. Factors such as the Patristic emphasis on the Mass as a sacrifice, the reaction against Arianism, and the severity of penances given in "private" confessions, all contributed towards a trend away from receiving holy communion. The fourth and fifth centuries saw the Mass less as a shared offering of thanksgiving, and more as an atonement offering for sin. Moreover the general populace, swelled by the Germanic conversions, tended to see the Mass more as a traditional religious ritual than as something calling for personal involvement.[15]

4. The Development of the "Private" Mass

The greatest single change in the West was the development of the "private" Mass. During the early centuries, the Mass had always been communitarian, and led by the bishop. But as the idea of the liturgy as sacrifice became dominant, the Eucharist tended to be offered for special reasons — such as for good weather, or for peace, and then for weddings, funerals and anniversaries. By the sixth century, these "votive" Masses outnumbered the regular liturgies.[16]

"Private" Masses, with no congregation at all, began in the monasteries. The monks had originally been laymen, but from the sixth century on, when they were sent out as missionaries to northern Europe, they tended to be ordained priests so that they would be able to take with them the Mass and the sacraments. Soon the monasteries were filled with many priests, saying Masses daily and privately, so that the "low" Mass became the norm through most of Europe — offered out of devotion, or for some special intention, even when no congregation was present. This practice was intensified by the giving of stipends and the establishment of Mass-saying benefices. Because most of these monks had no pastoral responsibilities, the priest came to be seen more and more as the one who was wholly concerned with the Mass and with offering sacrifice — without necessarily being attached to the Christian community.[17]

A further factor contributing to the priestly "privatizing" of the Mass was the retention of Latin as the sole liturgical language in the West. The Mass became something for the laity to watch rather than to be personally involved in. The priest "said Mass" on behalf of the people; the Mass was a sacrifice in which the Body and Blood of Christ were made present, were offered for their sins, and were consumed as holy communion.

5. The Effects of the Reaction Against Arianism

Part of the Patristic reaction to Arianism had been to emphasize the actual presence of God in the Eucharist. Augustine insisted, "No one should eat this flesh if he has not first adored it" (*On the Psalms* 98, 9).[18] One negative consequence of this emphasis was that laypeople began to have doubts about their worthiness to receive communion. John Chrysostom, who himself had called the altar "a table of holy fear," later complained: "We stand before the altar in vain; no one comes to partake" (*Homily on Ephesians* 3, 4).[19]

Through curious accidents of history this anti-Arian emphasis became more and more pervasive throughout the Church. In the earliest centuries, the rubrics retained great local variation: Spain, England, and France all had liturgical styles very different from Rome. The Roman liturgy had been somewhat simplified in the reforms made by Pope Gregory, but not elsewhere. In the seventh century, however, Roman missionaries took the Gregorian sacramentary to England, where it soon supplanted the older Celtic liturgy.

Then in AD 754 Pepin became King of the Franks. His son Charlemagne, in 784, imposed the Roman liturgy in an attempt to unify the Empire. However it was adapted by Alcuin of York, the chief scholar at the court, to the needs of the priests who were saying low Masses. Eventually only Milan retained a patristic liturgy — that of Ambrose.[20]

Because some of the southern tribes of Gaul had been Arian in the fourth and fifth centuries, the Gallic bishops emphasized the divine presence of Christ, and this "flavor" was now transferred to the Roman Mass. A ritual confession of sinfulness was added to the introductory rite, and the priests genuflected in adoration after the consecration. The canon was whispered — to protect and honor the mystery. The laity were discouraged from receiving communion too frequently, and certainly not with their hands! The creed of Nicaea was inserted between the Gospel and the Canon. The priest often prayed now with his hands joined in supplication, rather than outstretched in thanksgiving. Because the Mass was seen primarily as a sacrifice the sermon seemed to be increasingly superfluous.

By the tenth century, the cultural life of Rome was so low that it could not produce its own books — so the liturgy of northern

Europe now became the new liturgy of Rome by way of the liturgical books imported from the northern monasteries. The "Mass," in Church councils and canon law, was now seen as:

- — a liturgy of sacrifice and supplication (rather than communion and thanksgiving);
- — something performed by a single priest (rather than by a bishop surrounded by his college of presbyters);
- — something done "for" (rather than "with") the people;
- — spoken in Latin (rather than any living language);
- — whispered silently (rather than proclaimed aloud).[21]

These changes were also reflected in architecture. As early as the fourth century the notion that the priest "led" the people to God meant that altars were placed against the rear wall. This allowed the people to stand "behind" their leader, rather than "around" the altar for a sacrifice which they "all" offered. The people now "watched," and from an increasing distance, separated firstly by monastic stalls, then by ornate sanctuary screens, and then by communion rails at which people could kneel. With the twelfth century discovery of the pointed arch, cathedrals became even more spacious, and the people more distant.

The liturgy, which had once been a communal prayer, was now a clerical ritual, isolated by distance and language. Instead of casting light on the Christian mysteries, the liturgy itself had now become a mystery![22]

6. The Priesthood Increasingly Bound to the Eucharist

Throughout the entire period of the Middle Ages there was never any doubt that the supreme expression of the Church's life came not in political or intellectual triumph, but in the celebration of the Eucharist: "The noblest action in the Church is the simple consecration of the Eucharist" (Duns Scotus).[23] And it was for the celebration of the Eucharist that priests were primarily ordained, according to the constant teaching of medieval theologians and canonists.[24]

In the fourteenth century the "Black Death" took 25 million lives as the bubonic and subsequent plagues swept across Europe. Culture went into decline, trade dwindled, schools closed, and the great medieval theological renaissance came to an abrupt end.[25] In later centuries most treatises on the Mass were more concerned with canonical validity rather than with finer points of theology. The Mass had become an ecclesiastical ritual, with certain minimum requirements which had to be met in order to "produce" the sacrament. This meant that the Eucharistic celebrant had become before all else the agent for transubstantiation.

Receiving communion became increasingly rare for the laity, but worship of the "Blessed Sacrament" continued to grow. The feast of Corpus Christi, which had been established in France in the thirteenth century, spread rapidly throughout the Church.[26]

The Mass was now believed to produce spiritual benefits whether or not it was devoutly attended. "Private" Masses abounded: in December 1521 the City Council of Wittenberg proposed to the Elector Frederick that there be some control over "endowed Masses," since "many priests must say 5, 6, 7 or even more Masses daily."[27] By the fifteenth century, thousands of "altar priests" were being ordained just to say Masses — for the souls in purgatory, and for all manner of special intentions. The ratio of clergy to laity rose to almost 2% of the general population.[28] A city like Melbourne which in 1989 might have up to 2,000,000 Christians would have had 40,000 clerics! Nevertheless, as David Power notes, the impression one gains is not one of the clergy dominating the people, but rather of the people demanding these services of the clergy.[29]

By the end of the Middle Ages, the Mass had been transformed from an act of public worship into a form of clerical prayer. It had become "a good work," performed by priests for the spiritual benefit of the Church. This was the Mass the Reformers knew, and which many of them rejected.[30]

CHAPTER VIII

The Sixteenth Century

1. Introduction

Bernard Cooke writes that, apart from the formative second and third centuries, "no period of history is more critical to a study of Christian ministry and priesthood than is the sixteenth century."[1] André Lemaire agrees that much Reformation controversy centered around the question of ministry.[2] David Power reminds us that the principal magisterial statements on the ministerial priesthood still come from the Councils of Trent and Vatican II.[3] And the issues are far from dead. Alasdair Heron claims that ecumenical discussion today still stumbles at that point "where the Roman Catholic conception of the priesthood intersects with Eucharistic theology in the doctrine of the sacrifice of the Mass."[4] At the time of the Reformation, debates over the nature of the priesthood arose as part of a more basic challenge to the whole religious system of the time.[5]

2. The Call to Reform

For decades prior to the actual outbreak of the Reformation there had been continuing calls for reform "in head and members." At the heart of this movement was the urgent and obvious need among the ordinary people for dedicated spiritual leaders.

Despite official urgings and legislation, the level of theological education among both clergy and laity remained low.[6] The situation was not caused by any shortage of priests. But there was a general ignorance of Latin, catechesis was often lacking, attendance at Mass perfunctory, penance administered only "at the hour of death," and superstition was widespread.[7]

Bernard Cooke stresses that the contemporary discontent was to some extent the result of a clash of deeper intellectual movements. The new Humanism found expression in a more critical approach to the study of the Scriptures, prompted by a return to the original Greek and Hebrew texts. There was also a move to re-examine the writings of the Fathers, and a switch away from the allegorical and syllogistic methods which had begun to characterize Scholasticism.[8]

These changes were further complicated by the movement of Europe into the "modern" world with the rise of the *bourgeoisie*. As older aristocratic and feudal patterns of civilization were displaced, there was a reluctance on the part of Church officials to accept the growth of vernacular languages or national cultures.

(i) Martin Luther

Things came to a head when Albrecht of Brandenburg, brother of the Elector Joachim, was elected Bishop of Halberstadt, Archbishop of Magdeburg, and then Archbishop of Mainz as well. For the dispensation to hold three dioceses, Albrecht had to pay the Curia 10,000 golden ducats, plus another 14,000 to cover overdue pallium taxes for the See of Mainz. To meet these costs an agreement was made with the Curia to allow the "Peter's Indulgence" to be preached — on the understanding that half the money so raised would go to Albrecht, and the other half towards the construction of St. Peter's.[9]

When the Dominican Johann Tetzel began preaching indulgences, the young theology professor Martin Luther complained to his archbishop.

"Papal indulgences for the building of St. Peter's are being
hawked about under your illustrious sanction. . . I regret
that the faithful have conceived some erroneous notions
about them. These unhappy souls believe that if they buy a
letter of pardon they are sure of their salvation."[10]

On Oct. 31, 1517, he nailed his 95 theses to the door of the castle
church in Wittenberg and announced his intention to hold a
debate on the value of indulgences "for the love and the elucida-
tion of the truth."

After trying several times to persuade Luther to modify his
views, Pope Leo X, on June 15, 1520, issued the Bull of Excom-
munication *Exsurge Domine* in Rome — and Luther replied with
his famous treatises, written during that same year.

(ii) "We Are All Priests Alike"

In his *Appeal to the Christian Nobility of the German Nation*
Luther rejected the clergy-laity distinction, according to which
those exercising spiritual power claimed precedence over the
temporal authority.

"We are all consecrated priests by baptism (1 P 2:9). . . . If a
little company of pious Christian laymen were taken pri-
soners and carried away to a desert . . . and were there to
elect one of them . . . to baptize, to celebrate the Mass, to
absolve and to preach, this man would as truly be a priest
as if all the bishops and all the popes had consecrated
him."

"Since we are all priests alike, no man may . . . take upon
himself without our consent and election, to do that which
we have all alike power to do."

He rejected the whole notion of any permanent priestly
character:

"And if it should happen that a man were appointed to one of these offices and deposed for abuses, he would be just what he was before. . . . Therefore a priest is verily no longer a priest after deposition."[11]

(iii) The Attack on the Sacramental System

Luther followed his political appeal with a doctrinal attack on *The Babylonian Captivity of the Church*. This attacked the whole medieval sacramental system so radically that Erasmus believed it precluded all possibility of peace with the papacy.[12] Luther claimed that only baptism, penance, and Eucharist could really be shown to be instituted by the Lord. Henry VIII earned the title "Defender of the Faith" for his response to this treatise.[13]

Concerning the Lord's Supper, Luther argued for consubstantiation, and dismissed transubstantiation as a Thomistic or Aristotelian fiction. But his main concern was to attack the notion that "the Mass is a good work and a sacrifice." This belief, he claimed, had turned a divine sacrament into "an article of trade" — upon which priests and monks depended for their livelihood. In the midst of all this confusion the divine promise, that "he who believes and is baptized shall be saved," had been forgotten.[14]

Luther's great insight was his rediscovery of the scriptural notion of the "priesthood" of all the baptized.[15] Luther was not opposed to seeing the Lord's Supper as an act of worship — but he saw the "priesthood" exercised in this action as being that of the whole people. Because all Christians were equally "priests" through baptism, they all had an equal power to administer all the sacraments, including the Eucharist.

Luther agreed that within this priestly people, some may be designated to perform "ministries" of word and sacrament — but they were merely doing what anyone else in the community in fact could do. Any such "ordination rite" was merely a ceremony of delegation or appointment, and certainly not a sacrament. It did not confer any priestly character which had not previously been possessed. One consequence of Luther's position is that he never very clearly distinguishes between "priesthood" (common to all the baptized) and "ministry" (the function of the ordained).[16]

(iv) Later Reformation Views

Martin Bucer emphasizes the priesthood of all believers, yet also sees the offices of bishop, presbyter and deacon as "of divine origin."[17] Calvin believed that the ordained ministry does "come from God" and does not grow out of the universal priesthood — yet somewhat paradoxically he also rejects the distinction between clergy and laity.[18] John Wesley later will allow laymen to preach, but insists on ministerial ordination before one may administer the sacraments.[19]

Obviously there is a marked absence of any idea that the ordained person is placed on some special, sacred level of Christian existence. However, almost immediately the minister is seen as some sort of "official" Christian: a situation which still prevails today, although "illogically perhaps," according to Presbyterian Dr. John Nelson in his review of Vatican II's "Decree on the Ministry and Life of Priests."[20] But the minister certainly ceases being seen as a "sacrificing" cultic priest, and tends to be more of a "public functionary" in religious affairs.

(v) The "Private Mass" Repudiated

Luther had often condemned the greed of the clergy, and saw the fundamental abuse as being the "private Mass" system — that is, the belief that a Mass offered by an ordained priest was somehow a meritorious and propitiatory sacrifice, even when only the priest himself received communion. In their frequent attacks on the notion of a virtually infallible *ex opere operato* efficacy, it was usually to this practice that the Reformers were objecting.

In order to repudiate the "private" Mass the Reformers referred back to the need for justification by faith. They claimed that if the Mass could *ex opere operato* take away the sins of the living and the dead, then justification is by the Mass and not by faith.[21] They also saw the Eucharist as essentially a "proclamation" of the death of Christ, calling forth the faith required in order to approach holy communion. Thus they could not see how the Eucharist could be of benefit to non-communicants — and especially to the dead![22] Nor, for the same reason, could they see any point in having the Mass "proclaimed" in Latin.[23]

The Roman Catholic theology of the Mass certainly had become entangled with the computations of the Celtic penitential system — so that "twenty Masses," for example, might compensate for "seven months of penance."[24] Although the merits of Christ on the cross were of infinite value, it was believed that Masses could be repeated for the same intention — because one could never determine either the openness of the recipient to grace, or the devotion at any one time of either the celebrant or the congregation.[25]

It is important to stress, however, that the main Catholic apologists neither used nor defended this rather "quantitative" approach. Instead they spoke of the Mass as a mystical and sacramental offering, wholly related to the Cross, of which it is a memorial. But their theology did depend upon a belief in the real presence of Christ in the Eucharist. Although their explanations differed, they all concurred that Jesus, truly present, was offered to the Father.[26]

(vi) The Role of the Priest-Celebrant

The Protestants saw the Eucharist as a sacrifice of praise and thanksgiving performed in faith. In contrast to this spiritual offering by all the people, Catholics tended to emphasize the act of the priest-celebrant, who consecrated the bread and wine, and then offered them to the Father. David Power notes that all the conciliar arguments for the silent canon and the retention of Latin — namely that they aid the attention and reverence of the priest — manifest a view which saw the Mass as most particularly a prayer of the priest himself.[27]

Somehow, at the very heart of the Mass system, Catholics still found an understanding of sacrifice which they saw as fundamental to Eucharistic theology and practice — but which the Reformers could not accept. The Mass practices of the late Middle Ages were only one part of a whole religious construct. Within this there certainly were exaggerations, gross impieties, clerical negligence, and superstition. But there is still disagreement as to the basic health or otherwise of the whole system. Power claims that, despite the accusations of the Reformers, it did give coherence, meaning, and even hope — in an era when life was often precarious, and death always imminent.[28] The central question is whether Protestant and Roman Catholic reformers were really trying to salvage the same basic faith.

The Protestants saw as "abuses" the daily offering of the sacrifice of the Mass for the sins of the living and the dead; the practice of making payment for the celebration of Masses; the reception of communion by the priest alone; and the use of a "foreign" language.[29] The Protestant understanding of the Eucharist as a promise of God's forgiveness saw these practices as a blasphemous denial of the unique sacrifice of propitiation offered once and for all by Christ at Calvary.[30]

3. The Response of the Council of Trent (1545-1563)

Although too late to prevent the split between Catholicism and Protestantism, the Council of Trent did prove to be a very effective instrument for implementing much needed reforms within Catholicism. Its overwhelming bias was pastoral. Lectureships in Holy Scripture were to be established (Session V, ch. I). Bishops were instructed to reside within their dioceses (S. VI, ch. I), and were forbidden to hold more than one diocese (S. VII, ch. II). Seminaries were to be established for the proper training of clergy (S. XXIII, ch. XVIII), and parish priests were ordered to explain the Sacred Scriptures to their people at Mass (S. XXIV, ch. VII).[31]

(i) The Priesthood Reaffirmed

In response to Protestant criticisms, however, the Council only stressed even more emphatically the "cultic" nature of the ordained priesthood. Symptomatically, the practice of priests saying Mass without attendant congregations was defended rather than challenged:

> "The holy council . . . does not condemn as illicit those Masses in which the priest alone communicates sacramentally, but rather approves and commends them . . . because they are celebrated by a public minister of the Church." (S. XXII, ch. VI).[32]

Probably the most important statement in its Decree on the Sacrament of Order is its opening clause,

> "*Sacrificium et sacerdotium ita Dei ordinatione coniuncta sunt. . .*" ("Sacrifice and priesthood are thus conjoined by divine ordinance") (S. XXIII, ch. I).[33]

The ordained ministry is, "by divine ordinance," tied to sacrifice. It involves the power of consecrating, offering and administering the Eucharist, and linked to this is the power of absolution.

The Council dismissed Luther's claim that deposed priests could once again become laymen.[34]

> "The holy council justly condemns the opinion of those who say that the priests of the New Testament have only a temporary power. . . . And if anyone should assert that all Christians without distinction are priests of the New Testament . . . he seems to do nothing else than derange the ecclesiastical hierarchy, . . . as if, contrary to the teaching of St. Paul, all are apostles, all prophets, all evangelists, all pastors, all doctors" (S. XXIII, ch. IV).[35]

One constant is the Catholic belief that ordination confers a sacramental spiritual power which permanently distinguishes the priest. And what he does in the Eucharist he does by that power, and not by any delegation from the community. Thus any notion of a common priesthood which denies the essentially hierarchical structure of the Church is rejected. Priesthood is more than simply a "function" that can be given one day and taken away the next. The idea of sacramental character is central.[36]

(ii) "Concerning the Sacrifice of the Mass" (September, 1562)

In talking about the Sacrifice of the Mass itself, the Fathers begin by stating very clearly that redemption is accomplished solely through the Cross — so the Mass must be understood from that perspective (S. XXII, ch. I).

The second chapter connects the doctrine of sacrifice with that of the real presence: thus "the same Christ" who was offered on the cross is contained and immolated in an unbloody manner in the Mass. The Mass, therefore, is a propitiatory sacrifice — but its fruits are accessible only to those who approach God "with a true heart and with upright faith, with fear and reverence, contrite and penitent" (S. XXII, ch. II).[37] This was a response to the Reformers' accusations of automatic *ex opere operato* salvation.[38]

Luther's doctrine of consubstantiation was condemned:

"This holy council declares it anew, that by the consecration of the bread and wine a change is brought about *of the whole substance...*" (S. XIII, ch. IV).[39]

The Fathers give no very clear explanation of the "mechanics" of how the Mass "worked," and precisely how it connected with Calvary — because theologians could come to no agreement on such issues. They therefore do not elucidate on just "how" the Mass benefits both the living and the dead: they simply affirm that it does (S. XXII, ch. II & III).[40]

(iii) Assessing the Council of Trent

David Power argues that the theologians and Fathers at
Trent were really simply trying to defend traditional Catholic
"practice" — that is, the current *status quo*. The "practice" was that
Masses were commonly said for a stipend. The Mass therefore was
seen to consist of a *priestly* offering of propitiation, and this was
believed to be advantageous to all, both the living and the
dead.[41] According to Power, what Trent's dogmas and doctrines
explained was a way of worshiping that took the mediation of the
ordained priest as an essential factor in the celebration of the
Mass.

> "Left without this form of priesthood, it seemed as though
> the Catholic faithful would be left without the possibility of
> benefitting from Christ's once and for all sacrifice."[42]

We should, however, be wary of seeing the defence of
"practice" as being the sole motivation for the conciliar decrees.
The Reformers, after all, felt no reluctance about changing the
"practice" of centuries. And the Fathers themselves also altered
many "practices" — including that which had allowed Albrecht of
Brandenburg to take possession of more than one diocese in the
first place! (S. VII, ch. II).[43]

David Power makes reference to an article in which Piet
Fransen argues that placing something under an anathema was
merely equivalent to placing a curse on people who were disturb-
ing the peace.[44] Fransen argues that it was a strategy to defend
the "customary practices within the Church" (*consuetudines ec-
clesiasticae*).[45] He claims that the Tridentine teaching on sacramental character, for example, amounts to a declaration that such
a belief is "not contrary" to divine revelation — but it does not
mean that such a belief is somehow "intrinsic" to that revelation.[46]

Jean Galot, however, maintains that the theologians at Trent
were preoccupied with more than simply defining what was "current" teaching. In their discussions they often made very clear
distinctions between what was believed to be "erroneous," what

was held to be "heretical," and what was simply proposed as an "opinion."[47]

In considering the topic of sacramental character itself, some theologians held that to deny its existence was heretical; others said that to hold this belief was simply to maintain a "less probable" opinion. But the Council decided by a clear majority that such a view was in fact heretical. Galot concludes that there is nothing to indicate that the Fathers at Trent believed they were there simply to discuss "customary practices": they were trying to decide very specifically whether certain views were, or were not, heretical. This, moreover, is the light in which theologians in subsequent centuries have always read the Council texts.[48]

4. Conclusion

However we may assess the decrees of Trent, the stature of that Council meant that its teachings have exercised a lasting influence on the Catholic understanding of the ordained priesthood.

The consistent use of religious orders to implement the decrees of the Council led to yet another "monastic" revitalization of the priesthood. There was a determined effort to develop a spirituality for the diocesan priest which would be as lofty as, and preferably loftier than, that of religious. At the center of this movement was the so-called "French" School of men such as Pierre de Bérulle, Jean-Jacques Olier, and Vincent de Paul, whose followers were to be so influential in implementing the Council's call to establish seminaries.[49]

The inheritance of Trent was a priesthood that was more than ever linked to cult — *sacrificium et sacerdotium ita Dei ordinatione coniuncta sunt*. The great achievement of the Second Vatican Council, to which we must now turn our attention, was to liberate the presbyterate from the limitations of this definition — and to free the notion of ministerial service in the Church from being exclusively the prerogative of the clergy. It will be in the light of these new perspectives that we must work towards trying to create a contemporary theology of the presbyterate.

CHAPTER IX

The Second Vatican Council (1962-1965)

1. Introduction

Because the First Vatican Council (1869-1870) did not deal with the presbyterate we must move forward into our own century to find an Ecumenical Council once again turning its attention to the priesthood. Vatican II is characterized by a "rediscovery" of sources, and by a distancing of itself from the polemics of the Counter-Reformation. The result is that it tries to integrate Trent into a broader and more coherent tradition. To appreciate fully Vatican II's insights with regard to the presbyterate, it is necessary to have some idea of the developments which had already taken place in the course of the Council before the Fathers turned their attention to this topic.

2. The Dogmatic Constitution on the Church: "Lumen Gentium"

When Pope John XXIII in 1959 announced his intention to call an Ecumenical Council, it was generally presumed that the Church herself would be its major theme. Vatican I had planned a lengthy "Constitution on the Church of Christ," but its deliberations had been cut short by the Franco-Prussian War and the invasion of the Papal States by the Piedmontese armies. Instead of the planned fifteen chapters that Council enacted only four, on the primacy and infallibility of the Pope. When taken on their own, without reference to the planned treatment of bishops and other members of the Church, Avery Dulles notes that these chapters gave a curiously unbalanced picture of the Church as some kind of absolute monarchy.[1]

The balance had been somewhat redressed by subsequent papal teachings, such as Pope Pius XII's encyclical *Mystici Corporis* (1943). However Pope Paul VI in his first encyclical, *Ecclesiam Suam* (1964) agreed that the Church was indeed "the principal object of attention of the Second Vatican Ecumenical Council" (art. 33).[2]

The ecclesiology of the manuals had been dominated by a juridical viewpoint, and focused on the authority structures of the Church. This had come about partly in reaction to the Reformers' preaching of the "hidden" Church of the Predestined. It was in response to such views that Cardinal Bellarmine had made his famous claim that the Church was "as visible and tangible as the union of the Roman people, or the Kingdom of France, or the Republic of Venice"![3]

The original schema for the key "Dogmatic Constitution" on the Church (*Lumen Gentium*) thus predictably laid heavy emphasis on the hierarchical and juridical aspects of the Church. The first three (of twelve) chapters were:

I) The Nature of the Church Militant.

II) The Members of the Church, and the Necessity of the Church for Salvation.

III) The Episcopate as the Highest Grade of the Sacrament of Holy Orders; The Priesthood.[4]

At the First Session (December 1962) the Council Fathers expressed concern that the Mystical Body of Christ and the Roman Catholic Church were being too closely identified. They called for a presentation which would be more biblical, more historical, and more dynamic. That this request was taken seriously can be seen from the number of patristic and scriptural footnotes that appeared in the final documents. Where Trent's Decree on the Sacrament of Orders, for example, had only 10 quotations from the Scriptures, Vatican II's "Decree on the Ministry and Life of Priests" (*Presbyterorum Ordinis*) has 153![5]

The final version of *Lumen Gentium* shows marked changes from the draft initially proposed. Its first five (of eight) chapters are headed as follows:

    I) The Mystery of the Church (1-8)
   II) The People of God (9-17)
 III) The Hierarchical Structure of the Church, with Special Reference to the Episcopate (18-29)
 IV) The Laity (30-38)
  V) The Call of the Whole Church to Holiness (39-42)

In view of our interest in the presbyterate it is important to notice that the Council, with a renewed appreciation of the primordial value of baptism, deals firstly with the whole People of God before considering the hierarchy. It is also significant that the Council had already developed a theology of the episcopate before turning its attention to the presbyterate. These two factors meant that the Fathers could produce a far richer theology of the presbyterate than the Church had now known for many centuries. We will need to look at these two areas before we turn our attention to the presbyterate itself.

3. The People of God: A "Priestly People"

Undoubtedly one of the great achievements of the Council was its retrieval of the "priestly" identity of all the baptized (1 P 2:9). There was considerable discussion at the Council as to how to distinguish the "priestly" laity from the "priestly" hierarchy. The Theological Commission eventually settled on the term "common priesthood" — because it is shared by all the baptized, and is not eliminated in those consecrated to the "ministerial" priesthood.[6] However, to avoid any repetition of Luther's denial of the latter, the Fathers did make the point that the two priesthoods "differ from one another in essence and not only in degree" (LG 10).[7]

But the first concern of the Council was to acknowledge that the whole Mystical Body comprises a holy and royal priesthood. "Hence there is no member who does not have a part in the mission of the whole Body" (PO 2).[8] All are empowered to enter the sanctuary by the blood of Jesus, to speak freely with the Father, and to offer their lives to him in sacrifice.

To appreciate fully this notion of the common priesthood, Yves Congar notes that it is important to recall the uniqueness of the Christian cult. Jesus's own ministry stands very much in the line of the prophets — who were often pitted against the priesthood. With the Levitical priesthood, "the sacred" was something "set apart" — and this "apartness" was preserved by layers of detailed legislation. Many good Israelites undoubtedly followed these prescriptions faithfully and joined the offering of their own lives to their temple sacrifices, but the constant danger in this priestly faith was formalism.[9]

The prophets ceaselessly reminded the people that there must be no separation between secular and sacred:

> "I am sick of holocausts of rams
> and the fat of calves.
> The blood of bulls and of goats revolts me.
> . . . Cease to do evil. Learn to do good,
> search for justice, help the oppressed. . . ." (Is 1:11, 17)

In the New Testament this love of neighbor is spoken of in cult terms: "Keep doing good works and sharing your resources, for these are *sacrifices* that please God" (Heb 13:16; cf. also Ph 4:18, 1 Cor 9:12). In the Eucharist, the poor sacrifice of our own lives — of which each of us is the fragile priest — is united to the perfect sacrifice of Jesus. And within this "priestly" community, the ordained ministers exercise, as presidents of the assemblies, the cult of the Body as a whole: "Acting in the person of Christ, he brings about the Eucharistic Sacrifice, and offers it to God in the name of all the people" (LG 10).[10] This strong emphasis on the "priestly" nature of the People of God colors all the teaching of the Council. Gerard Philips has noted that in the original draft of the Decree on the Church, the chapter on "The Call to Holiness in the Church" was intended to highlight the call to religious life.[11] In fact the Fathers did praise and encourage the outstanding value of the witness vowed religious give within the Church (LG 42-47), but they now also needed to stress the call to holiness as it applied to themselves, to their clergy, and to all the baptized.

For the same reason, Henri Le Sourd notes that Vatican II never uses the phrase "the priest, another Christ" (*sacerdos alter Christus*) which Popes had frequently used to express the traditional Catholic esteem for the ordained priesthood.[12] In fact, Vatican II quotes from an encyclical by Pius XI *(Ad Catholici Sacerdotii* — Dec. 20, 1935), but stops abruptly just before that phrase is quoted with approval (PO 12).[13] However it is not correct to claim, as does Hervé-Marie Legrand, that the notion is "so disputable that Vatican II completely ignored it."[14]

The difficulty of course is that each of the baptized is called to be an *alter Christus* — but the ordained priest is still expected to be so *par excellence*, and the Council specifies this in a series of other expressions which Le Sourd believes to be both more evocative and more technical.

> "Priests are configured to Christ the Priest so that as *ministers of the Head* and co-workers of the episcopal order they can build up and establish His whole Body. . . . They have become *living instruments of Christ* the eternal priest" (PO 12).[15]

Through their union with the Order of Bishops, the Order of Presbyters shares in that authority by which Christ himself builds up, sanctifies, and governs his Body, the Church (PO 2).

4. The Nature of the Episcopate

The next factor which helped to enrich the subsequent treatment of the presbyterate was the Council's teaching on the episcopate which had already been introduced in the third chapter of *Lumen Gentium.* Three major themes are introduced.

(i) The Sacramental Nature of Episcopal Consecration (LG 21)

Article 21 deliberately avoids the common claim that episcopal consecration is the "highest degree" of the priesthood. Thus the episcopate is not defined in terms of the (presbyteral) priesthood — as had been the norm through most of the Middle Ages. Instead, "this sacred Synod teaches that by episcopal consecration is conferred *the fullness of the sacrament of orders*" (LG 21).[16] The presbyterate, therefore, is treated as a limited share in this (episcopal) "fullness of the sacrament of orders."

This put an end, once and for all, to the old view that the bishop is simply a "priest" with greater powers of jurisdiction.[17] Episcopal consecration is the primary and comprehensive instance of sacramental ordination.

> "In the bisops, therefore, for whom presbyters are assistants, our Lord Jesus Christ, the supreme High Priest, is present in the midst of those who believe" (LG 21).[18]

Karl Rahner explains that this is why the consecration of a bishop is quite valid without any previous priestly ordination — as has happened many times through history. This fact also provided theological justification for the participation of titular and auxiliary bishops in the Council itself. The sacrament bestows on bishops a sacramental character which is a permanent and inalienable gift, involving powers to sanctify, teach, and govern. This was an important advance on the ordinary theology of the

Schools where the "power of orders" (*potestas ordinis*) was traditionally attributed to the Sacrament of Orders, and the "power of jurisdiction" (*potestas jurisdictionis*) to the "letter of appointment" (*missio canonica*) from the Pope — a view which could not demonstrate any intrinsic unity for the two elements.[19]

(ii) The Collegial Nature of the Episcopate (LG 22)

Article 22 explores another of these central conciliar themes — that of the "College" of Bishops:

> "Just as, by the Lord's will, St. Peter and the other apostles constituted one apostolic college, so in a similar way the Roman Pontiff as the successor of Peter, and the bishops as the successors of the apostles are joined together" (LG 22).[20]

A number of arguments are put forward for the existence of the College: the parallelism with the Apostolic College; the sense of permanent "communion" among the bishops of the early Church; and the ancient liturgical practice of having a number of bishops present to consecrate a new member to their College.

Rahner emphasizes that the College does not comprise the sum of the individual bishops and their powers. The College itself has an active infallibility in its ordinary magisterium (LG 25)[21] which, in view of the fallibility of the individual bishops, it cannot have if its teaching is regarded simply as the total of the teaching of the individual bishops. So its powers are not brought to the College by the individual bishops: rather the individual bishop's threefold office comes to him insofar as he is a member of the College.[22]

This whole "collegial" thrust will be carried through to the Council's treatment of the presbyterate. In contrast with Trent, which always speaks of "the priest" in the singular, Vatican II's references to "the presbyter" were all deliberately rewritten, in their final draft, in the plural. In Vatican II theology, "to become a

priest" is, more precisely, "to enter into the Order of Presbyters."
This change revives the ancient and venerable notion of the
presbyterion. It is this whole "Presbyteral Order" which is the co-
operator with the whole "Episcopal Order."[23]

(iii)   The Threefold Office of the Bishop (LG 25-27)

The third rather interesting innovation in Vatican II's treatment of the episcopacy is its use of the threefold division of
Prophet, Priest, and King, to describe the ministry of Jesus and
consequently of his followers. This threefold pattern dates from
the time of the Fathers, but does have a sound scriptural foundation — as for example in the Lord's final command to "make
disciples . . . baptize them . . . and teach them to observe all the
commands I gave you" (Mt 28:19f).[24]

Through all its documents, Vatican II builds its theology of
Orders around this concept — in an effort to retrieve especially
the presbyterate from its centuries-old restriction to the realm of
cult. In many ways this line of argumentation is ingenious and
successful, but it too has its limitations. Friedrich Wulf points out
that the three "offices" are really only partially distinguishable.[25]
And writers like Anton Houtepen would stress that this threefold
model is certainly not exhaustive: Scripture and tradition use
numerous other titles to try to express the richness of the mission
of Jesus.[26]

For these reasons Michael Richards has argued that "it is
misleading to divide the work of New Testament ministry into
these three Old Testament categories."[27] And Bernard Cooke, in
his book on Ministry, actually considers two further spheres of
ministerial activity: that of "helping others" and of "passing
judgment."[28]

But whatever the limitations of the threefold model, one
interesting consequence is to see the very deliberate Prophet-
Priest-King sequence in which they are applied to the episcopate.
"Among the principal duties of bishops, the *preaching* of the
Gospel occupies an eminent place" (LG 25).[29] In second place,

"a bishop, marked with the fullness of the sacrament of orders, is 'the steward of the grace of the supreme *priesthood*,' especially in the Eucharist" (LG 26).[30] And finally, "bishops *govern* the particular churches entrusted to them as the vicars and ambassadors of Christ" (LG 27). [31]

Given the strongly cultic bias which the priesthood had had in recent history, one might have expected that precedence would be given to the "priestly" function for bishops. But the Fathers realized that unless the Gospel is first preached, the sacraments remain meaningless rituals. Then, because the Order of Presbyters is derived from the episcopate, and shares in a limited way the fullness of that sacrament possessed by the Bishop, presbyters have the same priority of functions: "presbyters, as co-workers with their bishop, have as *their primary duty the proclamation of the Gospel* of God to all" (PO 4).[32]

5. *The Primacy of the Concept of "Mission"*

Yves Congar has noted that one of the great achievements of Vatican II was to base its decisions not on externally imposed arguments of convenience, but rather on intrinsically sound theological principles. For example, its support for ecumenism was based on the unity we already enjoy in baptism, rather than on the "usefulness" of a united resistance to atheism. Its teachings on the role of the laity were not grounded in any shortage of clergy but in the very nature of Christian existence. And similarly, it balanced papal authority by developing a sound theology of the episcopacy which it constructed around the whole notion of "mission."[33]

In Scripture, "election" is always linked to "mission." God calls and consecrates — in order to send out. This was true of Abraham (Gn 12:1), Moses (Ex 3:10, 16), Amos (7:15), Isaiah (6:9, 42:6, 49:1-5, 61:1), Jeremiah (1:7), and Ezekiel (2:3-8). And it was true *par excellence* of Jesus: "The Son, therefore, came on mission from his Father" (LG 3).[34] So too, the apostles were "consecrated" and "sent out" into the world (Jn 17:17-19).

This link between consecration and mission becomes one of the major themes of the Council — and applies in turn to Jesus, to the Twelve, to the Apostles, to their successors, and to all the baptized.

> "Jesus Christ, the eternal Shepherd, established His holy Church by sending forth the apostles as He Himself had been sent by the Father (Jn 20:21). He willed that their successors, namely the bishops, should be shepherds in His Church even to the consummation of the world" (LG 18).[35]

This meant that right from the beginning the episcopacy was defined in terms of a broad apostolic commission, and so preserved from being too narrowly restricted to the realm of cult — as had happened so often in the past.

This also cleared the way for a more comprehensive appreciation of the presbyterate. At the Council there was a predictable attempt to define the priesthood in relation to the Eucharist, but the Fathers wanted to show more clearly the link between the ministry of priests and that of their bishops.[36] Thus the first chapter of *Presbyterorum Ordinis* firmly rivets the conciliar theology of the presbyterate to the apostolic commission entrusted to the episcopate, and to the even more basic mission which Jesus received from his Father:

> "they (priests) are co-workers of the episcopal order in the proper fulfillment of the apostolic mission entrusted to the latter order by Christ" (PO 2).[37]

One consequence of this missionary emphasis is that the presbyter is "set apart" from others — but not in the sense of being "separated" from the world. He is set apart for the service of the Gospel — just as Barnabas and Saul were "set apart" within the Church at Antioch (Ac 13:3). The Council quotes a classic text which had been used by all the recent popes:

"Every high priest has been taken out of mankind and is
appointed to act for men in their relations with God, to
offer gifts and sacrifices for sins" (Heb 5:1).

But the Fathers then conclude: "Hence they deal with other men
as with brothers" (PO 3).[38] The contrast with all preceding uses
which had emphasized the sacred "apartness" of the clergy, could
not be more striking.

For these reasons, and stemming also from the Council's
awareness of the dignity of all the baptized, there is the tendency
to present the presbyter more emphatically as a "brother" rather
than simply as a "father." St. Paul certainly claimed a spiritual
fatherhood over churches he had founded (1 Cor 4:15; Gal 4:19;
Phm 10). And the Council agrees that the presbyter is called to be
"a father and teacher among the People of God." But the same
paragraph continues:

"They are nevertheless, together with all of Christ's faithful, disciples of the Lord . . . brothers among brothers with
all those who have been reborn at the baptismal font" (PO
9).[39]

6. *The Recovery of the Title "Presbyter"*

A further indication of the Council's intention to free the
priesthood from being too narrowly identified with cult can be
seen in the retrieval of the scriptural term of "presbyter" ("elder").
That this was a deliberate decision can be seen from the alterations that were made to the title of the proposed Decree on the
Priesthood. It began as "De *Clericis*" ("Concerning *the Clergy*"), was
changed to "De *Sacerdotibus*" ("Concerning *Priests*"), and finally
ended up as "De *Presbyterorum* Ministerio et Vita" ("Concerning
the Ministry and Life of *Presbyters*").[40]

We have already seen how, for a variety of reasons, the
presbyters of the early Church came to be seen more and more as
"priests" — and that over the centuries this "sacerdotal" aspect of

both the presbyterate and the episcopate came to be seen as the essential and definitive element. Other dimensions, especially the commission to preach, fell disproportionately into the background.[41]

Friedrich Wulf writes that this exaggeration of the sacral character of sacramental ordination meant that priests were seen as "sacred" persons who had to keep at a distance from all profane things.[42] The great John Chrysostom (d. 407), patriarch of Constantinople, thus writes of priests:

> "As though already translated to Heaven, as though free from our human passions — so high, to such a dignity, have they been raised!"[43]

Vatican II tried to correct this line of development by avoiding terms such as "clergy" and "priest", and by returning to the New Testament expression "presbyter" with its collegial and fraternal associations.

Unfortunately the English translation of the Council Documents has effectively concealed the theological precision for which the Fathers were striving. As a general rule the conciliar texts try to follow the Scriptures and to restrict the word "priest" (*sacerdos*) to Jesus himself and to the "common priesthood" of the baptized; and when talking about the ordained they use the word "*presbyteros*." But the English translation uncritically translates both "*sacerdos*" and "*presbyteros*" as "priest." By way of illustration, the word "priest-priestly-priesthood" occurs 14 times in the English version of paragraph 2 of *Presbyterorum Ordinis*; on 10 of these occasions the Latin original has used the word "*presbyteros*"; "*sacerdos*" is used only 4 times — twice referring to Jesus, once to all the baptized, and only once with reference to the ordained priesthood.

Michael Richards has argued that the term "presbyter" *must* be used to designate that particular kind of priest which one becomes through the reception of Holy Orders. He maintains that the undue emphasis on the sacerdotal element in the make-up of the presbyter — at the expense of the other ingredients —

has for too long obscured the essential originality of the New Testament ministry.[44]

The "minister" of the New Testament is neither preacher nor priest nor ruler — he is, somewhat undermining the divisions which have for so long divided Christendom, all these at once. To focus exclusively on one of the categories is to restrict the ordained ministry.

> "In practice, the use of the word 'priest' leads to a narrowly ceremonial view of this vocation which is precisely the damaging limitation that has given rise to our present crisis."[45]

If the presbyter were simply called "prophet" or "king" we should be faced with an equally restricted and lop-sided view of his role.

7. The Contrast with the Council of Trent

(i) Trent Begins with Eucharist, Vatican II with "Mission"

The Council of Trent refers to the priesthood primarily in Sessions XXII (September, 1562: "Concerning the Sacrifice of the Mass") and XXIII (July, 1563: "Concerning the Sacrament of Order"). Thus Trent's starting point is very clearly Eucharistic, whereas Vatican II's is more broadly Christological and ecclesial. Trent will teach that since the Church has received from Christ the visible sacrifice of the Eucharist, "it must also be confessed that there is in that Church a new, visible and external priesthood" (XXIII, 1);[46] but Vatican II will talk instead of the Church as "one body, where all the members have not the same function" (PO 2).[47]

Vatican II begins with the "mission" of the Son. It teaches that as Jesus was sent by the Father so he in turn sent his apostles and their successors, the bishops, whose ministry is shared "in a limited degree" by presbyters (PO 2)[48] Trent, on the other hand, writes that the apostles, "and their successors in the priesthood," have been given "the power of consecrating, offering and administering His body and blood. . . ."(XXIII, 1).[49] While bishops are acknowledged to be superior to priests (XXIII, 4),[50] the Tridentine structure of priesthood still finds its fundamental identity in the power to confect the Eucharist.

According to the vision of Vatican II, the apostolic preaching of the Gospel convokes the whole People of God. They then offer themselves to God as "a living sacrifice." "Through the ministry of presbyters, the spiritual sacrifice of the faithful is made perfect in union with the sacrifice of Christ" as the Eucharist is offered in the name of the whole Church (PO 2).[51] Thus the Vatican II consideration of the presbyterate reaches its climax in the celebration of the Eucharist — which is, by contrast, the starting point for Trent's deliberations.

(ii) Content of Trent's Agenda Set by the Reformers

What Trent had to say about the Sacrament of Orders is a definitive and authentic expression of Catholic faith — but Henri Denis emphasizes that even the Fathers at Trent realized that it was far from being exhaustive.[52] They could just as easily, for example, have spoken of the priesthood in terms of the "care of souls" (cura animarum) but Trent's agenda was set in advance by the Reformers. Luther had condemned as "another scandal" the belief that "the Mass is a sacrifice which is offered to God."[53] The Council felt compelled to refute these Protestant views on the sacrifice of the Mass — and so ended up defining the priesthood in terms of the Eucharist. Thus it emphasized that there is one unique sacrifice of Christ, that this sacrifice is rendered visible within the Church, and that because there is a divinely willed connection between priesthood and sacrifice, a visible and external priesthood must therefore exist (Session XXIII).

Vatican II, by commencing with the mission of the whole People of God, somehow gives implicit recognition that this "common priesthood" is first in the ontological order.[54] Presbyters operate "within" this priestly people. The emphasis now is not on the visibility of the Eucharistic sacrifice, but on that of the Church herself. Trent had no intention of denying the popular "royal priesthood," but did not want to emphasize what the Reformers were not contesting: Trent's more urgent task was to protect the ordained priesthood. Henri Denis notes that Vatican II did not "add" to Trent's teaching on the priesthood, but rather "enfolds" it within a larger ecclesiological whole.[55]

Trent's greatest limitation was its reduction of New Testament priesthood to the power to confect the Eucharist: "sacrifice and priesthood are thus linked by divine ordinance" (XXIII, 1).[56] This lack of any reference to the episcopate at the beginning of its reflections on the Sacrament of Orders had important repercussions for the future of theology — until the bias was corrected at Vatican II. The great dogmatic texts of Trent limit the function of the presbyter to saying Mass and to absolving sins — although the views of the Fathers were obviously more comprehensive, and students in Tridentine seminaries certainly knew that they were also called to be "apostles." But somehow the "partial" presentation of the presbyterate at Trent was accepted as the full and complete teaching on the topic.

David Power maintains that a similar fate befell the Tridentine teaching on the Eucharist. In order to avoid giving the impression that they were presenting a complete teaching on the Eucharist (rather than simply a resolution of the essential conflict) the Fathers greatly shortened their Decree "Concerning the Sacrifice of the Mass" (S. XXII, September, 1562). They eliminated all their preliminaries about remembering the love of God, and concentrated simply on connecting the doctrine of sacrifice with that of the real presence.

> "For the victim is one and the same, the Same now offering by the ministry of priests who then offered Himself on the cross, the manner alone of offering being different" (XXII, 2).[57]

Power believes that this strategy did make their teaching very plain, but it also "backfired" — because contrary to the wishes of the Fathers, later generations also took Trent's teachings on the Eucharist as a "full" presentation of Catholic belief and practice.[58]

(iii) The Moment of Institution of the Presbyterate

With regard to the institution of the presbyterate, Trent taught that "If anyone says that by those words, *'Do this for a commemoration of me,'* Christ did not institute the Apostles priests . . . let him be anathema" (XXII, can. 2).[59] Despite this, Trent did not limit itself to the Last Supper as the place of institution — because it also alludes explicitly to the priestly mission of "forgiving and retaining sins" (XXIII, 1)[60] — a power which was not entrusted to the Twelve until after the Resurrection (Jn 20:23). Nevertheless the Last Supper still did assume a certain pre-eminence — following already ancient references in the liturgy — but always at the risk of isolating the Supper both from the rest of the Lord's life and even more especially from the paschal mystery and from Pentecost. The consequences of this "Holy Thursday" origin of the priesthood were a narrow (and exclusively Eucharistic) ecclesiology, an absence of any organic link between presbyterate and episcopate, a static rather than a mission-oriented notion of presbyterate, and an inability to explain the other "associated powers" of the presbyter.[61]

Vatican II makes no attempt to fix the "moment" when Christ "ordained" the first priests. The focus instead is on mission. Christ sent the Apostles as he himself had been sent: he let them share in his consecration and in his mission — they, and their successors, the bishops. This apostolic mission is then transmitted "in a limited degree" (*subordinato gradu*) to the Order of Presbyters (PO 2). When approached in this light, one cannot treat of the institution of the presbyterate without broaching the larger question of the "organic nature" of the hierarchical Order. This marks a highly significant advance on Trent. Moreover it has given the mission of the presbyter a universal scope: the only limitation is that it be exercised *"subordinato gradu,"* that is in dependence upon the episcopal college.

8. Yet the Eucharist Remains the "Chief Duty" of the Presbyter

We have now seen the extent to which Vatican II radically enriched the Church's understanding of the priesthood. Archbishop Guilford Young makes the point that "no longer is the focus almost exclusively on the priest as the 'cult man.' "[62] The Council emphasized this point by its recovery of the more ancient and less sacerdotal title of "Presbyter." Then because the Order of Presbyters shares, *"subordinato gradu,"* in the mission entrusted to the College of Bishops, it has as its "primary duty" the "proclamation of the Gospel of God to all" (PO 4)[63] — rather than "offering the Sacrifice of the Mass," as priests might previously have inferred from the Council of Trent's *"sacrificium et sacerdotium ita Dei ordinatione conjuncta sunt"* (XXIII, 1).

However, for all this "broadening" of our appreciation of the presbyterate, the Vatican Council still teaches that "the Eucharistic Sacrifice . . . is the center and root of the whole priestly life" (PO 14).[64]

Right from the beginning we are told that the key characteristic of the presbyters within the priestly People of God is that they are the ones who would be able (quoting Trent)

> "by the sacred power of their order to *offer sacrifice* and to remit sins. . . . *Through the ministry of presbyters*, the spiritual sacrifice of the faithful is made perfect in union with the sacrifice of Christ. . . . *Through the hands of priests*, and in the name of the whole Church, *the Lord's sacrifice is offered in the Eucharist* in an unbloody and sacramental manner until He Himself returns. *The ministry of presbyters is directed toward this work and is perfected in it"* (PO 2).[65]

The Tridentine doctrine on the real presence of Christ in the Eucharist is reaffirmed unequivocally: "for the most blessed Eucharist contains the Church's entire spiritual wealth, that is, Christ Himself, our Passover and living bread." Every work of the apostolate is linked with the holy Eucharist and is directed towards it. "Hence *the Eucharist shows itself to be the source and the apex of the whole work of preaching the Gospel*" (PO 5).[66] In talking of the pastoral ("kingly") role of the presbyter, the Council stresses that "*no Christian community . . . can be built up unless it has its basis and center in the celebration of the most Holy Eucharist*" (PO 6).[67]

In view of this strongly Eucharistic emphasis, it comes as no surprise to learn that "*priests fulfill their chief duty in the mystery of the Eucharistic Sacrifice.*" The traditional teaching is repeated: "For this reason, priests are strongly urged to celebrate Mass every day, *for even if the faithful are unable to be present, it is an act of Christ and the Church*" (PO 13).[68]

Thus, whatever newly retrieved insights Vatican II has to offer for a theology of the presbyterate, the Council still strongly reaffirms the tradition. Vatican II builds upon Trent, and inserts its teachings within a more comprehensive ecclesiological perspective.[69] But it very clearly does not reverse any Tridentine teachings.

David Power agrees, although in a more critical frame of mind. He points out that while Vatican II certainly encouraged more active lay participation within the liturgy, the Council still envisaged a "priestly system" which is virtually identical with that of Trent.[70] He maintains that if difficulties in ecumenical discussions are to be addressed, the Catholic Church still needs to reconsider the role of the priest and the language of sacrifice — and the possibility of doing this "in a differentiated historical continuity with Trent."[71]

Whatever we may think about Power's reservations, the bond between the presbyter and the Eucharist — to which he alludes — was strongly reaffirmed by Vatican II, and is constantly restated in documents issuing from Pope John Paul II.[72] This continuing emphasis will need to be kept clearly in mind in any attempt to express a contemporary Roman Catholic theology of the presbyterate.

9. *Conclusion*

With this review of the presbyteral theology of the Second Vatican Council we come to the end of our survey of the scriptural sources and the development of the presbyterate through the subsequent centuries. We began this journey in order to equip ourselves to address some of the questions currently being raised about the place and the significance of the ordained ministry within the Church. It is to this task that we must now turn our attention.

CHAPTER X

Re-Addressing The Present Problem

1. The Nature of the Problem

Now that we have concluded our survey of the scriptural and historical background to the presbyterate, and before we turn our attention to factors which seem to be significant in any re-examination of Roman Catholic theology in this regard, it is important to remember the context within which this study is being undertaken. It is not simply a theoretical exercise. The number of ordained presbyters continues to decline. Yet many parishes continue to grow in size and in ministerial demands.

There is still considerable disagreement as to the seriousness of the problem. Both Pope Paul VI (in 1976) and Pope John Paul II (in 1981) have bluntly called it a "crisis."[1] Bishops are seriously concerned as they strive to maintain parishes with a body of presbyters who are growing older, and fewer in number, with each succeeding year.

However, many Catholics also agree that the increased participation of laity in ministry is a positive move. Dioceses in all countries are finding more lay-people than ever before who are interested in serving within the Church. For this reason Eugene Kennedy sees no problem at all.[2] Dean Hoge cites 1985 surveys in the U.S.A. suggesting that lay-people certainly see access to the sacraments as important, but that they are also concerned to see more participatory forms of parish life established.[3]

Hoge, Professor of Sociology at the Catholic University of America, believes that the factors contributing to the vocations downturn — such as patterns of migration and suburbanization, methods of mate selection, and forms of recreation — are so pervasive and powerful that the Church can do little to counter them.[4]

But Hoge also believes that the problem facing the Catholic Church is basically an institutional one. As proof he notes that all middle-class Protestant denominations in the U.S.A. currently have a surplus of clergy — yet mainline Protestants and Catholics both live in the same mainstream American culture.[5] However he argues that as U.S. Catholics are further assimilated into mainstream American life they will come to resemble other religious groups "lying directly ahead on the assimilation path," namely the Episcopalians and more particularly the Lutherans.[6] But this appears to offer cold comfort because Hoge suspects that "their" problems ("membership is down . . . theological identity is in a situation of drift . . . a prospect of becoming mere culture religion") are certainly spiritual rather than institutional.[7] So the prognosis is not encouraging.

Hoge believes that there is no indication at parish level that the Catholic Church is dying: interest in Church life and in lay ministries remains high. However, Melbourne sociologist Michael Mason recently warned that the Church in Australia had lost more than a million practicing or nominal Catholics over a 15-year period from 1966-1981, and that "the body is bleeding, so to speak, at its growth points — youth, those entering mixed marriages and young parents."[8]

Hoge would see this as evidence of a "classic assimilation pattern"[9] — as Catholic institutional resistance to assimilation into mainline (American) culture finally collapsed during the 1960s.[10] Quite predictably the younger people are the first to assimilate to the surrounding culture: this involved decreases in church-going until their rate reached that of their Protestant age-mates, "a convergence which took place sometime after 1980."

While I suspect that many pastors would share Mason's concern over the health of the patient, a recent study by Andrew Greeley and Michael Hout supports Hoge's more optimistic views. Greeley and Hout argue that there was a dramatic drop in Catholic practice from the late Sixties to the mid Seventies (prompted, they believe, by the 1968 "birth control" encyclical of Paul VI), but that numbers have since stabilized again, and now remain constant.

"... young people attend church today in the same proportion, given the general Catholic decline in all age groups between 1965 and 1975, as their predecessors 20 years ago ... no evidence to support (the claims of a) gradual 'secularization' over the last 20 years."[11]

But however we may actually diagnose the problems, everyone seems agreed that at least for the forseeable future Catholics are going to have to cope with fewer priests. Any realistic reflection on the Roman Catholic theology of the presbyterate must take place within this contemporary context.

2. *Strategies for the Future*

(i) *The Eleven Options of Dean Hoge*

Dean Hoge has undertaken a helpful study of eleven options which, he claims, "exhaust the possibilities of responding to the priest shortage."[12] He divides them into four types:[13]

TYPE A OPTIONS:
REDUCE THE NEED FOR PRIESTS

1. Combine or restructure parishes, or re-educate Catholics to have lowered expectations of priestly services.

Numerous dioceses are now trying to make provision for the pastoral care of "priestless parishes." The Archdiocese of Baltimore is planning to recognize a new role, that of "pastoral leader."[14] In 1986 the Archbishop of Cincinnati advised his people that changes were inevitable, that parishes with a weekend Mass attendance of less than 1,800 would lose their associate pastors when their terms expired, and that the number of lay ministers in the diocese would need to double within a few years.[15]

TYPE B OPTIONS:
MORE PRIESTS, WITH EXISTING ELIGIBILITY CRITERIA

2. *Reassign or redistribute existing priests to get better utilization for parish leadership.*
3. *Get more parish priests from religious orders.*
4. *Get more priests from foreign nations.*
5. *Recruit more seminarians.*

Options 2, 3 and 4 are not regarded as being particularly viable. Few U.S. bishops now feel they have sufficient priests to loan to other dioceses, or to switch from specialized apostolates to parish work. Religious orders are even more drastically short of priests than are dioceses, and most have their own particular apostolates to maintain anyway. And no one is particularly keen to import priests from overseas because of difficulties in acculturation which have been experienced in the past.

Option 5, the recruitment of more seminarians, has been everyone's favorite for years. The problem is that it has not been working, and seminary enrolments continue to sag.[16] Hoge notes that for these reasons this option should not be pursued alone, to the exclusion of others.[17] Research indicates that the two key determinants of interest in priestly vocations are positively, the encouragement factor (by parents, peers, and priests), and negatively, the deterrence effect of celibacy. "A change in either one would affect the number of men entering the seminary."[18]

TYPE C OPTIONS:
GET MORE PRIESTS, WITH BROADENED
ELIGIBILITY CRITERIA

6. *Ordain married as well as celibate men.*
7. *Ordain women.*
8. *Institute a term of service for the priesthood, or institute an honorable discharge.*
9. *Utilize some resigned priests as sacramental ministers.*

Although these four options are being discussed among Catholics at present, some raise major theological problems, and none seems to be being seriously pursued by Vatican authorities. One interesting statistic to emerge with regard to option 6, however, is the revelation that 63% of all Catholic adults, and 63% of Catholic priests in a 1985 U.S. survey were in favor of the ordination of married men. Hoge believes that, since celibacy is seen as the single most important deterrent, if it were made optional the number of Catholic priests would probably increase "until it hit a financial limit."[19]

TYPE D OPTIONS:
EXPAND THE DIACONATE AND LAY MINSTRIES

10. *Expand and develop the permanent diaconate.*
11. *Expand and develop lay ministries.*

Hoge himself emphasizes that these two options are uniquely realistic, and "should" be pursued. He stresses that the restoration of the permanent diaconate (LG 29)[20] and the expansion of lay ministries by Vatican II were not simply a response to the priest shortage, but have a theological legitimacy in their own right.[21]

The restoration of the permanent diaconate began in the U.S.A. in 1968, and the first class was ordained in 1971. By the end of 1985 there were 7,425 permanent deacons in the U.S.A., with another 2,264 in training.[22] Because there are so many candidates, high standards can be maintained. Moreover the American experience is that deacons are inexpensive since most programs work by night classes. Most candidates come with long experience in parish involvement, and because they tend to have already retired from other professions, they are willing to work for much less than a professional wage.

However, for all these perceived advantages, the diaconate is under heavy fire in the U.S.A. today.[23] Because only 3% of U.S. deacons are employed fulltime, a common complaint is that deacons are not as useful as are other parish staff. Moreover, because the role of the deacon is inadequately defined, many deacons (54%) had no formal job description, and no formal working agreement with parishes or dioceses. In the same 1980 survey, deacons said that conflict with priests — who were not accustomed to sharing leadership — was their Number One frustration.[24]

Eugene Kennedy scathingly dismisses married deacons as

"a past, temporary accommodation with a clerically dominated Church. . . . They will be remembered as a significant transitional presence which helped condition the Church for its greater lay character."[25]

Anglican Archbishop Michael Ramsey expressed similar reservations:

"I doubt if the road leads very far, and I doubt whether we could tread it without stultifying the revival of lay service by reviving an unnecessary semi-clerical status."[26]

However, Donald McMonigle objects:

"Need lay ministry be championed to the expense of the permanent diaconate. . .? Would the servanthood of the whole people of God be compromised by such a sacramental sign if the permanent diaconate is restored?"[27]

After all, he observes, the Church has in the past managed to encourage the distinctive vocations of all Christians without seeing the need to abandon the other ordained ministries of bishop and presbyter.[28]

Permanent deacons would obviously be of great practical assistance in celebrating baptisms, conducting weddings, presiding at non-eucharistic liturgies, and generally assisting with the pastoral oversight of parish communities. One advantage would be that these tasks would then be fulfilled without undermining the traditional hierarchical structure of the Church.[29] The presence of a number of married deacons among the clergy of a diocese may modify any exaggerated clericalism. And one further attraction would be that the traditional threefold pattern of ministry would become a lived reality within the contemporary Church.

Option 11, the expansion and development of lay ministries, is already progressing rapidly. Many of these ministers are very experienced, and have just as much theological training as priests. Most in the U.S.A. (83% in 1981)[30] are women; the majority work in the areas of religious education and youth ministry, and tend to be found in larger and wealthier parishes.[31]

Experience to date shows that Catholics have little difficulty with the idea of hiring lay ministers for pastoral work. A 1980 Gallup poll also indicated that in the total population there is a high level of interest in religious work (6% of total population, 9% of those over age 50): it is seen as a desirable career.[32] Hoge's own 1985 college student survey leads him to estimate that the pool of young people interested in lay ministries is about fifty times as large as that interested in religious life.[33]

(ii) The Major Difficulty: No Eucharist

The major difficulty with all of Hoge's options, when assessed against the current discipline of the Church in ordaining only celibate men, is that Catholic communities in the future look destined to survive without any regular celebration of the sacraments. Richard McBrien expresses the fears of many in warning against the possibility of some new form of "high-church congregationalism," in which lay-people themselves take responsibility for Eucharistic leadership.[34]

Raymond Hickey, writing from Nigeria, warns that

"A Eucharist-less Catholic community will in time become a non-Eucharistic community scarcely distinguishable from the many Protestant churches which flourish in Africa. . . . A sacrificial priesthood and regular celebration of the Eucharist can be expected to become more and more irrelevant to a Christian community which has managed for long periods without them."[35]

Hickey's solution is to propose the establishment of "an auxiliary married priesthood" for the Latin rite of the Catholic Church.[36] He observes that "at every stage of her history there has been a married priesthood within the Roman Catholic Church,"[37] and reminds us of the encouragement offered to these married priests of the Eastern Churches at Vatican II:

"This most sacred Synod . . . lovingly exhorts all those who have received the priesthood after marriage to persevere in their sacred vocation, and to continue to spend their lives fully and generously for the flock committed to them" (PO 16).[38]

Hickey emphasizes that he is not proposing a change to the "Apostolic Rule" according to which a celibate priest may not marry after his ordination: this has been a constant tradition for both Catholic and Orthodox, in East and West, from the earliest times — and was reaffirmed both at Vatican II and at the 1971 Synod of Bishops.[39] An auxiliary married priesthood is not proposed in competition with a celibate priesthood. There is a need for both to remain — as in the East. However, he insists that the proposal for an auxiliary married priesthood should not be seen as an "innovation" in the Latin Church.[40]

But like the movement for a vernacular liturgy in the 1950s, Hickey's proposal will seem to many Catholics at this stage to be somewhat radical; he believes it is important at present simply to promote a dialogue — which may eventually lead to a consensus.[41] Until such a consensus has been achieved Hickey admits that it is unlikely that Rome would be prepared to initiate any changes[42] — although the 1971 Synod revealed that 44% of the bishops present were not averse to the idea.[43]

However, underlying both Hickey's proposal, and the objections raised against Hoge's suggestions, is the presumption that guaranteeing ready access to the Eucharist is the most urgent priority confronting contemporary Catholics. Is this, in fact, the case?

3. Should the Availability of the Eucharist Be Our First Priority?

Much discussion about future directions for the priesthood centers on the significance of the Eucharist. Pope John Paul II has claimed that

> "*There is no Church without the Eucharist*, but there is no Eucharist without priests. There can be no Church without priests. . . ."[44]

The documents of the Second Vatican Council speak similarly. The Decree on Priests talks of the Eucharist as "the *source and apex of the whole work of preaching the Gospel*" (PO 5),[45] and states that

> "no Christian community . . . can be built up unless it has its basis and center in the celebration of the most Holy Eucharist" (PO 6).[46]

This emphasis on the importance of the Eucharist certainly has a strong scriptural foundation. St. Paul (1 Cor 11:23f), and each of the synoptics (Mk 14:22f, Mt 26:26f, Lk 22:15f), records the institutional narrative. And Jesus himself had warned that "if you do not eat the flesh of the Son of Man and drink his blood, you will not have life in you" (Jn 6:53).

Our intention here, however, is not to challenge the inestimable worth of "the wonderful sacrament of the Eucharist by which the unity of the Church is both signified and brought about" (UR 2).[47] Our intention is simply to ask whether, in the present situation, the continued availability of the Eucharist should be our first priority. Two factors should make us hesitate: on the one hand, it is areas of the Church which are deprived of the Eucharist which seem to be showing the greatest vitality; and conversely, it is those regions which have been most blessed by the ready availability of the Eucharist which are most afflicted by that spiritual malaise which seems to be stifling the life of the Church.

Michael Mason has warned that the Australian Catholic Church appears to have lost one million adherents over the period 1966-1981[48] — and virtually all of these will have left parish communities in which the Eucharist was celebrated frequently. William J. O'Malley, who has taught theology to U.S. teenagers for 23 years, confirms that "a large number of our young people find the Mass neither meaningful, nor important, nor relevant to their lives."[49] Simply making the Eucharist more available in this situation is not going to achieve much.

O'Malley argues that we must recognize that most young people are baptized, *but unconverted.* The negative witness of departing priests and religious, and the not uncommon spectacle of religious professionals in open conflict, breeds scepticism. Catholicism is often seen in terms of prohibitions, and Christianity in terms of "doing nice little things" occasionally for the neighbor — but neither seems worth the effort of getting up for Church the morning after party night.[50]

Peter Chirico, while not addressing this specific topic, has still noted that "the first and most important" priority, "the purpose of all ministry," is "to facilitate the internalization of the enduring values of the Christian tradition."[51] Vatican II reminded presbyters that this "proclamation of the Gospel" was their "primary duty" (PO 4).[52]

The Eucharist undoubtedly is "the source and apex of the whole work of preaching the Gospel," and Michael Evans is right to warn us against seeing a priest-less and Eucharist-less Church as the norm, rather than as "an unfortunate situation of which we must make the most."[53] But the absolute prerequisite to our appreciation of the Eucharist is that the Gospel has actually been preached — and received. The diminishing number of available priests points perhaps to a need, not to maintain a weekly Eucharist in as many parishes as possible, but to undertake a far more basic re-evangelization of the Church. And the experience of the churches of Africa or Latin America suggests that maybe this is done by celebrating the Eucharist less frequently and concentrating instead on other forms of community worship.

During the past 25 years the Catholic population of Africa has increased by more than 300% — despite the fact that the Eucharist is not celebrated regularly in the great majority of Catholic communities.[54] During the 1950s the Church in Brazil began a "community evangelization movement"; this bred the famous "basic church communities" which were nourished through the efforts of lay catechists — so that "catechesis became the center of a community."[55] The result, writes Leonardo Boff, is that "the basic communities are generating a new ecclesiology."[56]

Boff notes that there was a time when people in the interior of Latin America gathered for worship only when a priest came to visit — sometimes just once or twice a year. Only during these times did they feel themselves to be part of the living Church, united together with their ordained minister by word and sacrament. But with the establishment of base communities, these same people began to meet at least once a week to celebrate the presence of the Risen Lord, to hear and meditate on his word, and to consider parish and diocesan affairs.[57] The 1968 Medellin Conference spoke of the Christian base community as "the first and fundamental ecclesiastical nucleus."[58]

It may be important, in trying to address the problems raised by our impending shortage of presbyters, to keep in mind the vitality of the frequently "priestless" churches of Africa or Latin America. They do challenge the common presupposition that our first priority must be to provide ready access to the Eucharist. If it is true, as O'Malley suggests, that most of our youth (and many of their parents) are in fact still "unconverted," the more urgent task is to turn our efforts to the work of basic evangelization, and to learn all we can from those areas where the Church now seems to be most vital.

4. Further Considerations

(i) Should We Be Promoting "Communion Services"?

In June 1988 the Vatican Congregation for Divine Worship acknowledged the growing shortage of priests by issuing its "Decree for Sunday Celebrations in the Absence of a Priest":

> "Among the forms of celebration found in liturgical tradition when Mass is not possible, a celebration of the word of God is particularly recommended, and also its completion, when possible, by Eucharistic communion" (para. 20).

The document repeatedly emphasizes that, "Any confusion between this kind of assembly and a Eucharistic celebration must be carefully avoided" (p. 22).[59] However, it is precisely the prospect of this sort of confusion which has liturgical experts extremely concerned.

Gerard Broccolo, Director of the Ministerial Formation Department for the Archdiocese of Chicago, has objected that the most radical change there can be is to have Christian communities without the centrality of the Eucharistic celebration. He describes the notion of a "Communion Service" as "a radical departure from our Catholic tradition."[60] Such services, warns Edward

Schillebeeckx, mean that "the Sunday celebration of the Eucharist is trivialized."[61] Gerard Austin writes that: "Receiving a previously consecrated host is a fine thing, but it is not what celebrating the Eucharist is about."[62]

Another liturgist, Gabe Huck, has emphasized the radical nature of this change of practice. Catholics have traditionally had a tremendous devotion to their Sunday Mass — but often had to be cajoled into receiving communion at least once a year. The present practice of opting for Communion Services seems to suggest that it does not matter if the Mass is not available, but that the really important thing is that everyone have the opportunity to receive communion.

"If we say that priestless Sundays are OK as long as we
have leaders for the word, the prayer of thanksgiving and
the communion service, then we have opted for Sundays
without Eucharist, Sundays without the human, sacramental bond which is ordained ministry in our church."[63]

Huck believes that it would be preferable to keep the Sunday assembly, but to gather for some devotion which is more firmly entrenched in our tradition — such as Morning Prayer, celebrated with song and gesture, along with the readings of the day. This would avoid the risk of switching to a radically novel rite which seems to give the impression that it does not matter whether we "do Eucharist" or not.

(ii) Do Christians Have a "Right" to the Eucharist?[64]

A further claim which is frequently made when discussing the future of the priesthood is that the baptized have a "right" to the celebration of the Eucharist, on the basis of the Lord's Eucharistic mandate to, "Do this as a memorial of me" (Lk 22:19). Schillebeeckx, for example, writes that "this apostolic right has priority over the criteria for admission which the Church can and may impose on its ministers." He adds that this right "may not be made null and void by the official Church."[65]

Scripture scholar Albert Vanhoye objects to Schillebeeckx's pitting of "the official Church" against "Christian communities." He argues that the New Testament does not talk in terms of "rights" — either to ministers or to the Eucharist. It tends rather to stress the opposition between what one may claim by "right," and what one receives by faith as God's gracious gift (Rm 4:4). The Latin liturgy still repeats the prayer of the centurion: "Lord, I am not worthy. . . ." (Mt 8:8).[66]

Part of the history of the Catholic Church in Australia records a "Holy House" in Sydney, where for 2 years after the 1818 deportation from the colony of Fr. Jeremiah O'Flynn, the Blessed Sacrament was reserved for the sick. This room, in the cottage of one William Davis, served as a secret center for the devotions of a small band of Catholics who for this period were six thousand miles from the nearest priest.[67] One cannot help but reflect on how strange this talk of a "right" to the Eucharist would have sounded to the ears of these early settlers — for whom, one suspects, it was seen more in terms of a "privilege" than as something they believed they could insist upon.

Schillebeeckx acknowledges this to some extent by frequently referring to the "right, *by grace*," to the Eucharist.[68] But he still clings to his talk of a "right," and in his second book attributes the idea to Thomas Aquinas: "those are not my words: *habent ius ad mensam Domini accedendi* (ST. III, 67, a. 2)."[69] Question 67, however, is discussing not the Eucharist, but the Sacrament of Baptism. The sentence quoted actually reads:

> "It is through baptism moreover, that a person becomes a partaker of the unity of the Church *and also receives the right to approach the table of the Lord* (*et accipit jus accedendi ad mensam Domini*)."[70]

St. Thomas is considering the privileges imparted at baptism, including the "*jus accedendi ad mensam Domini*." But whether he is saying, as Schillebeeckx suggests, that the baptized have a further right to "demand" the Eucharist is not quite so apparent.

(iii) Should the One Who Presides Over the Community also Preside Over the Eucharist?

With the increasing tendency to entrust the care of parishes to lay ministers, and the obvious difficulties faced by non-residential "circuit-riding" priests,[71] a number of theologians are arguing that in the primitive Church those who presided over the Eucharist did so precisely because they were the ones who presided over the community. The idea is expressed twice, parenthetically, in the *relatio* of Vatican II's Central Theological Commission on paragraph 28 of *Lumen Gentium*:

> "Now since in the New Testament and in the post-apostolic age the Eucharist was understood as a "sacrifice," *and presbyters as presiders (rectores) over the community were presiders (rectores) over the Eucharist*, the ministerial priesthood of the New Testament reveals its proper dignity as instituted by Christ. *The function of presiding over the community* appears linked with *the cultic function*."[72]

Should not, therefore, these "lay" ministers, who now "preside" over parish communities, also be commissioned to confect the Eucharist for these communities? Schillebeeckx believes that there can be "no community without ministry,"[73] and argues that the very notion of a "shortage of priests" is an "ecclesiological impossibility."[74]

Hervé Legrand, in a comprehensive survey of pre-Nicene writings, confirms that those who presided over the community (whether as Apostles, Prophets, Bishops or Presbyters) certainly were the ones who presided at the Eucharist. He thus concludes that the presidency of the Eucharist is a "liturgical dimension" of what is essentially a "pastoral charge."[75]

As a consequence of this insight Peter Chirico has questioned the current practice of promoting persons who do not preside at liturgy (e.g. pastoral workers) to an overseeing pastoral function.[76] Conversely, Legrand argues that once Christians are competent to preside over the upbuilding of their local church, they are likewise competent to receive the ordination which entitles them to preside at the Eucharist.[77] He asks whether, in the light of this ancient tradition, we are today taking seriously enough the relationship between Church and Eucharist.[78]

Legrand's question is obviously legitimate, and needs to be taken seriously. However, we must also ask whether Legrand himself has sufficiently explained the source of the authority which was recognized in these early leaders of the community. We may agree that these individuals presided at the Eucharist because they presided over the community. But how did they come to be "rulers of the community" (*rectores communitatis*) in the first place? Was it simply by way of some extrinsic appointment (as is now the situation with lay-ministers), or was it that some individuals were perceived to have been entrusted with an authority which came more directly from Christ?

Clement of Rome (d. 100?), for example, is emphatic that the Corinthians have no authority to dismiss presbyters who have been "serving Christ's flock in a humble, peaceable and disinterested way." His concern is that these men now have an authority which the community cannot rescind (*1 Clem* 44).[79] Clement tells us that the Apostles, as they went from region to region "appointed their first converts — after testing them by the Spirit — to be bishops and deacons for the believers of the future" (*1 Clem* 42).[80] One could argue that it is because of this authority that these individuals are the leaders of the community, and the presiders at the Eucharist, in the first place.

All recent Roman Catholic magisterial statements stress the point that the presbyter does *not* represent the community because the community has elected him. On the contrary he represents the community because — by virtue of his ordination — "he first represents Christ himself, who is the Head and Shepherd of the Church."[81]

In his efforts to uncover the "perennial, global tradition"[82] of the Church, Legrand ends up in the awkward position of having to challenge Vatican II's allusion to the priest's unique role in the Eucharist.[83] And this is all done in defense of an interpretation of the praxis of the first millennium which is not itself unchallenged. Even Legrand admits that this early period was characterized by "more than one" axis of understanding the presidency of the Eucharist.

> "The sacerdotal axis is ancient: *as early as the Carolingian period* specific actions such as *conficere, consecrare* and *immolare* ('confecting' [the Eucharist], 'consecrating,' and 'immolating') began to be attributed to priests."[84]

In order to determine a fully satisfactory theology of the presbyterate we must investigate in greater detail this awareness of the authority, or even the power, of the one who for that very reason presided over both the community and its celebration of the Eucharist. Scholastic theologians would speak of a priestly "character," but the underlying notion has roots in the Christian tradition which stem from the earliest centuries.

CHAPTER XI

The "Permanent" Aspect of the Sacrament of Orders

1. The Nature of the Distinction Between the Clergy and the Laity

The current shortage of priests, and proliferation of lay ministers, is very naturally prompting discussion of the nature of the "distinction" which the Roman Catholic theology of the presbyterate has consistently maintained between the "ordained" and "non-ordained" ministries.

Martin Luther, of course, rejected any such distinction. Because "all Christians are truly of the spiritual estate," and because "we are all consecrated as priests by baptism" (1 P 2:9), a ministerial "priest" is really simply doing

> "that which we have all alike power to do. . . . A priest should be nothing in Christendom but a functionary; as long as he holds his office, he has precedence; if he is deprived of it, he is a peasant or a citizen like the rest."[1]

A priest who never preaches the Word of God has stopped "functioning," do obviously ceases to be a priest.[2]

In our own time Edward Schillebeeckx, and other Roman Catholic theologians, are also questioning the permanence of presbyteral ordination,[3] and the traditional distinction between clergy and laity. Cyrille Vogel, to whom both Schillebeeckx[4] and Hervé Legrand[5] are indebted, has argued that when priests and bishops were deposed during the first millennium of the Church's history, such a deposition entailed a loss of priestly identity and a complete reintegration into the ranks of the laity. He finds proof for this in the fact that sacraments conferred by deposed clerics were frequently rejected as invalid, that such clerics were permitted to marry, and that they were thenceforth subject to civil rather than to ecclesiastical tribunals.[6] He goes on to claim that it was only in the twelfth century that a radical break occurred in the development of the tradition with the emergence of scholastic theories concerning a permanent sacramental character.[7]

The really significant question, however, is whether the Church during this first millennium actually repeated the sacrament of ordination — as in the case of a cleric who was deposed but later reinstated in office. And the universal practice, which Vogel himself is forced to admit, is that it did not.[8]

But Vogel insists that this was not because of any awareness of the "permanence" of a character.[9] Instead he theorizes that the act of deposition (and its reversal) is a "cultic" act which in these circumstances takes the place of the ordination ceremony:

> "In law, the deposed presbyter is able to be readmitted to his (Holy) Orders. And, in that case, the lifting of the deposition is sufficient for this readmission; *a second ordination is unnecessary*: not because the presbyteral state is 'maintained' despite the deposition, but because the lifting of the deposition is itself a religious and ecclesial action (and not purely juridical and coercive), and suffices to 'return' that which the deposition (another religious action) has withdrawn."[10]

Vogel's comments here seem to be extraordinarily tendentious, but Schillebeeckx finds them convincing.[11] Schillebeeckx concludes from them that the second millennium of the Church's history is out of step with the practices of the first — and that we have to decide which millennium we are going to accept as truly "Christian and apostolic."[12] During the first millennium, he claims,

> "a minister, who for any personal reason ceased to be the president of a community, 'ipso facto' returned to being a layman in the full sense of the word."[13]

2. The Sixth Canon of the Council of Chalcedon (AD 451)

Schillebeeckx hinges much of his argument on his reading of the famous sixth canon of the Council of Chalcedon (451), which states that:

> "No one shall be ordained at large, either to the presbyterate, or diaconate, or any place in the ecclesiastical order whatsoever; nor unless the person ordained be particularly designated to some church in a city, or village, or to some martyr's chapel, or monastery. And if any have been ordained without charge, *the holy synod has decreed such ordination to be null and nowhere operative*, to the reproach of the ordainer."[14]

From this canon Schillebeeckx draws two conclusions:

(1) that anyone whose ordination is judged to be "null and nowhere operative" by that very fact returns to "being a layman in the full sense of the word";[15]

(2) that any *"absolute"* ordination ("one in which hands are laid on someone *without his being asked by a particular community* to be its leader") is null and void.[16]

For Schillebeeckx, the laying-on of hands by neighboring bishops (in the case of the ordination of a bishop) is simply "an expression of the communion of all the Christian communities with one another." But the absolute *sine qua non* for any ordination is not this ceremony, but rather the election by the community concerned.[17]

Henri Crouzel agrees with Schillebeeckx that conciliar canons from the fourth and fifth centuries do emphasize the election by the people in the ordination of any new bishop. But Crouzel maintains that the bishops of the province, often led by their metropolitan, played a more active role than Schillebeeckx suggests. It was they who actually "presided" over the election, and ensured the "apostolic succession." Moreover, while there are clear precedents for the community's involvement in the election of a new bishop, there is little historical evidence that the community ever played such a significant part in the choice of candidates for the presbyterate or diaconate.[18]

But more to our point, we must ask whether the sixth canon of Chalcedon is really as significant as Schillebeeckx maintains. In fact, there is virtually no evidence to suggest that those who had once been ordained could subsequently return to the lay-state. On the contrary, even Cyrille Vogel acknowledges the consistent refusal to reordain a deposed minister if he is reappointed to office.[19] During the fourth and fifth centuries, bishops who converted from Donatism to Catholicism always retained their episcopal dignity — even if it meant that there were sometimes two bishops in the same diocese. Even Ambrose (d. 397) never queried the episcopal dignity of his Arian adversary Auxentius.[20]

Chalcedon itself, in its twelfth session (October 30, 451), had deposed two rival bishops of Ephesus and instructed the other bishops of the province to elect someone completely new to the post. However both Bassianus and Stephen, the two bishops concerned, were to receive an annual salary from the See of Ephesus, and there is no indication that the Council believed either of them had lost his episcopal status.[21]

Schillebeeckx also reads the sixth canon to say that candidates must be called by a community. However, it is difficult to see how a martyr's shrine, or even a monastery, could be seen as a "community" in the sense that Schillebeeckx is suggesting. Moreover, Crouzel writes that there is ample evidence, prior to Chalcedon, for the existence of "absolute" ordinations (i.e. without any "call" from a community), and in most cases there is not the slightest indication that they met with any disapproval.[22]

One can also argue quite cogently that Chalcedon was not making any statement whatsoever about a candidate for orders having to be "elected" by a community. The Council's real concern was to ensure that no one be ordained without some provision being made for his livelihood; the Fathers wanted to prevent the scandal of having unattached clerics roaming the countryside in search of employment. The Council had already had to deal with this sort of a predicament in Ephesus, and canons four and five are both directed against these vagrant monks and clerics.[23] Understood in this sense, as a prohibition on the ordination of "vagrants," the sixth canon was explicitly reaffirmed at Trent (S. XXIII, Reform Ch. XVI)[24] and the same commonsense precautions still apply in the Church's current canon law.[25]

3. The Permanent Effect of Priestly Ordination

The whole weight of the tradition — in both millennia! — bears witness to a belief that some of the sacraments produce a permanent effect on the recipient — and for this reason could never be repeated. Martin Luther realized, in challenging the traditional distinction between clergy and laity, that it was this idea of the permanence of the priesthood that he had to attack. Of the "Romanists" he wrote:

> "They have invented *characteres indelibiles* ("indelible characters"), and pretend that a priest after deprivation still differs from a mere layman. . . . All this is nothing but mere talk and a figment of human invention."[26]

The response at Trent was predictable:

> "If anyone says that in three sacraments, namely, baptism, confirmation and order, there is not imprinted on the soul a character, that is, a certain spiritual and indelible mark, by reason of which they cannot be repeated, let him be anathema" (S. VII, can. 9).[27]

Of the nature of priestly character they decreed that

> "since in the sacrament of order, as also in baptism and confirmation, a character is imprinted which can neither be effaced nor taken away, the holy Council justly condemns the opinion of those who say that the priests of the New Testament have only a temporary power, and that those who have once been rightly ordained can again become laymen if they do not exercise the ministry of the word of God" (S. XXIII, ch. IV).[28]

Vatican II reaffirmed this belief that there was a difference *"in essence and not only in degree"* between clergy and laity (LG 10),[29] and taught that presbyters were *"marked with a special character"* at the moment of their ordination (PO 2).[30]

In using this language of "character" both Trent and Vatican II (and Luther!) were alluding to something which has deep roots in the tradition, and finds support even in the New Testament. In Greek, a *"character"* was analogous to a *"sphragis"*: it meant initially whatever "produces" an imprint, and then the "imprint" itself. In Latin, the ineffaceable tattoo a soldier received when enlisting was called either a *"signaculum,"* or a *"character."*[31]

4. The Idea of the "Sphragis" in Scripture and the Fathers

In the Gospel of John, Jesus urges the people to work for food which endures to eternal life, the kind of food the Son of

Man was offering, "for on him the Father, God himself, *has set his seal (esphragisen)*" (Jn 6:27). Later Jesus will claim that *"to have seen me is to have seen the Father"* (Jn 14:9). The Letter to the Hebrews describes the Son as "the radiant light of God's glory, and *the perfect copy* of his nature (*charaktēr tēs hypostaseōs autou*)" (Heb 1:3).

St. Paul writes to the Corinthians that "God has anointed us, marking us with his seal (*sphragisamenos*)" (2 Cor 1:22). He reminds the Ephesians that they have been *"stamped with the seal (esphragisthēte)* of the Holy Spirit of the Promise" (Ep 1:13, 4:30). And the Book of Revelation talks of a future "sealing (*sphragida*)" as part of some great eschatological drama (Rv 7:2, 9:4).

The early Church Fathers very naturally adopted this vocabulary. They realized that just as a material *"sphragis"* might be used to identify the sheep of a flock or the soldiers in an army, so baptism produced a spiritual *"sphragis"* by which God could identify his own.[32] And from the fourth century on there is already a strong tendency to see this spiritual *"sphragis"* as being indestructible. Cyril of Jerusalem (d. 386) talks of baptism as producing the "ineffaceable *'sphragis'* of the Holy Spirit." And John Chrysostom (d. 407) observes that the material *"sphragis"* branded on an enlisting soldier obviously remains even if he should become a deserter.[33] That this mark was seen to persist even in the unworthy brings out the distinction between *"sphragis"* and grace.

With regard to priestly ordination, Augustine (d. 430) is the first to assert that it too entails the impression of a permanent character — for which reason it too can never be repeated.[34] But Jean Galot writes that Augustine is drawing on an even earlier tradition which had already emphasized the parallels between the "sacrament of baptism" and the "sacrament for the administration of baptism."[35] Gregory of Nyssa (d. 395) had gone so far as to compare the "transformation" wrought in the soul of a priest to that wrought in the Eucharistic species at the moment of consecration.[36]

One interesting feature of Augustine's thought is that the existence of a sacramental character is not inferred as a "consequence" of the non-repetition of particular sacraments. Augustine's reasoning works in the opposite direction: certain sacraments are not repeated because they have already imprinted a character, and any attempt to repeat them would be to do "injury" to the sacrament.[37]

5. The Theological Notion of "Character"

Augustine's writings on sacramental character were never a question of serene speculative reflection undertaken for its own sake. Instead, he was constantly searching for the most striking and most concrete images he could use to oppose any suggestion that converts from Donatism should be rebaptized. St. Thomas Aquinas repeats, with approval, Augustine's rhetorical question: "Are Christian sacraments less lasting than this military brand in the flesh?"[38] Augustine's great achievement was his insight into the clear distinction between "grace" and "sacrament" (i.e. "character").

But it was not until the Middle Ages that theologians tried to analyze just what the nature of "character" was. Bonaventure (d. 1274) details four aspects:

(i)   as something which prepares for grace, it is the principle of life (*principium vitae*).

(ii) as something which distinguishes the Lord's flock, it is a seal (*sigillum*).

(iii) as something which remains indelibly, it is a guard (*custodia*).

(iv) as something which especially disposes one for faith, it is called an illumination of the mind (*illuminatio mentis*).[39]

Aquinas (d. 1274), however, was determined to preserve Augustine's insight into the distinction between "grace" and "character." He could accept that the character produced a "seal" which marked out the flock of the Lord, or a "guard" which guaranteed indelibility; but he rejected Bonaventure's teaching that the character constituted a "principle of life" which opened the soul to grace, or an "illumination of the mind" which disposed the subject to faith. Aquinas argued that the character gave a "power/potential" (*potentia*) to perform particular actions, but that it had no intrinsic predisposition towards moral goodness — because this last quality was a product of grace, not of the character itself. The sacerdotal character, for example, gave a priest the "*potentia*" to consecrate, but it had no bearing on whether he did so worthily or not.[40]

This precision of thought led Aquinas to distinguish between the "internal" realm of grace and the "external" sphere of "participation-in-the-sacraments," to which character belonged. Thomas saw character as a dynamic "*potentia*" to participate in the sacraments and so to influence the spiritual life.[41] This led Aquinas to recognize the character of orders, which so obviously imparted a "*potentia*" to participate in cultic activities, as his "prime analogue": as the sacramental character which gave the clearest insight into the nature of character itself.[42]

Galot observes, however, that while Thomas's definition of character as a "*potentia*" directed towards cult finds its most perfect expression in that of orders, its adaptation to the sacraments of baptism and confirmation is not quite so smooth. He sees baptism as conferring a predominantly passive "*potentia*" — to "receive" the other sacraments; and confirmation as being a more active "*potentia*" — enabling the recipient to grasp spiritual truths and to courageously profess the faith.[43]

However, Thomas's great achievement was his recognition that character comprised a real power for acting, which was not to be confused with the power for accomplishing meritorious actions. He thus gave character a dynamic significance, and its own proper field for efficacy — in cultic action.

6. *The Dogmatic Weight of the Teaching on Indelible Character*

Much contemporary debate on character centers particularly on the theological weight of the Tridentine definition: is it a dogmatic truth, and therefore of the essence of our faith (*fides divina*), or is it simply a belief of the Church (*fides ecclesiastica*)?[44] Piet Fransen argues that the placing of an anathema on some view was merely a strategy to preserve current Church teachings or practices which were deemed to be under attack — and was never seen as constituting a formal "*de fide*" definition of Catholic doctrine.[45] Hervé Legrand accepts Fransen's argument and, bearing in mind the canonical principle (can. 1323, art. 3) that dogmatic definitions should be understood to state "only that which authority manifestly wished to define," concludes that "one would be expressly disloyal to the intentions of the doctrinal authority of the Catholic Church were one to consider the doctrine of the 'character' as dogma."[46]

But the Theological Commission which met prior to the 1971 Synod of Bishops evidently thought otherwise, and approved a declaration in which they claimed that there were no valid reasons to question the normative doctrinal teaching of tradition, especially as expressed at Trent, concerning the existence and permanency through life of the sacramental character of the ordained minister.[47] David Power writes that Trent simply affirms that the existence of character belongs to the Christian tradition, and thus cannot be denied with impunity.[48] Jean Galot, however, argues that the denial of character was explicitly condemned as heretical;[49] and that Trent did intend to affirm, as a truth integral to the faith, the existence of the sacramental character — defined as "a certain spiritual and indelible mark" (S. VII, can. 9).[50]

Everyone agrees, however, that Trent's definition was extremely nuanced. The Fathers were reluctant to adduce any scriptural "proof-texts," because the validity of these arguments was disputed among the Fathers.[51] Nor did they wish to endorse any particular scholastic theory: not even St. Thomas's notion of character as a "cultic empowerment" was officially sanctioned.[52] Consensus was finally achieved in terms of what had already been declared by the magisterium of the Church.[53] Thus the Council simply reproduced, without added precision, what had been asserted in the Decree for the Armenians — which had been published in the Council of Florence (1439) by Pope Eugene IV in an attempt to bring about the reunion of the Armenian Church with the Catholic Church.

7. Sacramental Character and the Structure of the Church

Peter Kenny maintains that the doctrine concerning sacramental character is often not fully appreciated because it is so frequently presented in an impersonal and "dehydrated" manner.[54] In fact, suggests Kenny, the baptismal character is the very "anchor" of salvation which keeps even a person in serious sin (and thus deprived of grace) still linked with the Body of Christ: as Augustine had stressed to his Donatist adversaries, it had never been the practice of the Church to rebaptize public sinners on the occasion of their repentance.[55]

Aquinas had distinguished two different sorts of sacredness: that of "grace" (which is private, personal, and unseen), and that of "consecration" (which is public, impersonal, and visible).[56] One can never know the personal level of "holiness" of a particular individual, but because of the public nature of the ceremonies concerned, one can determine whether or not a church, a priest, or a Christian, has in fact been "consecrated."[57] David persistently refused to do any harm to King Saul, because he realized that Saul's sacredness, as the Lord's anointed, still remained even though he had lost God's favor through his disobedience (1 S 24:7). Similarly St. Paul has no hesitation in writing to the "holy" people of Jesus Christ at Corinth (1 Cor 1:2), even though it is clear that some of these "saints" are in a state of serious sin (1 Cor 5:1, 6:1, 11:20).

Perhaps the most striking feature of the doctrine of sacramental character is that it gives structural stability to the Church. Without it the visibility of the Church, and the value of the Liturgy and the Eucharist would all be undermined.[58] The Church would be reduced to an indeterminate group of those who were living in the state of grace. Like the converting Donatists of old, we would not know whether or not we had "retained" our baptism. And we would never know on any particular occasion whether a priest had performed a valid baptism, a valid absolution, or a valid Eucharist. The three sacramental characters therefore establish the public nature of the Church: our reliance upon the valid performance both of the Liturgy and of the sacraments turns upon them. Without character, concludes Kenny, there is "no Mass, no Sacrament, no Church, no Christian."[59]

8. The Meaning and Value of the Priestly Character

The existence of a priestly character means that the Church does not have to depend upon shepherds who can be appointed or dismissed as the community pleases. The doctrine of sacramental character expresses the belief that the plan of God for each individual "in Christ" is somehow "imprinted" onto the personal self.[60] In the character of order, as in that of baptism and confirmation, a new creation is entailed. The Semitic mind would have sensed something of this in the change of names experienced by both Peter and Paul (Mt 16:18; Ac 13:9). And Galot perceives an echo of Genesis in the language of Mark: "He *made* Twelve of them. He *made* the Twelve (*epoiēsen*)" (Mk 3:14, 16).[61]

The notion of priestly character is certainly ontological, but also dynamic. We have previously seen how strongly the theology of Vatican II linked "consecration" with "mission": "the Son, therefore, came on *mission* from his Father" (LG 3).[62] In a similar fashion, the priestly character impresses upon the being of the baptized person an orientation which commits the whole self to the mission of the priest — so that it may be realized "from within." It influences the actions of a priest precisely because it has already engaged him more deeply at the level of being.[63]

Authority accrues to the ordained priest not because the community has appointed him, but because the sacerdotal character has etched upon his soul the image of Christ the Shepherd.[64] This identification of the priest with Christ is expressed most obviously in the words of consecration: "*This is my body. . . . This is my blood.*" However, Karl Rahner has stressed that

> "we have no right to connect the character only to the cultic and sacramental empowerment of the priest — to the exclusion of the empowerment that goes hand in hand with his mission."[65]

Only the most comprehensive theology of the priesthood can do justice to the responsibilities entrusted to the Shepherd.

9. Conclusion

David Power notes appropriately that contemporary theology would be less inclined to treat the character of baptism as "passively" as did Aquinas — because of our appreciation of the fundamental significance of that sacrament.[66] Power also explores rather imaginatively the possibility of viewing the sacramental character in terms of a "relationship." He notes that the Church has always affirmed the necessity of at least an "intention" on the part of the subject which is in conformity with the intention of the Church in conferring a sacrament: thus one could never, for example, validly baptize a sleeping adult who had never expressed any desire for baptism. Hence Power defines a character as a "reciprocal relationship" between the Church and an individual, stemming from the initiative of the first and the acceptance of the second. And from the side of the Church the relationship remains thenceforth permanently open.[67]

However, Power's application of his theory to the priestly character is less convincing. He suggests that it too be seen as a

"reciprocal relationship," and as such capable of numerous mod-
ifications, but always sustained by the permanency of the
Church's call to minister. But, in considering the contemporary
question as to whether the "basic grounding" of this relationship
may itself be revoked, Power maintains that no definitive answer
to this question is possible at present.[68] Power's response here
seems to be at odds with the traditional refusal to repeat the rite of
ordination, and would seem to confirm the fears of critics that the
use of "relational" terms fails to give sacramental character sufficient ontological reality.[69]

   Jean Galot believes that modern critics of the idea of character are usually trying to make the point that the priesthood is
simply a function.[70] Schillebeeckx writes that "in the earliest understanding, ministry is not a status but in fact *a function*,"[71] — and
complains that even Vatican II at times confuses "the ontological
level of the baptism of the Spirit, and *the functional level of the
ministry*."[72] Similarly, Piet Schoonenberg describes the priestly
ministry as a "profession like that of the physician, the engineer,
or the plumber."[73] Thomas O'Meara stresses that "*ministry is
not . . . a state but an action. . . .* Is one truly a bishop who cannot
preach or does not preach?"[74]

   Such comments do raise the question as to whether the presbyterate is seen most appropriately as a "ministry," which by
definition tends to be function-oriented. Bernard Cooke observes
several times in his study that the presbyterate somehow constantly eludes such a "functional" categorization.[75]

   Galot warns that this "purely operational conception of
character" does pave the way to a new type of priest. The priest is
no longer a man who, in the image of Christ, is "a priest forever,"
but is instead a man whom the community designates, for a
specified period, as the person best qualified to lead it. One
cannot help wondering whether someone like St. Paul would
really have been happy with such a definition. The end result
certainly is "a new type of priesthood" which is notably different
from that previously known in the Catholic Church.[76]

CHAPTER XII

The Identity of the Presbyter

1. Introduction

As we now finally reach this stage of trying to determine very specifically some "key" to the identity of the presbyter, we inevitably return to the issue that was raised at the very start of this study — the challenge of trying to distinguish between "pastors" who are ordained, and that growing number of Roman Catholic "pastors" who are non-ordained. Until this issue is satisfactorily resolved the clergy seem fated to struggle on in what Michael Evans has called "a theological vacuum" — caught somewhere between that exaggerated "clericalism" of the past, which reserved all significant activity in the Church to the clergy, and a modern "anti-clericalism" where the priest is seen simply as a representative of the community and the servant of all.[1]

The challenge now facing the Church, believes Thomas O'Meara, is certainly "to explain and guide positively the expansion of the ministry"; but also "to heighten the importance of the traditional ministries of presbyter and bishop even as they are complemented by other fulltime services."[2] Jean Galot agrees that since the Church teaches that there is an "essential" difference between the universal and the ministerial priesthood, the nature of the latter certainly requires clarification.[3] It is to this question that we must now turn our attention. What is the "specific quality" which synthesizes the distinctive features of the presbyterate in the midst of what O'Meara has called a veritable "explosion" of ministry?[4]

2. The Presbyter as
"The One Who Presides Over the Community"

Seattle theologian Peter Chirico believes that, owing to the "complexifications" of modern life and the immense increase in knowledge, "we can expect the number of specialized ministries in the Church to keep increasing."[5] He argues that this increase of specializations is going to force the average pastor to switch from being a "one-man band" who dealt personally with most of his parishioners, into being the "orchestra leader" for a team of specialists.[6] The change of roles is similar to that experienced by the "bishops" (*episkopoi*) of the patristic Church who had to hand over to their "presbyters" many of the tasks through which they had previously personally served their people — in order to be free to assume the greater responsibility of "overseeing" their growing dioceses.

In his survey of "constant" features of the Church's ministry, Chirico writes that "one ministry must always exist": that of "leadership of the whole people of God."[7] This is a unifying ministry which coordinates and facilitates all other ministries. Classically, this is the role of the bishop (*episkopos*). Chirico also emphasizes the point made by Hervé Legrand,[8] namely that the one who presides over the community (be he bishop or parish priest) also presides over that community's celebration of the Liturgy "in the same way that the Head of State presides over official state functions."[9]

Chirico argues that "specialized persons should not be ordained to the pastoral priesthood" — because "a specialist does not lead the community."[10] For this reason he emphasizes that the ministry of overseeing the life of the community must not be seen simply as "one ministry among others." People must be helped to recognize "the prime importance of the overseeing pastoral ministry . . . because of its greater value to the life of the community" — just as the one who accepts the role of being Head of State is making a more valuable contribution than, for example, a machinist in a factory.[11]

Chirico's definition of the presbyter as the one who "presides over the community," or "leads the orchestra," or even "heads the State," can sound extremely flattering. But, as Chirico himself notes, it holds little appeal for countless presbyters who had entered the ministry with the intention of "serving the faithful in a personal way" — by celebrating the Eucharist, baptizing new Christians, hearing confessions, anointing the sick, and visiting parishioners.[12]

A further difficulty with Chirico's position is that it does not help to distinguish the ordained presbyter from the non-ordained parish worker who may already have been entrusted with the pastoral oversight of some particular community. Moreover Chirico's very "functional" bias does not seem capable of explaining the "permanent" aspect of the sacrament of orders which the tradition has consistently honored: presbyters are never re-ordained, but "orchestra leaders" or "Heads of State" can always relinquish the position or seek reappointment at some later date. Chirico's view also undermines the identity of ordained presbyters who do not in any very apparent manner "preside" over some particular community of faith — whether they be priests engaged in non-parochial apostolates, or simply the ordinary "assistant" priest in a parish.

3. The Inadequacy of Defining the Presbyterate in Terms of the Community

A recent article by Jesuit John W. O'Malley provides a useful perspective from which to highlight the limitations of Chirico's viewpoint. O'Malley complains that most histories of priesthood and ministry tend now to examine the biblical and patristic periods with great detail, but then to leap across the intervening 1500 years before focusing again on the teachings of Vatican II

and the modern era.[13] As a consequence of this, they generally
tend to overlook the extraordinary variety of ways in which the
presbyteral ministry has been exercised through history, particularly within the great "active" religious orders.[14]

The interesting feature of O'Malley's article for us is the
reminder it gives that much presbyteral ministry through the ages
cannot be reduced simply to the function of "presiding over a
community." The Celtic Church, for example, which was responsible for so much of the re-evangelization of Europe during
the seventh and eighth centuries, was predominantly a monastic
Church which was governed by abbots. The monks were not
necessarily operating as "parish" priests.[15] Similarly the great
mendicant orders of the thirteenth century were actually founded
to respond to ministerial needs which seemed to be outside the
capabilities of pastoral structures then normatively in place. In
many cases they did not "preside" over any fixed local community.[16] The same can also be said of the "presbyters" who
belonged to the new orders of the sixteenth and seventeenth
centuries — such as the Jesuits or the Vincentians. They
pioneered many "new" forms of ministry. The rural "missions" of
this period, which were without either medieval or patristic prece-
dent, combined preaching, adult education and sacramental
practice with such success that they were soon adapted to the cities
as well.[17]

The point O'Malley is trying to make is that from the sixth
century through to well after Trent the parish church was only
one element in a vast and lumbering array of "devotional centers"
which ranged from monasteries, shrines and manor chapels, to
guilds, confraternities and schools. Involvement in many of these
was voluntary — a fact which helped to impart to the medieval
Church its great vitality.[18]

In the light of this extraordinarily diversified past, O'Malley
wonders if perhaps Vatican II's model of the priesthood is too
limited. He argues that the Decree on the Priesthood is based on
the analogue of the contemporary diocesan clergy, and more
remotely on the structure of the patristic Church. It makes three
basic assumptions with regard to the presbyter: (i) that his

ministry is primarily one of Word and Sacrament, and is exercised normatively within a stable parish community; (ii) that he works mostly amid the faithful; and (iii) that he works in hierarchical communion with his bishop.[19]

The Church of an Ambrose or an Augustine certainly comprised a close-knit community of clergy around their bishops, and a stable community of the faithful, living in a world of Christian emperors. The only problem with making this model too normative, says O'Malley, is that it is a model which was unknown in New Testament times, and which has likewise been unknown to us virtually since the sixth century.[20]

O'Malley believes that there have been two quite distinct traditions of ministry which have given shape to the reality of priesthood in the Church: one has served as pastor within a stable "parish" community, the other has concentrated largely on alternative strategies for proclaiming the Gospel. Both can claim New Testament roots, and both can boast of a venerable history. They are separated by more than simple differences in spirituality. There have always been tensions between them. But the genius of Catholicism, claims O'Malley, has been its ability to contain both — and not to settle for neat resolutions or a single Church order for ministry.[21]

We might add too that Chirico's "singular" approach to the presbyterate overlooks the collegial principle which was so heavily emphasized at Vatican II. The Council stressed the collegial nature of the episcopate (LG 22),[22] and went on to teach that

> "no priest can in isolation or singlehandedly accomplish
> his mission in a satisfactory way . . . all priests are united
> among themselves in an intimate sacramental brother-
> hood" (PO 7, 8).[23]

Galot notes that this collegiality makes a division of labor possible and facilitates a distribution of the members of the college according to the needs of the apostolate and the talents of the individuals involved.[24]

In the light of all these reservations, Chirico's definition of the presbyter as the one who "presides over the community" seems less than adequate. It overlooks centuries of involvement by priests, especially those in religious orders, in apostolates which have ranged from schools to soup kitchens, from writing books to street preaching — countless evangelical initiatives, directed not simply to "the community of faith," but also to heretics, pagans and public sinners.[25] Somehow the "key" to the identity of the ordained presbyter cannot be satisfactorily reduced to his role as a community leader.

4. The Presbyter as "The Celebrant of the Eucharist"

One very obvious "constant" from the history of the Church is that it has been exclusively to the presbyter or the bishop, from the earliest centuries, that the celebration of the Eucharist has been entrusted. David Power notes that this role of the priest in the Eucharist has emerged as one of the primary concerns of the Roman Catholic magisterium in recent decades.[26]

Pope Pius XII in "Mediator Dei" (1947) taught that all the faithful celebrate the Eucharist — but not in the same way as the priest:

"the unbloody immolation . . . is performed by the priest alone, and by the priest insofar as he acts in the name of Christ, not insofar as he represents the faithful" (art. 96).

The faithful offer the sacrifice "through" and "with" the priest. The Eucharist involves the whole Christ: Head, together with members, offering the whole Christ, Head and members, to the Father. In this act of offering the priest alone "acts in the person of Christ considered as Head" (art. 97).[27]

The Second Vatican Council emphasized that "though all the faithful can baptize, the priest alone can complete the building up of the Body in the Eucharistic Sacrifice" (LG 17).[28] Today Power notes that both Pope John Paul II, and the Congregation for the Doctrine of the Faith (CDF), are anxious to encourage lay participation in the Eucharist, but not at the expense of obscuring the role of the priest.[29]

Pope John Paul II wrote in *"Dominicae Cenae"* (1980) that the Sacrifice of the Eucharist is that of the Church, but that it is confided in the first place to bishops and priests; in fact it is "the primary exercise of their ministry," in which they act *"in persona Christi."*[30] The CDF, in its response to the Statement on Ministry and Ordination by the Anglican-Roman Catholic International Commission, singled out the action of the priest in the Eucharist as "the" sacramental act whereby Christ became present and acted.[31] Similarly, in its 1987 Response to the World Council of Churches' "Lima Statement" on Baptism, Eucharist and Ministry, the CDF again stressed that the ordained minister "represents Christ in a personal and sacramental way."[32]

We have already seen in previous chapters the heavily Eucharistic bias of the presbyterate — epitomized in the Tridentine definition of the priesthood as a "power of consecrating and offering the true Body and Blood of the Lord and of forgiving and retaining sins" (S. XXIII, ch. I).[33] Vatican II "liberated" the presbyterate from being too exclusively linked to the Eucharist: presbyters, sharing "in a limited degree" (PO 2) in the mission entrusted to the College of Bishops, share with their bishops the same "primary duty", namely the "proclamation of the Gospel of God to all" (PO 4).[34]

Although Vatican II also insisted that "priests fulfill their chief duty in the mystery of the Eucharistic Sacrifice" (PO 13),[35] the Council's broader perspective ensured that this function could no longer be considered in isolation.[36] But seeing the presbyter as "the one who presides at the Eucharist," for all its limitations, certainly seems to be more satisfactory than the attempt to see him simply as "the one who presides over the community." Can we, however, specify the nature of this ordained ministry still further?

5. *The Presbyter as "The Shepherd of the Flock"*

We have previously noted Vatican II's use of the threefold division of Prophet, Priest and King, to describe the ministry of Jesus and consequently of his followers. However Friedrich Wulf points out that although the threefold pattern proved particularly helpful in freeing the presbyterate from its centuries-old restriction to the realm of cult, the three "offices" are really only partially distinguishable.[37] Kenan Osborne notes that "the format itself can only be seen as a theological aid, not a part of revelation itself" — since neither Scripture, nor the early Church, nor even the scholastics used it. Biblical scholars today apply the three titles to Jesus only in a very nuanced manner.[38]

For these reasons Jean Galot agrees that "to reduce ministry to only one of its three traditional functions entails an impoverishment."[39] Instead, he finds in Christ's own image of the Shepherd "a principle of unity."[40] The Good Shepherd leads the flock by the word he speaks (Jn 10:16), and finally guarantees the truth of his teaching by laying down his life for his sheep (Jn 10:15). According to this model the tasks of preaching, sacrificing and leading, all become expressions of the Shepherd's love for his sheep. And it is this image which shapes the Lord's commission to Peter: "Feed my lambs . . . Feed my sheep" (Jn 21:15-17).

The distinctive characteristic of the Shepherd image is that it implies authority over the flock. Vatican II taught that all the baptized share in the priestly, prophetic and kingly mission of Christ (LG 34-36).[41] But it is to the ordained ministers that the pastoral authority is reserved: ". . . priests exercise the office of Christ the Head and the Shepherd" (PO 6).[42]

Friedrich Wulf claims that, in view of the renewed emphasis on the common priesthood of all the faithful, the image of the Good Shepherd connotes too inappropriately a traditional "folk Church" comprising "the leaders and the led." He would prefer a more mature "Church of the faithful" where both priests and laity are entrusted with the same mission, and work together as brothers and sisters.[43] This criticism seems to lack a poetic sensitivity, especially since the image of the Shepherd is so deeply rooted in the Scriptures. But it does remind us of the difficulty we face in trying to distinguish between "Shepherds" who are ordained, and those who are not.

Michael Winstanly contests, however, that the image of the Shepherd is a thoroughly acceptable "paradigm" for Christian ministry.[44] And Michael Evans appreciates the particular insight it gives into the permanency of the priesthood.[45] The Shepherd in the Scriptures is not a "hired man" (Jn 10:12) who takes on some temporary or part-time responsibility.

6. *The Presbyter as "A Witness to Mystery"*

Peter Fink writes that he has suffered sufficiently at the hands of poor celebrants to welcome the contemporary emphasis on the need for functional skills in candidates for the priesthood. However, he maintains, and I believe correctly, that "the functional description of the priesthood" is of itself insufficient to capture the reality that is lived by individual priests, and that is described in Church teaching. This "other side" of the priesthood, formerly highlighted in almost "mythical" images, reflects the "unfolding mystery of Jesus Christ."[46]

Fink gives the humbling example of a homilist who preaches a superb sermon, and then finds that some member of the congregation was indeed deeply moved — but by some phrase that seemed so insignificant to the homilist that he could not actually remember having said it! Fink talks of a resulting "sense of awe," a sense of having been "in the presence of One without whose presence we make absolutely no sense as Church."[47] The Church has tried to give expression to this phenomenon by talking of the priest as somehow standing "*in persona Christi*": as the one who is "asked by the Church to be a sacrament of this Christ — as a ministry to its own prayer."[48]

Fink observes that "the grand myth" of the priesthood may have disappeared from our conversation, but "the grand reality" it tried to identify continues to unfold.[49] The problem with reducing the rhetoric of the priesthood to the functional is that it can tend to give the impression that "skills" are really all that the ordained priesthood is about. Yet somewhat ironically, these very "skills" lose their relevance if priest or people lose touch with the mystery of Christ which those functions serve. Perhaps significantly it is this very point which is also stressed in the Discussion Paper issued for the 1990 Synod of Bishops. The *Lineamenta* talks of the priest as pre-eminently "a witness to Mystery" (p. 7).[50]

James A. Fischer likewise emphasizes this "mystery" dimension.[51] He writes that the priest is the one who interprets in all the events of everyday life what Karl Rahner calls "the silent coming of God."[52] Fischer sees the priest as called to be a "comedian":

> "Tragedy is logic at its saddest, the inevitable destruction of the hero. . . . But the priest, who sees the story from a more-distant viewpoint, knows that it is a comedy."[53]

However we may finally describe the priest — as dispenser of mysteries or as sealed with a character, as spiritual Shepherd, or even comedian — "we are always dealing with the same distinctive characteristic. There is a mystery which inhabits these men."[54]

7. *The Need for a "High" Theology of the Presbyterate*

Michael Evans believes that a problem with priestly identity is almost inevitable if ordained ministry is seen in purely functional rather than ontological terms.[55] He notes with reference to Christology that theologians can approach the mystery of the Person of Christ either "from above" — stressing his divinity — or "from below" — emphasizing his humanity.[56] Where they begin their investigation does not matter, but unless they eventually end up with a "high" Christology which firmly acknowledges the divinity of Christ they undermine any real point in being a Christian. And, coining a new word in the process, Evans argues that a similar "Chalcedon-like" balance must be achieved in "ministeriology." Unless one eventually arrives at a "high" ministeriology it is difficult to see any particular worth in being a priest at all.[57]

The present trend in theology is to approach the priesthood "from below" and to see the priest primarily as a representative of the community. Thus David Power writes:

> "It is because he acts in the name of the Church, and by his actions mediates its faith, that the priest also represents and acts in the person of Christ . . . the priest therefore, by being a symbol of the Church in its dependency on Christ's headship, is a symbol of the headship itself."[58]

Evans's only comment is that this seems a rather "convoluted" way of reaching "from below" to a "high"ministeriology.[59]

Vatican II certainly presents an unequivocally "high" theology of the priesthood. The priest "shares in the authority by which Christ himself builds up, sanctifies and rules his body" (PO 2).[60] Priests are "so configured to Christ the priest that they can act in the person of Christ the Head" (PO 2).[61] Indeed "every priest in his own way represents the person of Christ himself" (PO 12).[62] He is "father and teacher among the people of God and for them" (PO 9).[63] Priests become "living instruments of Christ the eternal priest" (PO 12).[64]

Evans notes that this idea of the priest as being "the representative of Christ" is at the heart of all official Catholic theology since Vatican II.[65] In its 1976 Declaration on "Women and the Priesthood" the Sacred Congregation for the Doctrine of the Faith warned against reducing "*in persona Christi*" to "*in persona Ecclesiae*":

> "It is true that the priest represents the Church, which is the Body of Christ. But if he does so, it is precisely because he first represents Christ himself, who is the Head and Shepherd of the Church" (p. 5).[66]

Evans claims that a "low" ministeriology depicts the priest as being something like baptismal water: ordinary water which has been blessed and set aside for special use — but able to be replaced by any water in emergency situations. In contrast, a "high" ministeriology suggests that "perhaps there is more in common between the ordained man and the consecrated bread than with the baptismal water."[67] Interestingly, this image which is proposed so diffidently by Evans is precisely the one adopted centuries previously by Gregory of Nyssa (d. 395) to make the same point.[68]

8. A Pauline Starting-Point for a "High" Theology of the Presbyterate

Michael Evans turns to the theology of St. Paul to ground his argument for a high ministeriology.[69] The Pauline writings delicately balance the "servant" and the "authority" aspects of ministerial oversight. Paul is a servant of the Gospel (Ep 3:7), of the Church (Col 1:25), and of Jesus Christ (Ph 1:1). He is "the slave of everyone" (1 Cor 9:19). Yet he is also the steward of the mysteries of God (1 Cor 4:1), the envoy of God (2 Cor 2:17), and the ambassador of Christ (2 Cor 5:20). Paul believes he is able to serve the Church precisely because of the authority he possesses:

"Maybe I do boast rather too much about our authority, but the Lord gave it to me for building you up and not for pulling you down, and I shall not be ashamed of it" (2 Cor 10:8).

To understand the precise nature of the authority of the ordained presbyter we need to return to St. Paul's theology of the Church as the Body of Christ. Paul talks about the Body in two sets of texts. In the first (Romans and Corinthians) Paul stresses the diversity of the gifts which make up the one body: "Just as a human body, though it is made up of many parts, is a single unit because all these parts, though many, make up one body, so it is with Christ" (1 Cor 12:12). In the second set of texts (Ephesians and Colossians) the emphasis is on Christ himself as Head of the Body, the source of the community's life and unity: "Now the Church is his body, he is its head" (Col 1:18).

The priest is clearly a member of the Body — one of the many parts which make up the whole. But what is "essentially different" about his place in the Body is that it is he alone who represents Christ as Head of the Body — to the Body itself. The priest is not the only one to "represent" Christ — because all the baptized have that function. But his special vocation is to represent Christ "as Head" — to the rest of the faithful who are themselves "the fullness" of Christ (Ep 1:23).

Christ is present and active in his Church in many ways, but as Head of the Church he makes his presence manifest through the ordained ministry. Even Schillebeeckx once observed that "priestly acts are the personal acts of Christ himself made visible in sacramental form."[70] Writing of the celebration of the Eucharist, Schillebeeckx referred to the priest as the one who takes Christ's place in the visibility of the Church: "the priest is the 'sacramental Christ,' *alter Christus*, here present for the faithful."[71]

It is from this that the presbyter's authority comes — as the ambassador of Christ to his Church, the authorized representative of the Lord, speaking and acting in his name. Thus Paul claimed to speak for the Lord Jesus and "in Christ" (Rm 9:1), appealing in the Lord Jesus (1 Th 4:1), and giving orders in the Lord's name (1 Th 5:27; 2 Th 3:12) as a "father" in Christ (1 Cor 4:15).

One consequence of this, which David Power has noted, is that for all the fluctuations with regard to priestly functions or activities, one "constant" throughout history has been the personal qualities expected of the ordained minister. The ordination prayers of every era express the expectation that the priest be *"forma gregis"* (1 P 5:3): an "example to the flock."[72] Every age has expected him to be an elder in wisdom and virtue, as much concerned with living the Gospel himself as with preaching it to others.

9. An Ecumenical Postscript

Evans finds it perplexing that so many Catholic theologians are today drifting towards a "low" theology of the ministry precisely at a time when Protestant theologians are moving in the opposite direction. In ecumenical dialogue there is increasing unanimity in seeing the minister as "representative of Christ to the Church."[73]

The Anglican-Roman Catholic International Commission's 1973 Canterbury statement on Ministry and Ordination spoke of the minister: "As herald and ambassador, he is *an authorized representative of Christ*" (art. 8).[74] The 1982 Lima text of the World Council of Churches is almost identical: "As heralds and ambassadors, ordained ministers are *representatives of Jesus Christ* to the community. . . ." (art. 11).[75] Max Thurian, writing as a Protestant member of the Taizé community, states that it is above all in the Eucharist that the pastor "fulfills supremely his function of *ambassador of the head of the Church* and as the *sign of Christ the high priest*. . . ."[76]

We may note in conclusion that it is true that priests are called to serve, but they serve precisely by exercising leadership among God's people in Christ's name — as his ambassadors and his vicars. It is true that presbyters are "only the earthenware jars that hold this treasure" (2 Cor 4:7), but it is a treasure that they do indeed hold — as "living instruments of Christ the eternal priest" (PO 12).[77]

CHAPTER XIII

Conclusion

---

1. What is the Nature of the Church?

At an early stage in his book on the priesthood, Kenan Osborne makes the point that the "key" to any individual's understanding of the ordained ministry will inevitably lie in his or her prior understanding of the nature of the Church. Did Jesus, for example, himself establish certain "Church" structures, or did these all take shape only after the Resurrection?[1]

The importance of this "ecclesiological presupposition" is acknowledged in the Vatican response to the World Council of Churches' 1982 "Lima Statement":

> "The recognition of ordained ministry cannot be isolated from its ecclesiological context."[2]

Again and again the Vatican Response emphasizes the importance of ecclesiology.

> "The *study of ecclesiology must come more and more into the center* of the ecumenical dialogue.... Faith and Order *must focus more directly on ecclesiology*."[3]

This emphasis on ecclesiology stems partly from the need to know who (if anyone!) finally speaks with authority in addressing disputed questions. The "Lima Statement," for example, mentions the differences concerning the place and forms of the ordained ministry in the different Christian denominations, but then goes on itself to ask the question,

> "How, according to the will of God and under the guidance of the Holy Spirit, is the life of the Church to be understood and ordered, so that the Gospel may be spread and the community built up in love?" (M. p. 6).[4]

The Vatican Secretariat responds that this question

> "cannot be answered conclusively as long as the questions of who will decide, who will discern God's will in various developments, and with what authority, are left open. We believe in fact that certain people are commissioned in the Church with a God-given authority to exercise such ministry of decision."[5]

2. Towards an "Authentically Catholic" Ecclesiology

Cardinal Joseph Ratzinger, the Prefect of the Congregation for the Doctrine of the Faith, fears that the "authentically Catholic" meaning of the reality "Church" is tacitly disappearing.[6] In his 1984 interviews with Italian writer Vittorio Messori (*The Ratzinger Report*), Ratzinger expressed his concern that

> "even with some theologians, the Church appears to be a human construction, an instrument created by us and one which we ourselves can freely re-organize according to the requirements of the moment."[7]

For a Catholic, says Ratzinger, the fundamental structures of the Church are willed by God, and are therefore inviolable:

> "behind the human exterior stands the mystery of a more than human reality, in which reformers, sociologists, organizers have no authority whatsoever."[8]

Ratzinger is concerned that the emphasis on the Church as "People of God" has come to dominate many post-conciliar ecclesiologies. He argues that this model gives expression to the Church's continuity with Israel, but that taken on its own it is an inadequate expression of the full New Testament understanding of the Church — which Paul's image of the "Body of Christ" communicates more effectively.

> "The Church does not exhaust herself in the 'collective' of the believers: being the 'Body of Christ' she is much more than the simple sum of her members."[9]

Ratzinger emphasizes that if "we alone" are the Church and if her structures are not willed by Christ, then it is no longer possible to conceive of the existence of a hierarchy as a service to the baptized established by the Lord himself. Hierarchy then becomes not an authority willed by God, but an authority which has its legitimation in the consensus of the majority of the members. But, counters Ratzinger, the Church's "deep and permanent structure" is not "democratic": rather, it is "sacramental," and consequently "hierarchical."[10]

Ratzinger pleads for a return to "the authentic texts of the original Vatican II."[11] He fears that "Vatican II today stands in a twilight."[12] Progressives feel it has been surpassed, while conservatives see it as a dilution of Vatican I and Trent. To both criticisms, Ratzinger stresses that "Vatican II is upheld by the same authority as Vatican I and the Council of Trent, namely, *the Pope and the College of Bishops in communion with him.*" It is impossible, he believes, for a Catholic to be "for" one Council, but "against" another.[13] Ratzinger is very critical of any talk of a "pre-" or "post-" Vatican II Church, and notes that the documents of the Council "do nothing but reaffirm the continuity of Catholicism."[14]

3. The Teaching Authority of the Church

In Chapters III and IV, we have already drawn attention to the tendency of Edward Schillebeeckx and Hans Küng (to name but two) to critique later New Testament writings in the light of those which came earlier.[15] Thus Schillebeeckx, for example, prefers the radical equality of the Letter to the Galatians ("you are all one in Christ Jesus" — Gal 3:28)[16] to what he sees as the "non-Christian," and even "pagan," ministerial patterns of the Pastoral Epistles or 1 Peter.[17]

Our response to both Schillebeeckx and Küng must be to query the grounds upon which they make this preference. What is the underlying premise which leads them to prefer one book of the Bible over another, especially when an Ecumenical Council (Vatican II) teaches that "the books of both the Old and New Testament *in their entirety* . . . are sacred and canonical" (DV 11).[18]

A fully "Catholic" ecclesiology sees the Sacred Scriptures as somehow "belonging" to the Church. As a written expression of the teaching of the Apostles, the authoritative interpretation of these sacred writings is now entrusted to the successors of these same Apostles.

> "It is clear, therefore, that *sacred tradition, sacred Scriptures*, and the *teaching authority of the Church*, in accord with God's most wise design, are so linked and joined together that *one cannot stand without the others*. . . ." (DV 10).[19]

Vatican II clearly states its own "ecclesiological presuppositions."

> "This most sacred Synod, following in the footsteps of the First Vatican Council, teaches and declares with that Council that Jesus Christ . . . established His holy Church

by sending forth the apostles as He Himself had been sent
by the Father (Jn 20:21). He willed that their successors,
namely the bishops, should be shepherds in His Church
even to the consummation of the world" (LG 18).[20]

4. The Seeming Inadequacy of Schillebeeckx's Ecclesiology

It is this appreciation of the Church — as something instituted and hierarchically structured by Christ himself — which
seems to be most lacking in much current reflection on the presbyterate by Roman Catholic writers.

It is the lack of this appreciation which leads Schillebeeckx,
on the basis of Cyrille Vogel's research,[21] to the bizarre conclusion that twentieth-century Christians must make a choice between accepting "the practice and the views" of the Church either
in the first millennium or in the second millennium as being truly
"Christian and apostolic."[22] It also means that Schillebeeckx, for
whom the sixth canon of the Council of Chalcedon (451) becomes
so significant,[23] can simply ignore a totally different interpretation of the same canon which was explicitly reaffirmed in the
sixteenth century at the Council of Trent (S. XXIII, Ref. Ch.
XVI).[24]

John O'Malley notes appropriately that ultimately "the future of ministry in the Church is hidden in the mind of
God."[25] But we must also add that whatever proposals are made
for the future directions of ministry in the Roman Catholic
Church, none can really be taken seriously if it ignores the essentially hierarchical structure of the Church which was so clearly
reiterated at Vatican II. Ratzinger states of Vatican II that "its
authentic reception has not yet begun."[26] Until Catholics have
become fully conversant with the theology of this most recent of
the Church's Ecumenical Councils, a fully satisfactory theology of
the presbyterate will certainly continue to elude us.

5. *The Enduring Mystery of the Priesthood*

But if we do accept the ecclesiology of Vatican II we emerge with an unremittingly "high" theology of the presbyterate. As "co-workers of the episcopal order" (PO 2),[27] presbyters share in the original apostolic mission. Like St. Paul, the presbyter is called to be a "servant of the Gospel" (Ep 3:7), a "servant of the Church" (Col 1:25), a "servant of Jesus Christ" (Ph 1:1), and "the slave of everyone" (1 Cor 9:19). But he is also called to be the "steward of the mysteries of God" (1 Cor 4:1), the "envoy of God" (2 Cor 2:17), and the "ambassador of Christ" (2 Cor 5:20).

Because of the privileged position he holds, the presbyter is called to be a "father and teacher among the people of God" (PO 9),[28] the "living instrument of Christ the eternal priest" (PO 12).[29] He is expected to be *forma gregis*, an "example" to the flock (1 P 5:3) of which he is the Shepherd (PO 6).[30] Marked by an indelible character at the time of his ordination, the presbyter is empowered to act "in the person of Christ the Head" (PO 2).[31] He fulfills this role pre-eminently "in the mystery of the Eucharistic sacrifice" (PO 13).[32]

Jean Marie Vianney (1786-1859) was, for 41 years, the *"Curé"* of Ars. When he arrived at Ars in 1818, this French parish comprised about 50 families.[33] He set out through personal prayer and penances to "convert" his parish.[34] He was fascinated by the mystery of Christ's presence in the Eucharist, and spent long hours before the tabernacle in silent adoration. He is most famous, however, as the priest who eventually spent 10 to 15 hours each day in the confessional. During the final years of his life, 80,000 pilgrims annually flocked to his parish.[35] Pope Pius XI, in 1925, formally recognized his sanctity in the solemn ceremony of canonization, and 10 years later in his Encyclical *"Ad Catholici Sacerdotii"* named him "Heavenly Patron" of all parish priest.[36]

In the Introduction we alluded to "the power and the glory" of the priesthood by referring to the whisky priest in Graham Greene's novel. It seems appropriate to close our considerations by allowing *"Monsieur le Curé"* to share some of his own reflections on the topic.

"At the sight of a steeple you can say, 'What's in there?' The Body of our Lord. 'Why is he there?' Because a priest has passed by and said the Holy Mass."[37]

"Without the priest, the death and passion of our Lord would be of no use. It is the priest who continues the work of Redemption on earth."[38]

"How great is the priest! The priest will only be understood in heaven. Were he understood on earth, people would die, not of fear, but of love."[39]

"Oh, the priest is something great! If he knew it he would die."[40]

CHAPTER XIV

A Postscript on the Ordination of Women

1. Introduction

The main aim of this book has been to take a closer look at the legitimacy of the clergy-laity distinction within the Church, especially in the light of what we find both in Scripture and in Tradition.

However, any contemporary discussion concerning the priesthood now almost unavoidably leads to a consideration of the possibility of priestly ordination for women. Despite the 1976 Vatican Declaration, "*Inter Insigniores*," which stated that the Catholic Church does not consider herself "authorized" to admit women to the priesthood,[1] there remains a widespread perception that such a step is both imminent and inevitable.

It therefore seems important that we not conclude our consideration of the theology of the presbyterate without some examination of this topic.

2. The Usual Starting-Point

(i) The Attitude of Christ

The usual starting-point for any discussion on the ordination of women has been to consider the practice of Jesus himself, and in this the 1976 Declaration on "Women and the Priesthood" is no exception.[2]

Jesus did not call any women to be his apostles (Mk 3:13-19). Yet St. Luke does tell us that on his journeys the Lord was accompanied not only by the Twelve, but also by certain women: "Mary surnamed the Magdalene, from whom seven demons had gone out, Joanna the wife of Herod's steward Chuza, Susanna, and several others who provided for them out of their own resources" (Lk 8:2-3).

Moreover, in many respects Jesus showed no hesitation in disregarding the prevailing religious and cultural attitudes of his contemporaries in relating to women. He ignores the state of legal impurity suffered by the woman with the haemorrhage (Mt 9:20f), allows himself to be approached by the sinful woman in the house of Simon the Pharisee (Lk 7:37f), takes the side of an adultress (Jn 8:11), and challenges even the Mosaic Law by defending the equal rights of men and women with regard to the marriage bond (Mk 10:2f; Mt 19:3f). He shows his capacity for empathy with the world of women in such parables as that of the woman with the lost drachma (Lk 15:8-10), or the widow with the unscrupulous judge (Lk 18:1-8).

Women serve faithfully as his disciples all the way to the foot of the Cross (Mk 15:40-41). And on Easter morning it was to women that Jesus entrusted the responsibility of first proclaiming the paschal mystery to the Apostles themselves (Mt 28:7f; Lk 24:9f; Jn 20:11f).

Yet despite all this, women were not present at the Last Supper, which Jesus ate in the exclusive company of the Twelve (Mk 14:17f). The absence of women from this meal is all the more striking when one remembers that the Passover more than any other was a "family" supper, at which women and children were invariably present (Ex 12:1-14).

(ii)   The Practice of the Apostles

The apostolic community remained faithful to the practice of Jesus in relying solely on male office-bearers. Although Mary occupied a position of honor in their midst (Ac 1:14), there was never any suggestion that she should take the place of Judas as one of the Twelve (Ac 1:15-26). And on the Day of Pentecost, although the Holy Spirit was poured forth upon both men and women (Ac 1:13-14), it was "Peter and the Eleven" who undertook the initial preaching of the Gospel (Ac 2:1, 14).

What we know of St. Paul is especially enlightening. He relied upon and appreciated the assistance of women, perhaps to an even greater extent than did Jesus. From Paul we know of Phoebe and of her service in the Church at Cenchreae, but also of many other women who cooperated in his work (Rm 16:1-16). He was a close friend of Prisca (or Priscilla) and her husband Aquila (Rm 16:3) who took it upon themselves to complete the instruction of Apollos in Ephesus (Ac 18:26). And even the formidable Paul is lost for words when Lydia insists that he accept her hospitality at Philippi (Ac 16:14f)! Paul seems to take it for granted that women, along with men, will "pray" and "prophesy" when the community gathers for public worship (1 Cor 11:4-5, 13).

(iii)   The Pauline "Subordination" Texts

Yet it is from Paul that we also have the great New Testament texts on the "subordination" of women. In writing to the Corinthians, Paul states that:

> "What I want you to understand is that Christ is the head of every man, *man is the head of woman*, and God is the head of Christ. . . *a* man . . . is the image of God and reflects God's glory; but woman is the reflection of man's glory . . . and man was not created for the sake of woman, but woman was created for the sake of man. . . .
>
> "*However*, though woman cannot do without man, neither can man do without woman, in the Lord; woman may come from man, but man is born of woman — *both come from God*" (1 Cor 11:3, 7-8, 11-12).

When stressing the need to regulate spiritual gifts, Paul insists that:

> "*Women are to remain quiet at meetings* since they have no permission to speak; they must keep in the background as the Law itself lays it down. . . . Anyone who claims to be a prophet or inspired ought to recognize that what I am writing to you is *a command from the Lord*" (1 Cor 14:34, 37).

It is a message that he repeats to Timothy:

> "*During instruction a woman should be quiet* and respectful. I am not giving permission for a woman to teach or to tell a man what to do. A woman ought not to speak, because Adam was formed first and Eve afterwards, and it was not Adam who was led astray but the woman who was led astray and fell into sin. . . ." (1 Tm 2:11-14).

Paul returns to the same theme when writing on marriage:

> "Wives should regard their husbands as they regard the Lord, since *as Christ is head of the Church* and saves the whole body, *so is a husband the head of his wife*; and as the Church submits to Christ, so should wives to their husbands, in everything. Husbands should love their wives as Christ loved the Church and sacrificed himself for her, to make her holy. . . .
>
> "*In the same way husbands must love their wives* as they love their own bodies; for a man to love his wife is for him to love himself. A man never hates his own body, but he feeds it and looks after it; and that is how Christ treats the Church, because it is his body — and we are its living parts. . . .
>
> "*This mystery* has many implications; but I am saying it *applies to Christ and the Church*" (Ep 5:22-25, 28-32).

A closer examination of the texts concerned seems to indicate that while Paul had no difficulty with instruction being given by a woman (as in the case of Priscilla with Apollos), he was anxious to ensure that women not be permitted to give the official teaching usually associated with presiding at the liturgy. Paul sees this prescription as being somehow bound up with the divine order of creation (1 Cor 11:7; Gn 2:18-24). He also acknowledges some specific "command from the Lord" (1 Cor 14:37).

The "command from the Lord," although unknown to us, should not be too lightly dismissed. All though Paul's writings, Christ is seen as the author of a body of religious knowledge that must be passed on in exact detail, and that is to be preserved through those who serve as teachers (1 Cor 11:23, 15:1-2; 2 Tm 1:13). In Corinth Paul was exposed to severe attacks on his person and his office (1 Cor 1:12, 4:3; 2 Cor 10-12). If he had claimed support from some non-existent "command from the Lord," he would sooner or later have been convicted of untruth.

(iv) The Present-day Reaction

The Pauline texts today tend to arouse either incredulity or anger. It is argued that neither the example of Jesus nor the teaching of Paul, insofar as it concerns the role of women, can be regarded as normative for the Church in the twentieth century. Since both Jesus and Paul were obviously formed by the values of first-century Judaism, we have to "filter" from their words and actions the prejudices of that particular milieu before they can have relevance for us. As Schillebeeckx insists with regard to social history, "there are no such things as 'facts' . . . there are only interpreted facts."[3]

However, if we accept that both Jesus and Paul were subject to the prejudices of their own socio-cultural milieu, we must expect that our own views too will be equally suspect. And, indeed, two contemporary presuppositions do seem to be especially deserving of critical scrutiny.

One common assumption today is that the past was oppressively "patriarchal." Another is that the differences between the sexes, apart from the obvious bio-genital roles, are predominantly the result of social conditioning. This latter belief has led some modern Christians to claim that the radical equality of the sexes is a Gospel value. We noted earlier Edward Schillebeeckx's predilection for Paul's instruction to the Galatians:

> ". . . and there are no more distinctions between Jew and Greek, slave and free, male and female, but all of you are one in Christ Jesus" (Gal 3:28).[4]

Although Paul's concern is for the "unity" of the Church rather than for the equality of the sexes ("you are *one* in Christ Jesus"), Schillebeeckx sees the passage instead as proof of some primitive "egalitarian ecclesiology."[5]

It may be helpful for us to ask quite seriously just how "patriarchal" the past actually was, and secondly whether to some extent we may be underestimating the differences between the sexes.

3. How "Patriarchal" Was the Past?

(i) Ancient Israel

The larger social context of ancient Israel was undeniably patriarchal. The Ten Commandments include a man's wife in the category of property — along with his servants, his ox and his donkey (Ex 20:17). A husband could divorce his wife simply by handing her a writ of dismissal (Dt 24:1) — a practice which sounds ruthless to us until we realize that it is not strikingly different from modern divorce practice, which causes no less anguish for innocent parties.

There is, however, no evidence that women in Israel cried out in bondage as the whole people had done previously in Egypt. It was specifically forbidden that a wife be simply sold as a slave (Dt 21:14). Like Abigail with Nabal, a wife often had *de facto* control over her husband's property (1 S 25:18-19). Children were expected to show equal respect to both father and mother (Ex 20:12). There are also clear indications that the love between husband and wife was frequently as tender as it can be today. When the prophet Ezekiel is told that his wife — "the delight of your eyes" — is to die, he is instructed by God as a prophetic sign to avoid manifesting in public his natural inclination to lament, to weep, and to let his tears "run down" (Ezk 24:15-16). Similarly the dialogue between bride and groom in the Song of Songs is as romantic as that between young lovers in any age:

> (*Groom*): "How beautiful you are, my love,
> How beautiful you are!
> Your eyes are doves. . . ."

> (*Bride*): "How beautiful you are, my beloved,
> And how delightful!
> All green is our bed." (Sg 1:15-16)

The Old Testament records the deeds of countless outstanding women. Huldah the prophetess was respectfully consulted by the king (2 K 22:14-20); Deborah guided the destiny of Israel during particularly difficult times (Jg 4:4f); and Miriam, the sister of Moses and Aaron, was in her own right a leader for her people (Ex 15:20f). Women also participated in the kingly office, especially when there was no male regent — as when the ruthless Athaliah seized power on the death of her son Ahaziah (2 K 11:1f). The Queen Mother was usually accorded a place of particular honor (1 K 2:13, 19f).

Such examples suffice to show that any sweeping thesis about the inferior position of women in Old Testament times cannot be accepted too uncritically. Yet one curiously striking feature remains: the total exclusion of women from the offices of priest and Levite despite the presence of women priests in contemporary

Canaanite society which was presumably just as "patriarchal" or otherwise as was that of Israel.[6]

(ii) The Position of Women in Hellenistic Times

Nor was the Hellenistic world of Paul's era as oppressively "patriarchal" as is today sometimes imagined. Although traditional Greek (Athenian) culture had excluded women from public affairs, the widespread restriction of women to the domestic sphere in ancient Greece had been transformed by a virtual emancipation that took place in most of the Roman Empire during the imperial period. Women's rights with regard to property, marriage, and even occupations, were equal to those of men. There are reports of female goldsmiths, doctors (especially in Asia Minor) and estate owners. Pythagorean and Epicurean philosophers both advocated the ideal of equality, and many women were highly educated.[7] If Paul had chosen female colleagues instead of Barnabas or Timothy, it would have caused no offense among the Greeks. The behavior of women in public, especially in the cities, was increasingly similar to that of men. In sports, women even participated in chariot-racing, hunting, fencing and wrestling.[8]

Priests of both sexes were relatively common in Greek regions. The participation of women in religious leadership positions was further strengthened by the rise of powerful mystery religions such as the cults of Dionysus or Isis. One popular hymn used in the latter claimed of Isis that she had "given women the same power as men." The emancipatory practices against which Paul takes a stand in his "subordination" texts (e.g. 1 Cor 11:2-16, 14:33-38) spring from this socio-cultural milieu. Corinth was the city of Aphrodite, and home to a whole range of mystery religions.[9]

(iii) The Fathers of the Church

The Fathers of the Church were androcentric in the sense that they generally saw males as the measure of being "human."

However, the Church's refusal to countenance divorce was a move for the rights of women which reached all classes of society. And the Christian veneration for Mary and for female saints, as well as the esteem in which martyrdom and virginity were held, indicate that women were in no way seen as being morally inferior to men.

Although Roman Law excluded women from public office, actual practice, especially during the Imperial Age, was much more liberal. There seemed to be no obstacle to a woman's becoming empress. Theodora (d. 548) or Irene (d. 802) both ruled the Empire and both came from Christian houses.[10]

Theologically educated women were well known to the Church Fathers, and were encouraged by them. Clement of Alexandria (d. 215?) encouraged women to pursue philosophy. Origen's (d. 254) lectures in the same city were particularly well attended by women. Gregory of Nyssa (d. 395) received his basic religious instruction from his sister Macrina, to whom he remained grateful all his life. Although Jerome (d. 420), like Paul, regarded it as unnatural for a woman to speak at a gathering of men,[11] he himself dedicated his biblical commentaries to educated women, and conducted Scripture and Hebrew classes for them.[12]

These holy and educated women, especially virgins and widows who were not restricted by family commitments, were obviously potential women priests — yet that possibility was seen to be expressly closed to them by the statements of Paul and the behavior of Jesus.[13]

(iv) The Position of Women in the Middle Ages

In the Middle Ages, Thomas Aquinas (d. 1274) takes over from Aristotle the notion that woman is in some sense an "imperfect man." This biologically deficient notion arose from the assumption that the seed of a father would in itself produce a child of the male sex — like the father. It was believed that a girl was conceived as a result of a weakness in the active force of the seed, and as a result of such negative external forces as, for example, the sultry midday winds! (STh I q92 al ad1).[14]

To this extent Thomas is obviously "androcentric." Yet he never intends any devaluation of the personal relationship between husband and wife, which he regards as the greatest and most intense friendship conceivable between human beings. (ScG III 123)[15] At one stage he cites with approval the popular interpretation of the story of creation:

> "Woman should not be the master of man: therefore she was not formed out of his head. She should also not be disdained by man and slavishly subject to him: therefore, she was not formed out of his feet, but out of his side." (STh I q92 a3).

Thomas's contemporary, Berthold von Regensburg, adds: "God took her from your heart, and thus she should be close to you."[16]

A high estimation of women seems to have increased rather than declined during the Middle Ages. This was the era of chivalry, when knights chose noble women as their "ladies." Women were seen as beautiful and good, and men as needing to be educated. Esteem for women had its effects in every marriage because of the Church's strong stand against divorce. Another significant feature of the period was the constant popularity of Marian devotion, which was fostered so strongly by figures such as Bernard of Claivaux (d. 1153).

The most influential women in the history of the Church are to be found in these centuries. Without Catherine of Siena (d. 1380) the stay of the Popes in Avignon would not have ended as soon as it did. The Middle Ages saw nothing unusual or offensive in wordly rule by women. Numerous biographies from the 10th and 11th centuries tell us how highly queens and empresses were respected. Medieval abbesses often attended imperial diets and synods.[17]

Under the influence of Jerome (d. 420) and Ambrose (d. 397), theological education of extremely high standards was achieved in medieval convents. Lioba (d. 780), the sister(?) of Boniface (d. 755), was reputed to have known the Bible virtually by heart, and had studied Church Fathers, councils and canon law. Princes and bishops came to be instructed by her. The English Abbess Hilda (d. 680) produced five bishops from her school at Whitby Abbey. The clergy, members of religious orders, *and women*, frequently comprised the educated classes of the Middle Ages. Women are documented as doctors, pharmacists and teachers.[18]

That the sociological conditions of the Middle Ages were not sufficient to account for the strict exclusion of women from the priesthood is demonstrated by the ordination of women as priests in certain sects. The Waldensians and the Catharists, for example, both had women preachers, and in both sects women celebrated the Eucharist. Aquinas (d. 1274) would have been aware of this since his order was specifically founded to oppose heretics.[19]

(v) Conclusion

What holds true for the patristic Church holds also for the medieval Church: women were not admitted to ordination, even though social conditions would, at times, have been more than favorable. The problem for the Church was not that women were morally inferior, but that the two sexes were perceived as having quite distinct roles in the plan of creation and redemption. It was for this reason that each of the three great Scholastics (Aquinas, Bonaventure and Scotus) saw women as incapable of receiving ordination.[20] Yet it is the nature of these differences between the sexes which tends to be most thoroughly disputed in the present day.

4. How "Distinct" Are Male and Female?

(i) The Contemporary Trend Towards Androgyny

The other contemporary prejudice of which we should try to be aware — besides that of perhaps too lightly dismissing past civilizations as irredeemably "patriarchal" — is our tendency to minimize the differences between the sexes. Particularly in view of the threats to family life and the vulnerability of marriages in most Western societies today, we must ask ourselves just how healthy our own perception of sex roles actually is.

The present debate on the ordination of women has arisen not so much because of advances in theological knowledge, but largely because of deeper changes within our society. One very obvious factor since the 1960s has been the progress of the "contraceptive revolution" which has given women control over fertility and freedom from the "burden" of motherhood — to such an extent that most Western nations now have a rate of population growth which is below replacement level. They face the bleak prospect of having to support an increasingly elderly population with a diminishing number of young workers.

These changes, however, have been undergirded by certain philosophical and political movements which generally seem to have little to do with Gospel values.

Karl Marx, for example, argued that the ultimate goal for socialism must be to create a "new man" who would live for nothing but the social collective. Any biological or psychological obstacles to this must be overcome since man is nothing more than an "ensemble of social relationships."[21] Friedrich Engels observed that women must be liberated from the constraints of raising children and doing housework. Since mankind becomes truly human only through socially productive labor, "the liberation of woman" has as its main precondition "the reintegration of the whole female sex into the public industrial sector."[22]

Liberalism, which shares Marxism's concern for the abolition of power structures, usually rejects the violent imposition of collectivist ideals, but draws its inspiration from the "liberty-equality-fraternity" ideals of the French Revolution. The central concern here is for individual "freedom," as proposed for example in the writings of the French existentialist Jean-Paul Sartre. Sartre's lifelong companion, Simone de Beauvoir, applied this existentialism to the situation of women in her book, *The Second Sex*. She saw young girls as

"thwarted boys, that is, children that are not permitted to be boys,"

and represents the adult woman as an "abortive man."[23] Her conclusions finally imply that women can achieve emancipation only by freeing themselves from their femininity.

Contemporary debate on the relationship between men and women tends to proceed on the assumption that the differences between the sexes are predominantly sociological, and based on largely interchangeable social "roles." The longterm goal seems to be an "androgynous utopia" in which there is a full equivalence between the tasks and duties of men and women.[24] Evelyne Sullerot, who holds a chair in the sociology of women at the Sorbonne (Paris), argues, however, that an excessive lack of social differentiation between the sexes is not the mark of a higher stage in human development, but rather a fall back into primitive conditions.[25]

(ii) The Rejection of Biology

The pursuit of an "androgynous utopia" does tend to overlook the basic biological fact that there is no single cell in the human body (with the exception of the gametes) which is not sexually imprinted as either male or female.

The differences in the physical appearance of men and women are often divided into primary and secondary sex characteristics. The primary sex characteristics serve the interest of coitus, in which the female naturally has the role of receiving, and the male that of imparting. The process within the female is "centripetal," directed from the outside inwards towards the center of life; for the male the process is "centrifugal," directed from the center of life outwards.[26]

Secondary sex characteristics are closely bound up with the primary ones. Bone structure in women tends, on average, to be weaker, and musculature to be less strongly developed than in men. Men are thus better suited than women to overcoming physical resistance. Women's skin is softer, less hairy, and consequently more sensitive to tactile stimuli. Even the "style of movement" of the sexes differs: men tend to move "smartly," whereas the movements of women are more "flowing."

The basic "eccentricity" of males, and the corresponding "centrality" of females, is found also in the animal world. Even Aristotle noted that female creatures behave differently from their male counterparts[27] — a strong indication that the basic differences between the sexes are rooted firmly in biological nature.

These anatomical differences seem to carry over into qualities of mind and soul. Women are more naturally religious, because "receptive" devotedness towards God accords more easily with them than with men. Women tend to be guided more strongly by intuition and feeling, while men are more likely to critically analyze ideas.

These assertions will be seen as quite offensive by many sincere feminists. Yet countless other men and women would insist, with the French, "*Vive la différence!*" And while no gentleman would ever like to admit it, the exasperated Henry Higgins of *My Fair Lady* fame still seems to strike a familiar chord in most male hearts: "*Why can't a woman be more like a man?*"

Whether we like it or not, the overwhelming majority of human societies evince a clear preponderance of men in positions of social leadership.[28] This situation tends to continue even in highly technologized societies. The United Nations, for example, has women as 50% of its personnel; yet 80% of its higher positions are filled by men. In the USSR, 75% of teachers are women, but 75% of educational administrators are men.[29]

(iii) The Significance of Religious Symbols

The sacred heaven-earth duality is one of the central motifs of general mythology — and in this duality heaven is always representative of the masculine, and earth of the feminine.[30] The heavens, with their endless horizons, are seen as the abode of majestic power and as the source of life-giving and masculinely-procreative rains. The earth then "receives" the rain and brings forth abundant growth. In a similar way, the sun is always seen as masculine, and the moon as feminine.

These "masculine" and "feminine" traits are expressed over and over again in markedly different cultural contexts. The remarkable consistency of these associations suggest that they derive from an appreciation of male and female differences which stems from the depths of the unconscious — and which is so firmly impressed on the very fabric of our being that attempts at the conscious level to alter the sociological roles of men and women will have as little longterm impact as the surface waves on the depths of the ocean.[31]

Anglican lay theologian C.S. Lewis, writing of the power of these archetypal male and female symbols, argued that

"We have no authority to take the living and sensitive
figures that God has painted on the canvas of our nature
and shift them about as if they were mere geometrical
figures."[32]

The 1976 Vatican Declaration on "Women and the Priesthood" also emphasizes the power of these symbols, and alludes particularly to the nuptial imagery which pervades both the Old and the New Testaments (para. 5).[33]

5. The Teaching of the Church

The question of the ordination of women is obviously not going to be quickly resolved. But it can be helpful for us to have a clear grasp of basic Roman Catholic presuppositions.

(i) Sexual Differentiation Willed by God

The first of these is that the Church sees the sexual differentiation of mankind as something willed by God (Gn 1:1-24, 2:4-25). Both sexes are formed, in equal measure, "in the image of God." They are equal, but not the same. There does seem to be a certain order of succession: woman is created after man, and receives her name from him (Gn 2:18-25). But the Yahwist author does not see subordination as implying inferiority of woman to man — because all the preceding emphasis has been on the basic "sameness-in-kind" and "equality-of-worth" of the two sexes. It is only after the Fall that such an arrangement can degenerate into oppression: "Your desire shall be for your husband, and he shall rule over you" (Gn 3:16).

Anglican theologian E.L. Mascall writes that it would be "very strange" if these deep-rooted and God-willed differences between men and women were to be restricted to the order of creation, and to have no parallel role in the order of redemption.[34]

(ii) The "Subordination" of Wife to Husband

Although formal references to the scriptural "subordination" of wife to husband are generally avoided in post-conciliar Church documents, the thought content behind the term has not been abandoned.[35] Writing of this nuptial subordination, Paul says that "This mystery . . . applies to Christ and the Church" (Ep 5:32). In Paul's thought, a denial of the subordination of wife to husband in Christ, would amount to a denial of the subordination of the Church to Christ himself.

Pius XI, in his 1930 encyclical on marriage, "*Casti Connubii*," stressed the "equality of rights" of husband and wife. But he also noted that

"there must be a certain inequality . . . which is demanded by the good of the family and the right ordering and unity and stability of home life" (para. 77).

The Pope stressed that this "hierarchical" structure of marriage still implies no degradation of women, "for if the man is the head, the woman is the heart" of the family (para. 27f).[36]

Pius XII similarly stressed that each sex has special characteristics that must be taken into consideration, particularly the social leadership responsibility of men, and the maternal qualities of women.[37]

Vatican II's "Declaration on Christian Education" urges that the differences between the sexes be consciously accepted and developed. It states of teachers that they should

"pay due regard in every educational activity to sexual differences and to the special role which divine Providence allots to each sex in family life and in society" (GE 8).[38]

(iii) "Subordination" Not the Same as "Inferiority"

It is important, however, to emphasize that "subordination," in the scriptural sense, does not mean "inferiority." In Trinitarian theology, the Son is in a position of subordination to the Father, and seeks only to do the Father's will (Mt 26:39). Yet this in no way means that he does not share equally the divine nature: "The Father and I are one" (Jn 10:30).

We all have the experience of being in "subordination" to others. As a diocesan priest, I may be in a position of "subordination" to my bishop. As a son or a daughter I will be in a position of "subordination" to my parents. As a citizen I am in a position of "subordination" to my President or my Prime Minister. In no case does this mean that I am "inferior" to those to whom I am in subordination. Yet I accept this position for the sake of the harmony of the whole — whether it be of my diocese, or my family, or my nation.

(iv) Ordination of Women Not Necessarily a Sign of Esteem

It is worth emphasizing too that the ordination of women to the priesthood in the past was not always an indication that women were being appreciated for their specifically feminine gifts. The followers of the second-century heretic Marcion, along with the adherents of the Gnostic systems of the same period, all accepted the ordination of women. Yet neither group did so because they esteemed women as such. On the contrary, they ordained women because they dismissed merely biological differences, and frequently had a positively hostile attitude towards the realm of the body. In both groups there was often a repudiation of marriage and child-bearing, and an exaggerated abstention from food.[39] Paul's ban on teaching by women was grounded, by contrast, in an appreciation of the very real differences between men and women (1 Cor 11:12f).

The "androgynous ideal" so frequently proposed now by feminist theologians is often characterized by a "flight from the feminine" which is not unlike that of these second century supporters of the ordination of women. One could argue by contrast that the non-ordination of women is grounded in a high estimation of the specifically female nature.

(v) The Use of Marriage Imagery in the Scriptures

"Inter Insigniores" tries to take the discussion of women priests beyond a mere consideration of the attitude of Christ or the practice of the Apostles, and to situate it more fully within the mystery of Christ and of the Church (para. 5-6).[40] In this context, the significance of the marriage imagery in the Scriptures is especially important.

Marriage is the most central symbol from anthropology. It is more intimate than the bond between parents and children. From the time of the Old Testament prophets onwards the salvation offered by God to humankind was often depicted in the form of a nuptial mystery. God's Chosen People is seen as his ardently loved spouse. The deep and intimate nature of this love is most clearly presented in the Song of Songs. The Divine Bridegroom will remain faithful even when the bride betrays his love, when Israel is unfaithful to God (Ho 1-3, Jr 2).

This nuptial mystery, proclaimed in the Old Testament, reaches its fulfillment in the New Dispensation. There Christ is the Bridegroom, and the Church is his Bride, whom he loves. Henceforth he is inseparable from her.

This nuptial theme is present in the writings of St. Paul (2 Cor 11:2; Ep 5:22-23) and St. John (Jn 3:29; Rv 19:7, 9), but also in the Synoptic Gospels. The bridegroom's friends must not fast while he is still with them (Mk 2:19). The Kingdom of Heaven is compared to a king who gave a feast for his son's wedding (Mt 22:1-14, 25:1-13).

The 1976 Declaration notes that it is through this scriptural language, "all interwoven with symbols," that there is revealed to us the utterly unfathomable mystery of God and Christ. The images of Bride=Israel/Church and Bridegroom=God/Christ are not interchangeable. Israel, or the Church (the Bride), is *always* in a position of subordination to God, or Christ (the Bridegroom). Christ and the Church are never on the same level. And it is in the light of this marriage metaphor that we can never ignore the fact that Christ (the Bridegroom) is a man (para. 5)[41]

The symbolic ascendency of the husband retains its enduring value, even in the modern age. Paul attributes to the husband a primacy not of oppression, but of love and service:

"*Husbands should love their wives* just *as Christ loved the Church* and *sacrificed himself for her* .... *This mystery* has many implications; but I am saying it *applies to Christ and the Church*" (Ep 5:25, 32).

(vi)   The Identity of the Presbyter in
Roman Catholic Theology

We have already seen in the course of this book that the Catholic Church, in contrast with some other Christian denominations, clings to a "high" theology of the presbyterate. The presbyter does represent the Church-community in the liturgy, but he does so only because "he first represents Christ Himself, who is the Head and Shepherd of the Church."[42]

Presbyters have been "marked with a special character and are so configured to Christ the Priest that they can act in the person of Christ the Head" (PO 2).[43] They exercise authority not because the community has appointed them, but because the sacerdotal character has etched upon their souls the image of Christ the Shepherd.[44] They speak "*in persona Ecclesiae*," but they do so only because they have first been empowered to act "*in persona Christi*."

This identification of the presbyter with Christ is expressed most dramatically during the words of consecration at the Eucharist: "*This is my Body . . . This is my Blood.*" St. Thomas says of sacramental signs that they must "represent what they signify by natural resemblance" (IV Sent. dist. 25, q2).[45] Thus there is no contradiction when Thomas expressly states that, in the worldly sphere (*in temporalibus*), a woman can quite well function as ruler, but not in priestly spiritual matters (*in sacerdotalibus*) (STh Sppl q39 al ad2/3).[46]

In this area of sacramental symbolism, the Church has never believed it had power over "the substance of the sacraments."[47] The Church, for example, would not believe it had the authority to celebrate the Eucharist with substances other than bread and wine. In the same way it holds, with regard to the presbyterate, that the role of Christ (the Bridegroom, the Head of the Church) must be taken by a man.[48] To ask a woman to fill this role would be as incongruous as asking a woman to play the part of Romeo in Shakespeare's tragic love story.

6. Conclusion

(i) A Constant Tradition

The ordination of women has been rejected in the Church with remarkable unanimity through two thousand years — although often in the face of widely popular "emancipatory" currents. During the second century the volume of Christian-Gnostic literature at times actually exceeded that of orthodox Catholicism.[49]

But whenever the subject of ordaining women was raised it was rejected not simply as a breach of Church discipline, but as heresy. This occurs explicitly in Tertullian (d. 220), Epiphanius of Salamis (d. 403), Augustine (d. 430) and John Damascene (d. 749). The Fathers saw the non-ordination of women as a secure "truth of faith."[50]

This attitude persisted into later times. Medieval canonists regarded the ordination of women not simply as illicit (as was the ordination of a slave), but as invalid.[51] All Scholastic theologians known to us by name who dealt with the subject agree that women may not, by divine law, validly receive priestly ordination.[52]

It was, therefore, not without some foundation that the Congregation for the Doctrine of the Faith, with the sanction of Pope Paul VI, decreed in 1976 that:

"The Church, in fidelity to the example of the Lord, does not consider herself authorized to admit women to priestly ordination."[53]

(ii) The Greatness of the Vocation of Women

It would be tragic, however, if women were to see their exclusion from priestly ordination as being in some sense a rejection by the Church. The final goal for any discussion on this topic should be to highlight the unique contribution each sex is called to make to enhance the mission the Lord has entrusted to us. And the Church looks primarily to women in every age to help remind her (and especially to remind men within the Church) of her essentially feminine nature.

To dedicate one's life as a presbyter is to follow a high calling. To be empowered to preach the Word is to fulfill an important role within the Church; but even more important is the role of those who *"hear the word of God and keep it"* (Lk 11:28). To distribute the Body and Blood of the Lord to one's brothers and sisters is to perform a noble act, but *to receive him with faith and love* is infinitely more important. And in this the youngest child is on the same level as the most learned theologian.

The most important people in the Church ultimately are not the clergy but the saints. And in honoring her saints throughout the centuries the Church's warmest esteem has always centered not on the male Apostles but rather on the woman who has so frequently been hailed as "Queen of Apostles." Mary is "she who believed that the promise made her by the Lord would be fulfilled" (Lk 1:45).

As the Church continues to place her trust in the promises "made her by the Lord" she manifests her fundamentally Marian and feminine character. Male office-bearers are called upon to "represent" the self-giving Lord of the Church — but they do so from "within" the "femininely" receptive Church. Thus Hans Urs von Balthasar writes that:

> "The Church is first of all — and this primacy is an enduring one — feminine, before she receives her supplementary masculine side in the form of ecclesiastical office."

He goes on to claim that:

> ". . . desire for ecclesiastical office in a woman (can) arise only from a misconception of her proper position of worth within the Church (as Church) . . . a misconception that levels down the mystery of the sexes instead of living it out in its open and consummate tension and fruitfulness."[54]

That Mary was not an Apostle is due to her central position in the redemptive process. For the same reason, writes the German woman theologian, Gertrud von le Fort:

> "The Church was not able to entrust the priesthood to women, since she would thereby have destroyed the proper significance of women in the Church — she would have destroyed a part of her own essence, that part whose symbolic representation was entrusted to women."[55]

Manfred Hauke concludes his impressive study on "Women and the Priesthood" by noting that the need of the hour is not for some "emancipatory war" between the sexes, but rather for a "cooperation" between men and women that takes its orientation from the orders both of creation and of redemption. The ultimate goal for any debate on the priestly ordination of women should be to bring out the greatness and beauty of the respective callings of both men and women within the mission of the Church.[56]

> "God created man in the image of himself,
> in the image of God he created him,
> male and female he created them. . . .
>
> God saw all he had made, and indeed it was very good."
> (Gn 1:27, 31)

Endnotes

Chapter I: INTRODUCTION

1 Walter M. Abbott, S.J., ed., *The Documents of Vatican II* (London: Geoffrey Chapman, 1972), p. 27.
2 Michael Evans, "In persona Christi — the key to priestly identity," *Clergy Review*, LXXI, No. 4 (April, 1986), p. 117.
3 The Congregation for the Doctrine of the Faith in its 1976 "Declaration on Women and the Priesthood," *Inter Insigniores*, states that the Church "does not consider herself authorized to admit women to priestly ordination" (London, CTS, 1976, p. 5). I have tried to elucidate this teaching in the final chapter. But for a comprehensive analysis and explanation of this position, which is being held so steadfastly by the Roman Catholic and the Orthodox Churches, see: Manfred Hauke, *Women in the Priesthood?: A Systematic Analysis in the Light of the Order of Creation and Redemption* (San Francisco: Ignatius Press, 1988).
4 Edward Schillebeeckx, O.P., *The Church with a Human Face: a New and Expanded Theology of Ministry* (New York: Crossroad, 1986), p. 40.
5 *Ibid.*, p. 41.
6 *Ibid.*, p. 41.
7 Graham Greene, *The Power and the Glory* (London: William Heinemann, 1971), p. 82.
8 *Ibid.*, p. 210.
9 *Ibid.*, p. 234.

Chapter II: THE PRIESTHOOD IN CRISIS

1 John Paul II, sermon of May 10, 1981. Cited in Dean Hoge, *Future of Catholic Leadership: Responses to the Priest Shortage* (Kansas City: Sheed & Ward, 1987), p. 16. Hereafter referred to as Hoge, *Catholic Leadership*.

2 See David N. Byers, ed., *Vocations and Future Church Leadership* (Washington, D.C., United States Catholic Conference, 1986).

3 The numbers of ordinations and resignations for secular and regular priests in Holland over a 20 year period are as follows:

YEAR	ORDINATIONS	RESIGNATIONS
1963	302	16
1964	271	18
1965	237	45
1966	227	74
1967	193	155
1968	143	202
1969	110	244
1970	47	243
1971	49	221
1972	27	164
1973	35	156
1974	29	134
1975	29	94
1976	16	58
1977	16	50
1978	15	26
1979	21	23
1980	16	26
1981	26	15
1982	20	22
1983	32	18

See J. Bots, *Documentation on Dutch Catholicism* (Washington, D.C., Human Life International, 1984), p. 77.

4 Jan Kerkhofs, "From Frustration to Liberation?", *Minister? Pastor? Prophet?*, ed. Lucas Grollenberg (London: SCM Press, 1980), p. 10.

5 Jacques Pohier, *God In Fragments* (London: SCM Press, 1985), p. 20.

6. Patrick Dunn, "Observations of a Vocations Director," *Zealandia Newspaper* (Auckland, N.Z.), February 7, 1988.

7 *Ibid.*

8 "Melbourne Priests Discuss the Future Church," *The Advocate* (Melbourne, Australia), July 14, 1988.

9 Leonard H. Welsh, "Vocation Statistics, Research and Action Plans," *Vocations and Future Church Leadership*, ed. David N. Byers (Washington, D.C., USCC, 1986), pp. 41-42.

10 Jan Kerkhofs, *art. cit.*, p. 9.

11 Terence Card, *Priesthood and Ministry in Crisis* (London: SCM Press, 1988), pp. 15-16.

12 Jacques Pohier, *op. cit.*, p. 25.

13 Robert Towler and A.P.M. Coxon, *The Fate of the Anglican Clergy: A Sociological Study* (London: MacMillan, 1979), p. 28.
14 *Ibid.*, p. 53.
15 J. Botts, *op. cit.*, p. 14.
16 Eugene Kennedy, *The Now and Future Church: The Psychology of Being an American Catholic* (New York: Image Books, 1986).
17 Neil Darragh, "The Church as Counter-Culture," *Australasian Catholic Record*, LXIV, (No. 3, 1987), p. 238.
18 J. Botts, *op. cit.*, p. 15.
19 *Ibid.*, p. 23.
20 Eugene Kennedy, *op. cit.*, p. 5.
21 *Ibid.*, p. 18.
22 Gerald Arbuckle, *Strategies for Growth in Religious Life* (New York: Alba House, 1986; Homebush, NSW, St. Paul's, 1987), p. xv.
23 *Ibid.*, p. 10.
24 For a perceptive account of how the "Cultural Revolution of the 1960s" perplexed even Frank Sheed, the great Catholic apologist of the 1950s, see Wilfred Sheed, *Frank and Maisie: A Memoir with Parents* (New York: Simon & Schuster, 1985).
25 Arbuckle, *op. cit.* p. 6.
26 Walter M. Abbott, S.J., ed. *The Documents of Vatican II* (London: Geoffrey Chapman, 1972), pp. 56-65.
27 Aloys Grillmeier, "Commentary on Lumen Gentium" in Vorgrimler, ed., *Commentary on the Documents of Vatican II, Vol. I* (London: Burns & Oates, 1967), p. 156.
28 Abbott, *op. cit.*, p. 144.
29 *Ibid.*, p. 27.
30 Walter Kasper, "The Mission of the Laity," *Theological Digest* Vol. 35, No. 2 (Summer, 1988), p. 135.
31 Paul J. Cordes, "Commentary on Presbyterorum Ordinis" in Vorgrimler, ed., *Commentary on the Documents of Vatican II, Vol. IV* (London: Burns & Oates, 1969), p. 256.
32 Abbott, *op. cit.*, p. 500.
33 *Ibid.*, p. 270.
34 Thomas F. O'Meara, O.P., *A Theology of Ministry* (New York: Paulist Press, 1983), pp. 150-151.
35 Hoge, *Catholic Leadership*, p. 93.
36 *Ibid.*, p. 97.
37 *Ibid.*, pp. 104-106.
38 O'Meara, *op. cit.*, p. 195.

*Chapter III: CONTEMPORARY QUESTIONS ABOUT
ORDAINED PRIESTHOOD*

1 Joseph Martos, *Doors to the Sacred: A Historical Introduction to Sacraments in the Christian Church* (London: SCM, 1981), p. 511.
2 See, for example, Anne Llewellyn Barstow, *Married Priests and the Reforming Papacy: the Eleventh Century Debates* (New York & Toronto: Edwin Mellen Press, 1982). Although she perhaps underestimates the antiquity of the tradition for a celibate clergy in the Western Church, Barstow has assembled some fascinating contemporary documentation.
3 Martos, *op. cit.*, p. 516.
4 *Ibid.*, p. 518.
5 Leonard Doohan, *The Lay-Centered Church* (Minneapolis: Winston Press, 1984), p. 23.
6 *Ibid.*, p. 24.
7 *Ibid.*, p. 27.
8 *Ibid.*, p.37.
9 *Ibid.*, p. 96.
10 *Ibid.*, p. 3.
11 *Ibid.*, p. 9.
12 Walter J. Abbott, S.J., ed., *The Documents of Vatican II* (London: Geoffrey Chapman, 1972), p. 27.
13 Richard P. McBrien, *Ministry* (San Francisco: Harper & Row, 1987), p. 30.
14 *Ibid.*, p. 33.
15 *Ibid.*, p. 38.
16 *Ibid.*, pp. 43, 44.
17 Thomas Franklin O'Meara, *Theology of Ministry* (Ramsey, New Jersey: Paulist Press, 1983), p. 163.
18 *Ibid.*, p. 142.
19 *Ibid.*, p. 136.
20 Robert Towler and A.P.M. Coxon, *The Fate of the Anglican Clergy: A Sociological Study* (London: MacMillan, 1979), p. 49.
21 Yves M.J. Congar, "Laïc et laïcat," *Dictionaire de spiritualité* 9 (Paris, 1976), p. 79. Cited in O'Meara, *op. cit.*, p. 164.
22 Yves M.J. Congar, *Lay People in the Church* (London: Bloomsbury Publishing Co., 1957), e.g. p. 108.
23 Yves M.J. Congar, *Ministères et communion ecclésiale* (Paris, 1971). Cited in O'Meara, *op. cit.*, p. 165.
24 O'Meara, *op. cit.*, p. 166.
25 *Ibid.*, p. 166.
26 *Ibid.*, p. 167.
27 Hans Küng, *Why Priests* (London: Collins, 1972), p. 13.
28 *Ibid.*, p. 24.
29 *Ibid.*, p. 28.

30 *Ibid.*, p. 80.
31 *Ibid.*, p. 66.
32 *Ibid.*, p. 32.
33 *Ibid.*, p. 44.
34 *Ibid.*, p. 36.
35 *Ibid.*, p. 36.
36 Raymond E. Brown, *Priest and Bishop* (London: Geoffrey Chapman, 1971), p. 28.
37 Lucas Grollenberg, ed., *Minister? Pastor? Prophet?* (London: SCM, 1980), p. 1.
38 *Ibid.*, p. 2.
39 Abbott, *op. cit.*, p. 542.
40 Anton Houtepen, "Gospel, Church, Ministry: A Theological Diagnosis of Present-Day Problems in the Ministry," in Grollenberg *op. cit.*, p. 21.
41 *Ibid.*, p. 24.
42 Houtepen, *op. cit.*, p. 27.
43 *Ibid.*, p. 29.
44 *Ibid.*, p. 32.
45 *Ibid.*, p. 36.
46 *Ibid.*, p. 38.
47 *Ibid.*, p. 40.

Chapter IV: THE WRITINGS OF EDWARD SCHILLEBEECKX

1 Edward Schillebeeckx, O.P., *The Church With A Human Face: A New and Expanded Theology of Ministry* (New York: Crossroad, 1985).

   Edward Schillebeeckx, *Ministry: Leadership in the Community of Jesus Christ* (New York: Crossroad, 1981).

2 Schillebeeckx, *Human Face*, p. 1.
3 *Ibid.*, p. 11.
4 *Ibid.*, p. 265.
5 *Ibid.*, p. 266.
6 *Ibid.*, p. 266.
7 *Ibid.*, p. 266.
8 World Council of Churches, *Baptism, Eucharist and Ministry* (Geneva: WCC, 1982), 25.
9 Schillebeeckx, *Human Face*, pp. 260-262.
10 *Ibid.*, p. 40.
11 *Ibid.*, p. 41.
12 Text quoted in Schillebeeckx, *Human Face*, p. 38.
13 Schillebeeckx, *Human Face*, p. 41.
14 *Ibid.*, p. 46.

15 *Ibid.*, p. 47.
16 *Ibid.*, p. 49.
17 *Ibid.*, p. 52.
18 *Ibid.*, p. 51.
19 *Ibid.*, p. 51.
20 *Ibid.*, p. 60.
21 *Ibid.*, p. 66.
22 *Ibid.*, p. 67.
23 *Ibid.*, p. 68.
24 *Ibid.*, pp. 66-67.
25 *Ibid.*, p. 71.
26 Hans Küng, *Why Priests?* (London: Collins, 1972), p. 44.
27 Walter M. Abbott, S.J., *The Documents of Vatican II* (London: Geoffrey Chapman, 1972), p. 118.
28 Schillebeeckx, *Ministry*, p. 5; *Human Face*, p. 74.
29 Schillebeeckx, *Ministry*, p. 5.
30 Albert Vanhoye, S.J., "Le ministère dans l'Église: les données du nouveau testament," *Nouvelle revue théologique*, 104 (1982), p. 724.
31 Schillebeeckx, *Ministry*, p. 8.
32 Schillebeeckx, *Ministry*, p. 6; *Human Face*, p. 75.
33 Schillebeeckx, *Ministry*, p. 7; *Human Face*, p. 76.
34 Schillebeeckx, *Ministry*, p. 6.
35 *Ibid.*, pp. 35-37.
36 Schillebeeckx, *Human Face*, p. 116.
37 Schillebeeckx, *Ministry*, p. 37.
38 Schillebeeckx, *Ministry*, p. 20; *Human Face*, p. 103.
39 Schillebeeckx, *Ministry*, p. 8.
40 *Ibid.*, p. 5.
41 Vanhoye, *op. cit.*, p. 729.
42 Schillebeeckx, *Ministry*, p. 9.
43 *Ibid.*, p. 8.
44 *Ibid.*, p. 20.
45 Schillebeeckx, *Human Face*, p. 2.
46 *Ibid.*, p. 40.
47 *Ibid.*, p. 210.
48 Schillebeeckx, *Ministry*, p. 5.
49 Joyce A. Little, Review of "The Church with a Human Face," *The Thomist*, Vol. 52, No. 1 (January 1988), p. 161.
50 Schillebeeckx, *Human Face*, p. 11.
51 Little, *op. cit.*, p. 161.
52 Schillebeeckx, *Human Face*, p. 40.
53 Little *op. cit.*, p. 162.
54 Schillebeeckx, *Human Face*, p. 18.
55 *Ibid.*, p. 38.

56 *Ibid.*, pp. 39, 47.
57 *Ibid.*, p. 10.
58 Little, *op. cit.*, p. 165.

Chapter V: MINISTRY AND "PRIESTLY" LANGUAGE IN THE NEW
        TESTAMENT

 1 André Lemaire, *Ministry in the Church* (London, SPCK, 1977), p. 92.
 2 Hans Küng, *Why Priests?* (London: Collins, 1972), p. 29.
 3 Raymond E. Brown, *Priest and Bishop* (London: Geoffrey Chapman, 1971),
    pp. 17-19.
 4 Jean Galot, S.J., *Theology of Priesthood* (San Francisco: Ignatius, 1985), p. 71.
 5 Lemaire, *op. cit.*, p. 4.
 6 Galot, *op. cit.*, p. 75.
 7 *Ibid.*, p. 76.
 8 *Ibid.*, p. 78.
 9 *Ibid.*, p. 83.
10 David N. Power, O.M.I., *The Christian Priest: Elder and Prophet* (London:
    Sheed & Ward, 1973), p. 25.
11 Galot, *op. cit.*, p.84.
12 *Ibid.*, p. 86.
13 *Ibid.*, p. 164.
14 Lemaire, *op. cit.*, p.49.
15 Galot, *op. cit.*, p. 160.
16 *Ibid.*, p. 162.
17 *Ibid.*, p. 163.
18 *Ibid.*, p. 163.
19 Lemaire, *op. cit.*, p.10.
20 Maxwell Staniforth, ed., *Early Christian Writings: The Apostolic Fathers* (Mid-
    dlesex: Penguin Books, 1968), pp. 232-234.
21 Lemaire, *op. cit.*, p. 11.
22 Staniforth, *op. cit.*, p. 232.
23 Bernard Cooke, *Ministry to Word and Sacrament* (Philadelphia: Fortress,
    1976), p. 532.
24 Lemaire, *op. cit.*, p. 13.
25 Staniforth, *op. cit.*, p.235.
26 Lemaire, *op. cit.*, p.35.
27 *Ibid.*, p. 16.
28 *Ibid.*, p. 92.
29 Cf. World Council of Churches, *Baptism, Eucharist, and Ministry* (Geneva,
    WCC, 1982), commentary para. 17, p. 23.   See also Anglican-Roman
    Catholic International Commission (ARCIC), *The Final Report* (London,
    CTS/SPCK, 1982), Statement on "Ministry and Ordination", p. 35.

204 PRIESTHOOD

30 Albert Vanhoye, S.J., *Our Priest is Christ: The Doctrine of the Epistle to the Hebrews* (Rome, P.I.B., 1977), pp. 27f.
31 *Ibid.*, pp. 32f.
32 Galot, *op. cit.*, p. 32.
33 Cooke, *op. cit.*, p. 526.
34 Galot, *op. cit.*, p.49.
35 *Ibid.*, p. 22.
36 Cooke, *op. cit.*, p. 528.
37 *Ibid.*, p. 529.
38 *Ibid.*, p. 530.
39 Lemaire, *op. cit.*, p. 19.
40 Albert Vanhoye, S.J., "Le ministère dans l'Église: réflexions à propos d'un ouvrage récent," *Nouvelle revue théologique*, Vol. 104, (1982), p. 733.
41 Edward Schillebeeckx, O.P., *Ministry: Leadership in the Community of Jesus Christ* (New York: Crossroad, 1981), p. 35.
42 *Ibid.*, p. 21.
43 Vanhoye, *Nouvelle revue*, p. 734.
44 Cooke, *op. cit.*, p.530.
45 Küng, *op. cit.*, p.29.
46 Walter M. Abbott, S.J., ed., *The Documents of Vatican II*, (London: Geoffrey Chapman, 1972), p. 534.

Chapter VI: THE PRE-NICENE CENTURIES

1 August Franzen and John P. Dolan, *A Concise History of the Church* (London: Burns & Oates, 1969), p. 61.
2 *Ibid.*, p. 63.
3 Richard P. McBrien, *Ministry: A Theological, Pastoral Handbook* (San Francisco: Harper & Row, 1987), p. 38.
4 Kenan B. Osborne, O.F.M., *Priesthood: A History of the Ordained Ministry in the Roman Catholic Church* (New York: Paulist, 1988), p. 128.
5 Edward Schillebeeckx, O.P., *The Church with a Human Face: A New and Expanded Theology of Ministry* (New York: Crossroad, 1985), p. 91.
6 Maxwell Staniforth, ed., *Early Christian Witings: The Apostolic Fathers* (Middlesex: Penguin, 1968), p. 46.
7 Quoted in Henry S. Bettenson, ed., *Documents of the Christian Church*, 2nd ed. (London: Oxford University Press, 1967), p. 4.
8 André Lemaire, *Ministry in the Church* (London: SPCK, 1977), p. 13.
9 Bernard Cooke, *Ministry to Word and Sacraments: History and Theology* (Philadelphia: Fortress, 1976), p. 61.
10 Cyprian, *Epist.* 14. Cited in Cooke, *op. cit.*, p. 427.
11 Lemaire, *op. cit.*, p. 46.

12 R.H. Connolly, *Didascalia Apostolorum* (Oxford: Clarendon Press, 1929), p. xxxviii. Cited in Osborne, *op. cit.*, p. 130.
13 Cooke, *op. cit.*, p. 59.
14 *Ibid.*, p. 65.
15 *Ibid.*, p. 66.
16 *Ibid.*, p. 245.
17 *Ibid.*, p. 242.
18 Staniforth, *op. cit.*, pp. 45-46.
19 Lemaire, *op. cit.*, pp. 51f.
20 Cooke, *op. cit.*, p. 62.
21 Ancyra draws a clear distinction between those "*ek tou clerou*" and "*alloi laikoi.*" See fn. 73: Cooke, *op. cit.*, p. 71.
22 See Lemaire, *op. cit.*, p. 49. For a full treatment on the subject of deaconesses, see Aimé Georges Marimort, *Deaconesses: An Historical Study* (San Francisco: Ignatius, 1986).
23 Eusebius, *Hist. Eccl.*, VI, 45, 11. See Thomas F. O'Meara, O.P., *A Theology of Ministry* (New York: Paulist, 1983), p. 99.
24 O' Meara, *op. cit.*, p. 99.
25 Cooke, *op. cit.*, p. 64.
26 *Ibid.*, p. 539.
27 "*Non in sacerdotio ordinatur, sed in ministerio episcopi. . .*" See Cooke, *op. cit.*, p.548, fn. 22.
28 Cooke, *op. cit.*, p.538.
29 *Ibid.*, p. 544.
30 *Ibid.*, p. 552, fn. 110.
31 *Ibid.*, p. 541.
32 Cyprian, Epist. 61. Cited in Cooke, *op. cit.*, p. 549, fn. 46.
33 Schillebeeckx, *Human Face*, p. 145.
34 David N. Power, O.M.I., *The Sacrifice We Offer: The Tridentine Dogma and Its Reinterpretation* (Edinburgh: T & T Clark, 1987), p. 176.
35 Schillebeeckx, *Human Face*, p. 146.
36 Henri Crouze, SJ, "Le ministère dans l'Église: témoinages de l'Église ancienne," *Nouvelle revue théologique*, 104 (1982), p. 744.
37 *Ibid.*
38 *Ibid.*
39 Cooke, *op. cit.*, p. 542.
40 Edward Schillebeeckx, O.P., *Ministry: Leadership in the Community of Jesus Christ* (New York: Crossroad, 1981), p. 48.
41 Staniforth, *op. cit.*, p. 44.
42 Crouzel, *op. cit.*, p. 743.
43 Schillebeeckx, *Human Face*, p. 85.
44 Crouzel, *op. cit.*, p.746.
45 Schillebeeckx, *Human Face*, p. 241.
46 Crouzel, *op. cit.*, p. 747.

47 David N. Power, O.M.I., *The Christian Priest: Elder and Prophet* (London: Sheed & Ward, 1973), p. 11.
48 Cooke, *op. cit.*, p.551, fn. 75.
49 Schillebeeckx, *Human Face*, pp. 130-131.
50 Cooke, *op. cit.*, p. 418.
51 *Ibid.*, p.419.
52 *Ibid.*, p. 553, fn. 120.
53 *Ibid.*, p. 426, fn. 94.

Chapter VII: *MEDIEVAL INFLUENCES ON UNDERSTANDING OF PRIESTHOOD*

1 August Franzen and John P. Dolan, *A Concise History of the Church* (London: Burns & Oates Ltd., 1969), p. 63.
2 Bernard Cooke, *Ministry to Word and Sacraments: History and Theology* (Philadelphia: Fortress, 1976), p. 559.
3 *Ibid.*, p. 435.
4 *Ibid.*, p. 79.
5 Jerome, *Epist. 146, Ad Evangelum* (P.L. 22, 1194). Cited in fn. 59, Cooke, *op. cit.*, p. 101.
6 Cooke, *op. cit.*, p. 80.
7 *Ibid.*, p. 558.
8 Quoted in Cooke, *op. cit.*, p. 568, fn. 65.
9 Alcuin, *De virtutibus et vitiis 6.* Cited in Cooke, *op. cit.*, p. 269, fn. 62.
10 John W. O'Malley, S.J., "Priesthood, Ministry, and Religious Life: some historical and historiographical considerations," *Theological Studies* 49 (June, 1988), p. 236.
11 Cooke, *op. cit.*, p. 90.
12 *Ibid.*, p. 261.
13 Joseph Martos, *Doors to the Sacred: A Historical Introduction to Sacraments in the Christian Church* (London: SCM, 1981), p. 179.
14 Cooke, *op. cit.*, p. 90.
15 Martos, *op. cit.*, p. 258.
16 *Ibid.*
17 *Ibid.*, p. 260.
18 *Ibid.*, p. 257.
19 *Ibid.*, p. 258.
20 *Ibid.*, p. 262.
21 *Ibid.*, p. 264.
22 *Ibid.*, p. 265.
23 "*Actus nobilissimus in Ecclesia simpliciter est consecratio Eucharistiae,*" Duns Scotus, *Ox.* 4, dist. 24, q. unica, n. 7. Cited in Cooke, *op. cit.*, p. 115.

24 *"Consecrare enim est principalis actus, ad quem sunt actus omnium ordinum. . ."* Albertus Magnus, *De Sacramentis*, tract. 8, q. 2, ad. 18. Cited in Cooke, *op. cit.*, p. 581.
25 Martos, *op. cit.*, p.91.
26 *Ibid.*, p. 277.
27 Cited in David N. Power, O.M.I., *The Sacrifice We Offer: The Tridentine Dogma and Its Reinterpretation* (Edinburgh: T & T Clark, 1987), p. 36, fn. 19.
28 Bernard Bickers, "Ministry or Ministries?" *Clergy Review*, Vol. LXXI, No. 4 (April, 1986), p. 116.
29 Power, *op. cit.*, p.38.
30 Martos, *op. cit.*, p. 278.

Chapter VIII: THE SIXTEENTH CENTURY

1 Bernard Cooke, *Ministry to Word and Sacraments: History and Theology* (Philadelphia: Fortress, 1976), p. 591.
2 André Lemaire, *Ministry in the Church* (London: SPCK, 1977), p. 70.
3 David N. Power, O.M.I., *The Christian Priest: Elder and Prophet* (London: Sheed & Ward, 1973), p. 19.
4 Aladair I.C. Heron, *Table and Tradition: Toward an Ecumenical Understanding of the Eucharist* (Philadelphia: Westminster Press, 1987), p. 174. Cited in David Power, *The Sacrifice We Offer: The Tridentine Dogma and Its Reinterpretation*, (Edinburgh: T. & T. Clark, 1987), p. xiv.
5 Cooke, *op. cit.*, p. 594.
6 *Ibid.*, p. 136.
7 *Ibid.*, p. 133.
8 *Ibid.*, p. 140.
9 John Dolan, "Martin Luther," *New Catholic Encyclopedia* (New York: McGraw Hill, 1967), Vol. VIII, p. 1087.
10 *Ibid.*
11 Martin Luther, "Appeal to the Christian nobility of the German nation." Cited in Henry S. Bettenson, ed., *Documents of the Christian Church*, 2nd Ed. (London: Oxford University Press, 1967), pp. 193-194.
12 Dolan, *op. cit.*, p.1088.
13 Bettenson, *op. cit.*, p. 197.
14 Martin Luther, "The Babylonian Captivity of the Church." Cited in Bettenson, *op. cit.*, pp. 197-199.
15 Cooke, *op. cit.*, p. 595.
16 D. Hollaz, *Examen theologicum acroamaticum.* Cited in Cooke, *op. cit.*, p. 616, fn. 55.
17 Cooke, *op. cit.*, p. 616, fn. 61.
18 *Ibid.*, p. 598.
19 *Ibid.*, p. 626.

20 Walter M. Abbott, S.J., ed., *The Documents of Vatican II* (London: Geoffrey Chapman, 1972), p. 579.

21 Power, *Sacrifice*, p. 29.

22 *Ibid.*, p. 48.

23 *Ibid.*, p. 54.

24 *Ibid.*, p. 43.

25 *Ibid.*, p. 41.

26 *Ibid.*, p. 44.

27 *Ibid.*, p. 65.

For many centuries the Eucharist tended to be seen as the personal prayer of the priest. Bernard Cooke, *op. cit.*, fn. 48, p. 630, quotes from J. Soettler's *De Officiis Sacerdotalibus et Pastoralibus* which appeared in the 18th century, but was reprinted in 1825 at the urging of Pope Leo XII. It stresses the sanctity and life-style of the priest, but interestingly lists the celebration of the Eucharist as an aspect of his "personal prayer." However, it does note that he does it to give "the Trinity praise and glory, the angels joy, the sinner forgiveness, the just grace, those in purgatory solace, the Church the spiritual benefits of Christ, and himself medicine against daily sins. . . ."

28 Power, *Sacrifice*, p. 39.

29 *Ibid.*, p. 36.

30 *Ibid.*, p. 45.

31 H.J. Schroeder, O.P., ed., *Canons and Decrees of the Council of Trent* (London: B. Herder Book Co., 1941), pp. vii-xx.

32 *Ibid.*, p. 147.

33 *Ibid.*, p. 432.

34 Luther, "Christian nobility." Cited in Bettenson, *op. cit.*, p. 194.

35 Schroeder, *op. cit.*, pp. 161-162.

36 Power, *Christian Priest*, p. 91.

37 ". . . *cum vero corde et recta fide, cum metu et reverentia, contriti ac poenitentes*." See Schroeder, *op. cit.*, p. 419.

38 Power, *Sacrifice*, p. 121.

39 Schroeder, *op. cit.*, p. 75.

40 Power, *Sacrifice*, p.115.

41 *Ibid.*, p. 52.

42 *Ibid.*, p.141.

43 Schroeder, *op. cit.*, p. 55.

44 Power, *Sacrifice*, p. 127.

45 The same article is cited in Jean Galot, SJ, "Le caractère sacerdotal selon le concile de Trente," *Nouvelle revue théologique*, Vol. 93 (1971), p. 943.

46 Galot, *op. cit.*, p. 943.

47 *Ibid.*, p. 944.

48 *Ibid.*, p. 945.

49 Cooke, *op. cit.*, p. 488.

Chapter IX: THE SECOND VATICAN COUNCIL (1962-1965)

1   Walter M. Abbott, S.J., ed., *The Documents of Vatican II* (London: Geoffrey Chapman, 1972), p. 9.
2   *Ibid.*, p. 10.
3   Hubert Vorgrimler, ed., *Commentary on the Documents of Vatican II, Vol. I* (London: Burns & Oates, 1967), p. 146.
4   *Ibid.*, p. 106.
5   André Weers, "Les citations scripturaires de décret sur le ministère et la vie des prêtres: 'Presbyterorum Ordinis' ", *Unam Sanctam 68: Vatican II — Les Prêtres* (Paris: Les Éditions Du Cerf, 1968), p. 328.
6   Vorgrimler, *op. cit.*, Vol. I, p. 157.
7   Abbott, *op. cit.*, p. 27.
8   *Ibid.*, p. 534.
9   Yves M.J. Congar, O.P., "Le sacerdoce du nouveau testament: mission et culte," *Unam Sanctam 68: Vatican II — Les Prêtres* (Paris: Les Éditions Du Cerf, 1968), p. 252.
10 Abbott, *op. cit.*, p. 27.
11 Vorgrimler, *op. cit.*, Vol. I, p. 121.
12 H. Le Sourd, "Un aggiornamento spirituel?", *Unam Sanctam 68: Vatican II — Les Prêtre* (Paris: Les Éditions Du Cerf, 1968), p. 295.
13 Abbott, *op. cit.*, p. 558. fn. 154.
14 Hervé-Marie Legrand, "The presidency of the Eucharist according to the ancient tradition," *Worship*, 53 (1979), p. 425.
15 Abbott, *op. cit.*, p. 558.
16 *Ibid.*, p. 41.
17 Bernard Cooke, *Ministry to Word and Sacraments: History and Theology* (Philadelphia: Fortress, 1976), p. 581.
18 Abbott, *op. cit.*, p. 40.
19 Vorgrimler, *op. cit.*, Vol. I, p. 193.
20 Abbott, *op. cit.*, p.42.
21 Abbott, *op. cit.*, p.49.
22 Vorgrimler, *op. cit.*, Vol. I, p. 196.
23 Henri Denis "La théologie du presbytérat de Trente à Vatican II," *Unam Sanctam 68: Vatican II — Les Prêtres* (Paris: Les Éditions Du Cerf, 1968), p. 225.
24 Vorgrimler, *op. cit.*, Vol. IV, p. 215.
25 *Ibid.*, p. 216.
26 Anton Houtepen, "Gospel, church, ministry: a theological diagnosis of present-day problems in the ministry," in Lucas Grollenberg ed., *Minister? Prophet? Pastor?* (London: SCM, 1980), p. 32.
27 Michael Richards, "Priest or presbyter? The Pope at Ars, October, 1986," *The Clergy Review*, LXXII, No. 1 (January, 1987), p. 31.
28 Cooke, *op. cit.*, p. ix.

29 Abbott, *op. cit.*, p. 47.
30 *Ibid.*, p. 50.
31 *Ibid.*, p. 51.
32 *Ibid.*, p. 538.
33 Yves Congar, *op. cit.*, p.242.
34 Abbott, *op. cit.*, p. 16.
35 *Ibid.*, p. 37.
36 Henri Denis, *op. cit.*, p.207, fn. 8.
37 Abbott, *op. cit.*, p.534.
38 *Ibid.*, p. 536.
39 *Ibid.*, p. 552.
40 Vorgrimler, *op. cit.*, Vol. IV, p. 210.
41 Cooke, *op. cit.*, p.278.
42 Vorgrimler, *op. cit.*, Vol. IV, p. 212.
43 *Ibid.*, p. 213, fn. 8.
44 Richards, *op. cit.*, pp. 30f.
45 Richards, *op. cit.*, p. 31.
46 H.J. Schroeder, O.P., ed., *Canons and Decrees of the Council of Trent* (London: B. Herder Book Co., 1941), p. 160.
47 Abbott, *op. cit.*, p. 534.
48 *Ibid.*
49 Schroeder, *op. cit.*, p.160.
50 *Ibid.*, p.162.
51 Abbott, *op. cit.*, p. 535.
52 Henri Denis, *op. cit.*, p.205.
53 Martin Luther, "The Babylonian Captivity of the Church," in Henry S. Bettenson, ed., *Documents of the Christian Church*, 2nd ed. (London: Oxford University Press, 1967), p. 198.
54 Henri Denis, *op. cit.*, p.206.
55 *Ibid.*, p. 207.
56 Schroeder, *op. cit.*, p. 432.
57 *Ibid.*, p. 146.
58 David N. Power, O.M.I., *The Sacrifice We Offer: The Tridentine Dogma and Its Reinterpretation* (Edinburgh: T. & T. Clark, 1987), p. 122.
59 Schroeder, *op. cit.*, p.149.
60 *Ibid.*, p. 160.
61 Henri Denis, *op. cit.*, p. 211.
62 Abbott, *op. cit.*, p. 527.
63 *Ibid.*, p. 539.
64 *Ibid.*, p. 563.
65 *Ibid.*, pp. 534-535.
66 *Ibid.*, pp. 541-542.
67 *Ibid.*, p. 545.
68 *Ibid.*, pp. 560-561.
69 Henri Denis, *op. cit.*, p. 196.

70 Power, *Sacrifice*, p. 196.
71 *Ibid.*, p. 161.
72 *Ibid.*, p. 21.

Chapter X: RE-ADDRESSING THE PRESENT PROBLEM

1 Dean R. Hoge, *Future of Catholic Leadership: Responses to the Priest Shortage*, (Kansas City: Sheed & Ward, 1987), p. 17.
2 Eugene Kennedy, *The Now and Future Church: The Psychology of Being an American Catholic* (New York: Image Books, 1985), p. 158.
3 Hoge, *op. cit.*, p.29.
4 *Ibid.*, p. 38.
5 *Ibid.*, p. xiii.
6 *Ibid.*, p. 47.
7 *Ibid.*, p. 48.
8 "Church sociologist warns priests about loss of faithful," *The Age*, Melbourne, 11 May 1989.
9 Hoge, *op. cit.*, p. 55.
10 *Ibid.*, p. 42.
11 Andrew Greeley and Michael Hout, "The secularization myth," *London Tablet*, 10 June 1989, p. 667.
12 Hoge, *op. cit.*, p. 36.
13 *Ibid.*, pp. 86-87.
14 *Ibid.*, p. 93.
15 *Ibid.*, p.96.
16 Corpus Christi College in Melbourne, Australia, for example, trains priests for five dioceses. In 1989 it had 55 students — in contrast to 90 in 1982, and 140 in 1972. Figures reported in *Melbourne Sunday Herald*, Sept. 10, 1989, p. 9.
17 Hoge, *op. cit.*, p. 119.

For the statistically-minded, Hoge reports that it takes 10,000 Catholics an average of six years to produce just one ordained priest — less than one-fourth of 1 percent of the boys born per year in the U.S. Catholic community! (p. 124).

18 Hoge, *op. cit.*, p. 132.
19 *Ibid.*, p. 145.
20 Walter M Abbott, S.J., ed., *The Documents of Vatican II* (London: Geoffrey Chapman, 1972), p. 56.
21 Hoge, *op. cit.*, p.184.
22 *Ibid.*, p. 193.
23 *Ibid.*, p. 194.
24 *Ibid.*, p. 196.

25 Kennedy, *op. cit.*, p. 171.
26 Donald W. McMonigle, *The Diaconate: Its History and Renewal in the Anglican Tradition* (Melbourne College of Divinity, unpublished thesis, 1988), p. 114, fn. 13.
27 *Ibid.*, p. 151.
28 *Ibid.*, p. 167.
29 Hoge, *op. cit.*, p.212.
30 *Ibid.*, p. 198.
31 *Ibid.*, p. 203.
32 *Ibid.*, p. 190.
33 *Ibid.*
34 *Ibid.*, p. vii.
35 Raymond Hickey, O.S.A., "Priesthood and the Church of the future: the case for an auxiliary married priesthood," *Clergy Review*, LXXI, No. 5 (May, 1986), p. 159.
36 *Ibid.*, p. 160.
37 *Ibid.*
38 Abbott, *op. cit.*, p. 565.
39 Hickey, *op. cit.*, p. 162.
40 Hickey, *op. cit.*, p.163.
41 *Ibid.*, p. 162.
42 *Ibid.*, p. 163.
43 *Ibid.*, p.160.
44 *Ibid.*, p. 164, fn. 1.
45 Abbott, *op. cit.*, p. 542.
46 *Ibid.*, p. 545.
47 *Ibid.*, p. 343.
48 Mason, *op. cit.*, (see fn. 8. above).
49 William J. O'Malley, S.J., "Mass and teen-agers," *America* (Oct. 8, 1988), p. 214.
50 *Ibid.*, p. 216.
51 Peter Chirico, S.S., "Pastoral ministry in the Church in the light of the critical priest shortage," *Clergy Review*, Vol. LXIX, No. 3 (March, 1984), p. 81.
52 Abbott, *op. cit.*, p. 538.
53 Michael Evans, "In persona Christ — the key to priestly identity," *Clergy Review*, Vol. LXXI, No. 4. (April, 1986), p. 118.
54 Hickey, *op. cit.*, p. 158.
55 Leonardo Boff, *Ecclesio-genesis: The Base Communities Reinvent the Church* (London: Collins, 1986), p. 3.
56 *Ibid.*, p. 2.
57 *Ibid.*, p. 13.
58 *Ibid.*, p. 15.
59 Congregation for Divine Worship, "Directory for Sunday celebrations in the absence of a priest." This text is from *Liturgy Magazine* (Auckland, NZ), Vol. 14 (1989) No. 2, p. 8.

60 Cited in Hoge, *op. cit.*, p. 213.
61 Edward Schillebeeckx, O.P., *The Church With a Human Face: A New and Expanded Theology of Ministry* (New York: Crossroad, 1985), p. 1.
62 Cited in Hoge, *op. cit.*, p.264, fn. 7.
63 Gabe Huck, "Priestless Sundays: are we looking or leaping?", *Liturgy 80* (Office of Divine Worship, Chicago), October, 1987, p. 5.
64 The question of the "right" of the baptized to the Eucharist actually has important ecumenical implications in terms of intercommunion and mutual recognition of ministries. See, for example, J. Peter Kenny, S.J., "Ministry: does priesthood command Eucharist or Eucharist priesthood?", *Compass*, Vol. 11, No. 1 14-33.

The context of this debate as it is currently being aired *within* the Roman Catholic Church is somewhat different. Edward Schillebeeckx is not talking about the rights of a full "ecclesial community," but about the rights of a "local" or "parish" community.
65 Edward Schillebeeckx, O.P., *Ministry: Leadership in the Community of Jesus Christ* (New York: Crossroad, 1981), p. 37.
66 Albert Vanhoye, S.J., "Le ministère dans l'Église: les données du nouveau testament," *Nouvelle revue théologique* 104 (1982), p. 736.
67 James G. Murtagh, *Australia: The Catholic Chapter* (New York: Sheed & Ward, 1946), pp. 16-17.
68 See, for example, Schillebeeckx, *Ministry*, p. 35; or *Human Face*, p. 118.
69 Schillebeeckx, *Human Face*, p. 118.
70 St. Thomas Aquinas, *Summa theologiae, Vol. 57, Baptism & Confirmation (3a, 66-72)*, Ed. and trans. by James J. Cunningham, O.P. (London: Blackfriars, 1975), pp. 58-59.
71 Hoge, *op. cit.*, pp. 105-106.
72 "Cum jam in Novo Testamento et in aevo post apostolico Eucharistia ut 'sacrificium' intelligatur, *et presbyteri ut rectores communitatis sint rectores eucharistiae*, sacerdotium ministeriale Novi Testamenti suam propriam dignitatem a Christo institutam ostendit. *Functio rectorum communitatis cum functione cultica coniuncta apparet.*" — Schema Constitutionis De Ecclesia (1964), relatio on number 28, pp. 101-102. Cited in Hervé-Marie Legrand, O.P., "The presidency of the Eucharist according to the ancient tradition," *Worship*, 53 (1979), p. 413, fn. 1.
73 Schillebeeckx, *Human Face*, p. 128.
74 *Ibid.*, p. 207.
75 Legrand, *op. cit.*, p. 428.
76 Chirico, *op. cit.*, p.82.
77 Legrand, *op. cit.*, p.437.
78 *Ibid.*, p. 438.
79 Maxwell Staniforth, ed., *Early Christian Writings: The Apostolic Fathers* (Middlesex: Penguin, 1968), p. 46.

80 *Ibid.*, p. 45.

81 Congregation for the Doctrine of the Faith, *Women and the Priesthood: Declaration on the Question of the Admission of Women to the Ministerial Priesthood (Inter Insigniores)* (London: Catholic Truth Society, 1976), para. 5, p. 15.

82 Legrand, *op. cit.*, p. 428.

83 *Ibid.*, p. 432.

84 *Ibid.*, p. 435, fn. 71.

*Chapter XI: THE "PERMANENT" ASPECT OF THE
            SACRAMENT OF ORDERS*

1   Martin Luther, "Appeal to the Christian nobility of the German nation," cited in Henry S. Bettenson, ed., *Documents of the Christian Church* 2nd ed. (London: Oxford University Press, 1967), pp. 193-194.

2   Martin Luther, "The Babylonian Captivity of the Church," cited in Jean Galot, "Le caractère sacerdotal selon le concile de Trente," *Nouvelle revue théologique*, Vol. 93 (1971), p. 934.

3   André Lemaire, *Ministry in the Church* (London: SPCK, 1977), p. 118, reasons that the current practice of asking bishops and priests to tender their resignations after reaching a certain age indicates a sensible realization that the proper fulfillment of any "function" demands that it be accepted only for a limited term.

4   Edward Schillebeeckx, O.P., *Ministry: Leadership in the Community of Jesus Christ* (New York: Crossroad, 1981), p. 149, fn. 13.

5   Hervé-Marie Legrand, O.P., "The presidency of the Eucharist according to the ancient tradition," *Worship*, 53 (1979), p. 431.

6   Cyrille Vogel, "Laica communione contentus: Le retour du presbytre au rang des laïcs," *Revue des sciences réligieuses* 47 (1973), pp. 67f.

7   *Ibid.*, p. 120.

8   *Ibid.*, pp. 67, 118.

9   *Ibid.*, p. 67.

10 My translation. Vogel's actual text reads:

"En droit, le presbytre déposé peut être réintégré dans son ordre et, dans ce cas, la levée de la déposition suffit à cette réintégration; *une seconde ordination est exclue*: non que la qualité presbytérale se soit 'maintenue' malgré la déposition, mais parce que la levée de la déposition est un acte religieux et ecclésial (et non purement juridique et coercitif), qui suffit à 'redonner' ce que la déposition, autre acte religieux, avait retiré."

See Vogel, *op. cit.*, p. 75.

11 Schillebeeckx, *Ministry*, p. 149, fn. 13.

12 *Ibid.*, p. 65.

13 *Ibid.*, p. 41.

14 "Translations and reprints from the original sources of European history" (1900); (reprint, Philadelphia: University of Pennsylvania, Department of History, n.d.), vol. 4, no. 2, p. 24. Cited in Leonardo Boff, *Ecclesio-genesis: The Base Communities Reinvent the Church* (London: Collins, 1986), p. 65.

15 Schillebeeckx, *Ministry*, p. 41.

16 *Ibid.*, p. 39.

17 *Ibid.*, p. 42.

18 Henri Crouzel, S.J., "Le ministère dans l'Église: témoinages de l'Église ancienne," *Nouvelle revue théologique*, 104 (1982), p. 740.

19 Vogel, *op. cit.*, p. 75.

20 Crouzel, *op. cit.*, pp. 742-743.

21 Charles Joseph Hefele and H. Leclerq, O.S.B., *Histoire des conciles: d'après les documents originaux*, II. B (Paris: Létouzey et Ané, 1908), pp. 755-761.

22 Crouzel, *op. cit.*, p. 741.

23 Canon 4 attempts to control roaming monks: they are not to construct monasteries or houses of prayer without the permission of the local bishop; nor are they to leave their monasteries unless the bishop explicitly entrusts some charge to them.

Canon 5 addresses the problem of bishops and clerics who shift from one city to another. All the ancient canons which govern such moves retain the force of Law.

See P.-Th. Camelot, OP, *Histoire des conciles oecuméniques. Vol. II: Éphèse et Chalcédoine* (Paris: Éditions de l'Orante, 1962), p. 229.

24 Chapter XVI of the Decrees Concerning Reform, during Session XXIII ("Concerning the Sacrament of Order") reads as follows:

"VAGRANTS AND PERSONS USELESS TO THE CHURCHES SHALL BE EXCLUDED FROM ORDERS.

Since no one ought to be ordained who in the judgment of his bishop is not useful or necessary to his churches, the holy council, *following the footsteps of the sixth canon of the Council of Chalcedon*, decrees that no one shall in the future be ordained who is not assigned to that church or pious place for the need or utility of which he is promoted, where he may discharge his duties and not wander about without any fixed abode. But if he shall desert that place without consulting the bishop, he shall be forbidden the exercise of the sacred orders. Furthermore, no cleric who is a stranger shall, without commendatory letters from his ordinary, be admitted by any bishop to celebrate the divine mysteries and to administer the sacraments."

Cited in H.J. Schroeder, O.P., ed., *Canons and Decrees of the Council of Trent* (London: Herder, 1941), pp. 173-4.

25 Canon Law Society of Great Britain and Ireland, ed., *The Code of Canon Law*, Eng. Transl. (London: Collins, 1983). See canons 1015-1023, on "The Celebration of Ordination."

26 Martin Luther, "Christian nobility." Cited in Bettenson, *op. cit.*, p. 194.

27 Schroeder, *op. cit.*, p.52.

28 *Ibid.*, p. 161.

29 Walter M. Abbott, S.J., ed., *The Documents of Vatican II* (London: Chapman, 1972), p. 27.

30 *Ibid.*, p. 535.

31 Jean Galot, S.J., *La nature du caractère sacramentel: étude de théologie médiévale* (Paris-Louvain, Desclée de Brouwer, 1958), p. 36.

32 *Ibid.*, p. 32.

33 *Ibid.*, p. 35.

34 *Ibid.*, p. 44.

35 Jean Galot, S.J., *Theology of the Priesthood* (San Francisco: Ignatius, 1985), p. 199.

36 J.-M. Garrigues, J.-J. Le Guillou, et A. Riou, "Le caractère sacerdotale dans la tradition despères grecs," *Nouvelle revue théologique*, Vol. 93 (1971), p. 809.

37 Galot, *Priesthood*, p. 200.

38 Thomas Aquinas, *Summa Theologica*, III, q. LXIII, I, c. Cited in J.P. Kenney, S.J., *The Sacramental Character* (Melbourne:ACTS, 1958), p. 19.

39 "Et tangitur quadruplex conditio characteris: (i) quia enim praeparat ad gratiam, ideo principium vitae; (ii) quia distinguit gregem Domini, sic sigillum; (iii) quia indelebilitur perseverat, sic custodia; (iv) quia specialiter disponit ad fidem, dicitur illuminatio mentis." Bonaventure, *Sent.*, IV, D. 3, P. 1, a. 1, q. 1. Cited in Galot, *Nature*, p. 172.

40 Aquinas, *Sent.*,IV, D. 4, Q. 1, a. 1: "Cum ergo character ordinetur ad aliquid simplicitur, non ad illud bene vel male, quia sacerdos potest conficere bene vel male, non potest esse quod qualitas quam fundatur relatio characteris sit habitus, sed magis potentia." Cited in Galot, *Nature*, p. 174.

41 Galot, *Nature*, p. 182.

42 Aquinas *Sent.*, IV, D. 24. Q. 1, q. 2, ad. 1: ". . . Illud quod res tantum non est de essentia sacramenti; quod est etiam sacramentum tantum, transit; et sacramentum manere dicitur. Unde relinquitur quod *character interior sit essentialiter et principaliter ipsum sacramentum ordinis*. Ad secundun dicendum quod baptismus, quamis in eo conferatur aliqua spiritualis potentia recipiendi ea sacramenta, ratione cujus characterem imprimit, non tamen hoc est principalis effectus, sed ablutio interior. . . . Sed *ordo potestatem principaliter importat*. . . ." Cited in Galot, *Nature*, p. 181.

43 Galot, *Nature*, p. 194.

44 David N. Power, O.M.I., *The Christian Priest: Elder and Prophet* (London: Sheed & Ward, 1973), p. 93.

45 Jean Galot, S.J., "Le caractère sacerdotal selon le concile de Trent," *Nouvelle revue théologique*, Vol. 93 (1971), p. 943.
46 Hervé-Marie Legran, O.P., "The 'indelible' character and the theology of ministry," *Concilium*, Vol. 4, No. 8 (April, 1972), p. 60.
47 Galot, *Priesthood*, p. 213, fn. 12.
48 Power, *Christian Priest*, p. 92.
49 Galot, "Le caractère sacerdotal," p. 943.
50 Schroeder, *op. cit.*, p. 52.
51 Power, *Christian Priest*, p. 91.
52 Galot, *Priesthood*, p. 197.
53 *Ibid.*
54 J.P. Kenny, S.J., *The Sacramental Character* (Melbourne: ACTS, 1958), p. 5.
55 *Ibid.*, p. 9.
56 S. Th. III, LXIII, 6, ad 2um.   Cited in Kenny, *op. cit.*, p. 30, fn. 21.
57 Kenny, *op. cit.*, p. 14.
58 *Ibid.*, p. 24.
59 *Ibid.*, p. 27.
60 Galot, *Priesthood*, p. 209.
61 *Ibid.*, p. 73.
62 Abbott, *op. cit.*, p. 16.
63 Galot, *Priesthood*, p. 202.
64 *Ibid.*, p. 207.
65 Karl Rahner, S.J., *Le prêtre et la paroisse*, p 105f.   Cited in Galot, *Priesthood*, p. 215.
66 Power, *Christian Priest*, p. 100.
67 *Ibid.*, p. 103.
68 *Ibid.*, p. 108.
69 *Ibid.*, p. 102.
70 Galot, *Priesthood*, p. 196.
71 Edward Schillebeeckx, O.P., *The Church with a Human Face: A New and Expanded Theology of Ministry* (New York: Crossroad, 1985), p. 120.
72 *Ibid.*, p. 106.
73 Piet Schoonenberg, "Quelques réflexions sur le sacrement de l'ordre, en particulier sur le caractère sacramentel," in *Le prêtre et le monde sécularisé*, p. 60. Cited in Galot, *Priesthood*, p. 196.
74 Thomas F. O'Meara, O.P., *A Theology of Ministry* (New York: Paulist, 1983), p. 144.
75 Bernard Cooke, *Ministry to Word and Sacraments: History and Theology* (Philadelphia: Fortress, 1976).   See, for example, p. 209 or p. 543.
76 Galot, *Priesthood*, p. 196.

Chapter XII: THE IDENTITY OF THE PRESBYTER

1 Michael Evans, "In persona Christi — the key to priestly identity," *Clergy Review*, Vol. LXXI, No. 4 (April, 1986), p. 117.
2 Thomas F. O'Meara, O.P., *A Theology of Ministry* (New York: Paulist Press, 1983), p. 12.
3 Jean Galot, S.J., *Theology of the Priesthood* (San Francisco: Ignatius Press, 1985), p. 129.
4 O'Meara, *op. cit.*, p. 4.
5 Peter Chirico, S.S., "Pastoral ministry in the church in the light of the critical priest shortage," *Clergy Review* Vol. LXIX, No. 3 (March, 1984), p. 84.
6 *Ibid.*, p. 84.
7 *Ibid.*, p.82.
8 Hervé Marie Legrand, O.P., "The presidency of the Eucharist according to the ancient tradition," *Worship*, 53 (1979), pp. 413-438.
9 Chirico, *op. cit.*, p. 82.
10 *Ibid.*, p. 85.
11 *Ibid.*, p. 86.
12 *Ibid.*, p. 79.
13 John W. O'Malley, S.J., "Priesthood, ministry, and religious life: some historical and historiographical considerations," *Theological Studies*, 49 (June, 1988), p. 225.
14 *Ibid.*, p. 227.
15 *Ibid.*, p. 236.
16 *Ibid.*, p. 231.
17 *Ibid.*, p. 240.
18 *Ibid.*, p. 247.
19 *Ibid.*, p. 250.
20 *Ibid.*
21 *Ibid.*, p. 255.
22 Walter M. Abbott, S.J., ed., *The Documents of Vatican II* (London: Geoffrey Chapman, 1972), p. 42.
23 *Ibid.*, p. 549.
24 Galot, *op. cit.*, p.150.
25 O'Malley, *op. cit.*, p.255.
26 David N. Power, O.M.I., *The Sacrifice We Offer: the Tridentine Dogma and Its Reinterpretation* (Edinburgh: T. & T. Clark, 1987), p. 21.
27 Pope Pius XII, *Mediator Dei* (1947), cited in Evans, *art. cit.*, p. 120.
28 Abbott, *op. cit.*, p. 36.
29 Power, *Sacrifice*, p. 21.
30 *Ibid.*
31 *Ibid.*, p. 23.

32 Max Thurian, ed., *Churches Respond to BEM, Vol. VI: official responses to the "Baptism, Eucharist and Ministry" text* (Geneva: World Council of Churches, 1988), p. 29.
33 H.J. Schroeder, O.P., ed., *Canons and Decrees of the Council of Trent* (London: B. Herder Book Co., 1941), p. 162.
34 Abbott, *op. cit.*, p. 539.
35 *Ibid.*, p. 560.
36 Galot, *op. cit.*, p. 141.
37 Hubert Vorgrimler, ed., *Commentary on the Documents of Vatican II, Vol. IV* (London: Burns & Oates, 1969), p. 216.
38 Kenan B. Osborne, O.F.M., *Priesthood: A History of the Ordained Ministry in the Roman Catholic Church* (New York: Paulist Press, 1988), p. 339.
39 Galot, *op. cit.*, p. 135.
40 *Ibid.*, p. 137.
41 Abbott, *op. cit.*, pp. 60-64.
42 *Ibid.*, p. 543.
43 Vorgrimler, *op. cit.*, pp. 225-227.
44 Michael T. Winstanley, S.D.B., "The shepherd image in the scriptures: a paradigm for Christian ministry," *Clergy Review*, Vol. LXXI, No. 6 (June, 1986), p. 204.
45 Evans, *art. cit.*, p. 122.
46 Peter E. Fink, "The other side of priesthood," *America* (April 11, 1981), p. 291.
47 *Ibid.*, p. 292.
48 *Ibid.*, p. 293.
49 *Ibid.*, p. 294.
50 Jan P. Schotte, ed., *The Formation of Priests in Circumstances of the Present Day: lineamenta for 1990 synod of bishops* (Vatican City, 1989), p. 12.
51 James A. Fischer, *Priests: Images, Ideals and Changing Roles* (New York: Dodd, Mead & Co., 1987), p. 124.
52 *Ibid.*, p. 175.
53 *Ibid.*, p. 178.
54 *Ibid.*, p. 179.
55 Evans, *art. cit.*, p. 119.
56 *Ibid.*, p. 118.
57 *Ibid.*, p. 119.
58 David N. Power, O.M.I., *The Christian Priest: Elder and Prophet* (London: Sheed & Ward, 1973), pp. 112-113.
59 Evans, *art. cit.*, p. 121.
60 Abbott, *op. cit.*, p. 535.
61 *Ibid.*
62 *Ibid.*, p. 558.
63 *Ibid.*, p. 552.
64 *Ibid.*, p. 558.

65 Evans, *art. cit.*, p. 121.
66 Congregation for the Doctrine of the Faith, *Women and the Priesthood: Declaration on the Question of the Admission of Women to the Ministerial Priesthood (Inter Insigniores)* (London: Catholic Truth Society, 1976), p. 15.
67 Evans, *art. cit.*, p. 122.
68 J.-M. Garrigues, M.-J. Le Guillou, and A. Riou, "Le caractère sacerdotal dans la tradition desperes grecs," *Nouvelle revue théologique*, Vol. 93 (1971), p. 809.
69 Evans, *art. cit.*, p. 119.
70 Edward Schilleebeeckx, O.P., *Christ the Sacrament* (London: Sheed & Ward, 1963), p. 212.
71 *Ibid.*, p. 213.
72 Power, *Christian Priest*, p. 7.
73 Evans, *art. cit.*, p. 123.
74 Anglican-Roman Catholic International Commission, *The Final Report* (London: CTS/SPCK, 1982), p. 33.
75 World Council of Churches, *Baptism, Eucharist and Ministry* (Geneva: WCC, 1982), p. 21.
76 Max Thurian, *Priesthood and Ministry: Ecumenical Research* (Oxford: Mowbray, 1983), p. 123.
77 Abbott, *op. cit.*, p. 558.

Chapter XIII: CONCLUSION

1 Kenan B. Osborne, O.F.M., *Priesthood: A History of the Ordained Ministry in the Roman Catholic Church* (New Jersey: Paulist Press, 1988), pp. 30f.
2 Max Thurian, ed., *Churches Respond to BEM, Vol. VI: official responses to the "Baptism, Eucharist and Ministry" text* (Geneva: WCC, 1988), p. 36.
3 *Ibid.*, p. 5.
4 World Council of Churches, *Baptism, Eucharist and Ministry* (Geneva: WCC, 1982), p. 20.
5 Thurian, *Churches Respond*, p. 28.
6 Vittorio Messori, *The Ratzinger Report* (San Francisco: Ignatius, 1985), p. 45.
7 *Ibid.*
8 *Ibid.*, p. 46.
9 *Ibid.*, p. 47.
10 *Ibid.*, p. 49.
11 *Ibid.*, p. 31.
12 *Ibid.*, p. 28.
13 *Ibid.*
14 *Ibid.*, p. 35.
15 Hans Küng, *Why Priests?* (London: Collins, 1972), p. 44.

16 Edward Schillebeeckx, O.P., *The Church with a Human Face: A New and Expanded Theology of Ministry* (New York: Crossroad, 1985), p. 16.

17 *Ibid.*, pp. 66-68.

18 Walter M. Abbott, S.J., ed., *The Documents of Vatican II* (London: Geoffrey Chapman, 1972), p. 118.

19 *Ibid.*

20 *Ibid.*, p. 37.

21 Cyrille Vogel, "Laica communione contentus: le retour du presbytre au rang des laîcs," *Revue des sciences réligieuses*, Vol. 47 (1973), pp. 56-122.

22 Edward Schillebeeckx, O.P., *Ministry: Leadership in the Community of Jesus Christ* (New York: Crossroad, 1981), p. 65.

23 *Ibid.*, pp. 38-41.

24 H.J. Schroeder, O.P., ed., *Canons and Decrees of the Council of Trent* (London: B. Herder Book Co., 1941), p. 174.

25 John W. O'Malley, S.J., "Priesthood, ministry, and religious life: some historical and historiographical considerations," *Theological Studies*, 49 (June, 1988), p. 257.

26 Messori, *op. cit.*, p. 40.

27 Abbott, *op. cit.*, p.534.

28 *Ibid.*, p. 552.

29 *Ibid.*, p. 558.

30 *Ibid.*, p. 543.

31 *Ibid.*, p. 535.

32 *Ibid.*, p. 560.

33 George William Rutler, *The Curé d'Ars Today: St. John Vianney* (San Francisco: Ignatius, 1988), p. 98.

34 *Ibid.*, p. 47.

35 *Ibid.*, p. 119.

36 Bartholomew J. O'Brien, *Secrets of a Parish Priest: a Biography of St. John Vianney* (Chicago: J.S. Paluch Co., 1956), p. 120.

37 Rutler, *op. cit.*, p. 89.

38 *Ibid.*, p. 250.

39 *Ibid.*, p. 88.

40 *Ibid.*, p. 252.

Chapter XIV: A POSTSCRIPT ON THE ORDINATION OF WOMEN

1 Congregation for the Doctrine of the Faith, *Declaration on Women and the Priesthood: Inter Insigniores* (London: Catholic Truth Society, 1976), Intro., p. 5.

2 *Ibid.*, para. 1-4.

3 Edward Schillebeeckx, O.P., *The Church with a Human Face: A New and Expanded Theology of Ministry* (New York: Crossroad, 1985)), p. 40.

4 *Ibid.*, pp. 38f.

5 *Ibid.*, p. 39.

6 For a discussion of the reasons for this exclusion, see: Manfred Hauke, *Women in the Priesthood?: A Systematic Analysis in the Light of the Order of Creation and Redemption* (San Francisco: Ignatius, 1988), pp. 212-215.

7 Hauke, *op. cit.*, p. 341.

8 *Ibid.*, p.342.

9 *Ibid.*, p. 344.

10 *Ibid.*, p.433.

11 Jerome, *In epistolam I ad Corinthios XIV: PL 30*, p. 762. Cited in Hauke, *op. cit.*, p. 432.

12 Hauke, *op. cit.*, p. 434.

13 *Ibid.*, p. 436.

14 Cited in Hauke, *op. cit.*, p. 458.

15 Cited in Hauke, *op. cit.*, p. 458.

16 Hauke, *op. cit.*, p. 460.

17 *Ibid.*, pp. 463-464.

18 *Ibid.*, p. 465.

19 *Ibid.*, p. 467.

20 *Ibid.*, p. 467.

21 Karl Marx, *Frühe Schriften II* (Stuttgart, 1971), p. 3.   Cited in Hauke, *op. cit.*, p. 30.

22 Friedrich Engels, *Der Ursprung der Familie des Privateigentums und des Staates*, 17th ed., (Stuttgart, 1919), p. 62.   Cited in Hauke, *op. cit.*, p. 31.

23 Simone de Beauvoir, *Das andere Geschlecht, Sitte und Sexus der Frau*, (Hamburg, 1952), pp. 310f.

24 Hauke, *op. cit.*, p. 43.

25 Evelyne Sullerot, *Die Frau in der modernen Gesellschaft* (Munich, 1971), p. 18.   Cited in Hauke, *op. cit.*, p. 107.

26 Hauke, *op. cit.*, p. 86.

27 *Ibid.*, p. 113.

28 See for example, Steven Goldberg, *Male Dominance: The Inevitability of Patriarchy* (London: Abacus, 1979).

29 Hauke, *op. cit.*, p. 104.

30 *Ibid.*, p. 134.

31 *Ibid.*, p. 144.

32 C.S. Lewis, "Priestesses in the Church?" in *Undeceptions: Essays on Theology and Ethics* (London, 1971), p. 195.   Cited in Hauke, *op. cit.*, p. 193.

33 *Inter Insigniores*, CTS ed., pp. 13-14.

34 E.L. Mascall, *Women Priests?* (Westminster, 1972), p. 12.   Cited in Hauke, *op. cit.*, p. 204.

35 Hauke, *op. cit.*, p. 59.

36 Pope Pius XI, *Casti Connubii* (1930).   Cited in Hauke, *op. cit.*, p. 56.

37 Cited in Hauke, *op. cit.*, p. 57.

38 Walter M. Abbott, S.J., ed., *The Documents of Vatican II* (London: Geoffrey Chapman, 1972), p. 647.

39 Hauke, *op. cit.*, p. 401.

40 *Inter Insigniores* CTS ed., pp. 12-18.

41 *Ibid.*, p. 14.

42 *Ibid.*, para. 5, p. 15.

43 Abbott, *op. cit.*, p. 535.

44 Jean Galot, S.J., *Theology of the Priesthood* (San Francisco: Ignatius, 1985), p. 207.

45 Cited in *Inter Insigniores*, CTS ed., p. 13, fn. 19.

46 Cited in Hauke, *op. cit.*, p. 449.

47 Pope Pius XII, *Apostolic Constitution Sacramentum ordinis* (30 Nov. 1947). Cited in *Inter Insigniores*, CTS ed., p. 10, fn. 13.

48 *Inter Insigniores*, CTS ed., para. 5, p. 14.

49 Hauke, *op. cit.*, p. 404.

50 *Ibid.*, p. 478.

51 *Ibid.*, p. 447.

52 *Ibid.*, p. 467.

53 *Inter Insigniores*, CTS ed., Intro., p. 5.

54 Hans Urs von Balthasar, "Epilog: Die Marianische Prägung der Kirche," in Wolfgang Beinert (ed.), *Maria heute ehren*, 2nd ed. (Freiburg: Basel & Vienna, 1977), p. 276.

55 Gertrud von le Fort, *Die ewige Frau* (Munich, 1963), p. 133. Cited in Hauke, *op. cit.*, p. 325.

56 Hauke, *op. cit.*, p. 481.

Bibliography

Abbott, Walter M., SJ, ed. *The Documents of Vatican II.* London: Geoffrey Chapman, 1972.

Anglican-Roman Catholic International Commission. *The Final Report.* London: CTS/SPCK, 1982.

Arbuckle, Gerald A., SM. *Strategies for Growth in Religious Life.* New York: Alba House, 1986; Homebush, NSW: St. Paul Publications, 1987.

Arbuckle, Gerald A., SM. "Chaos and creativity: refounding religious congregations." *East Asian Pastoral Review*, 1989, No. 1, pp. 73-84.

Armstrong, Karen. *The Gospel According to Woman: Christianity's Creation of the Sex War in the West.* London: Pan Books, 1987.

Barstow, Anne Llewellyn. *Married Priests and the Reforming Papacy: The Eleventh Century Debates.* New York & Toronto: Edwin Mellen Press, 1982.

Bernardin, Joseph L. *Called to Serve, Called to Lead: Reflections on the Ministerial Priesthood.* Cincinnati: St. Anthony Messenger Press, 1981.

Bettenson, Henry S., ed. *Documents of the Christian Church*, 2nd Edition. London: Oxford University Press, 1967.

Boff, Leonardo. *Ecclesio-genesis: The Base Communities Reinvent the Church.* London: Collins, 1986.

Bots, J., SJ. *Documentation on Dutch Catholicism on the Eve of the Papal Visit, 11-15 May 1985.* Washington: Human Life International (418 C Street NE, DC 20002), 1984.

Brown, Raymond E. *Priest and Bishop*. London: Geoffrey Chapman, 1971.

Bunnik, Ruud J. *Priests for Tomorrow: A Radical Examination of Christian Ministry*. New York: Holt, Rinehart & Winston, 1969.

Byers, David M., ed. *Vocations and Future Church Leadership: The Collegeville Papers, June 9-16, 1986*. Washington: United States Catholic Conference, 1986.

Cada, Lawrence et al. *Shaping the Coming Age of Religious Life*. New York: Seabury Press, 1979.

Callam, Daniel, CSB. "The frequency of Mass in the Latin Church ca. 400 AD." *Theology Studies*, 45, (1984), pp. 613-650.

Camelot, P.-Th., OP. *Histoire des conciles oecumeniques: Vol. II Éphèse et Chalcédoine*. Paris: Éditions de l'Orante, 1962.

Canon Law Society of Great Britain and Ireland, ed. *The Code of Canon Law*. London: Collins, 1983.

Card, Terence. *Priesthood and Ministry in Crisis*. London: SCM, 1988.

Chirico, Peter, SS. "Pastoral ministry in the Church in the light of the critical priest shortage." *Clergy Review*, Vol LXIX, No. 3 (March, 1984), pp. 79-87.

Clark, Stephen B. *Man and Woman in Christ: An Examination of the Roles of Men and Women in Light of Scripture and the Social Sciences*. Ann Arbor, Michigan: Servant Books, 1980.

Congar, Yves M.J., OP. *Lay People in the Church*. London: Bloomsbury, 1957.

Congar, Yves M.J., OP. "Le sacerdoce du nouveau testament: mission et culte." *Unam sanctam 68: Vatican II — Les Prêtres*. Paris: Les Editions Du Cerf, 1968. Pp. 233-256.

Congregation for Divine Worship. "Directory for Sunday celebrations in the absence of a priest." *Liturgy Magazine* (Auckland, NZ). Vol. 14 (1989) No. 2, pp. 2-16.

Congregation for the Doctrine of the Faith. *Women and the Priesthood: Declaration Inter Insigniores on the Question of the Admission of Women to the Ministerial Priesthood*. London: Catholic Truth Society, 1976.

Cooke, Bernard. *Ministry to Word and Sacraments: History and Theology.* Philadelphia: Fortress, 1976.

Crouzel, Henri, SJ. "Le Ministere dans l'Église: témoinages de l'Église ancienne." *Nouvelle revue theologique,* 104 (1982), pp. 738-748.

Darragh, Neil. "The Church as counter-culture." *Australasian Catholic Record,* LXIV (No. 3, 1987), pp. 235-246.

Denis, Henri, "La théologie du presbytérat de Trente à Vatican II". *Unam sanctam 68: Vatican II — Les Prêtres.* Paris: Les Editions Du Cerf, 1968, pp. 193-232.

Dolan, J.P. "Martin Luther." In *New Catholic Encyclopedia.* New York: McGraw Hill Book Co., 1967, Vol. VIII, pp. 1086-1091.

Doohan, Leonard. *The Lay-centered Church.* Minneapolis: Winston Press, 1984.

Dunn, Patrick J. "Observations of a vocations director, 1981-1987." *Zealandia Newspaper* (Auckland, N.Z.), February 7, 14, 21, 28, and March 7, 1988.

Evans, Michael. "In persona Christi — The key to priestly identity." *Clergy Review.* Vol. LXXI, No. 4. April, 1986, pp. 117-125.

Fink, Peter E. "The other side of priesthood." *America,* April 11, 1981, pp. 291-294.

Fischer, James A. *Priests: Images, Ideals and Changing Roles.* New York: Dodd, Mead & Co., 1987.

Franzen, August, and John P. Dolan. *A Concise History of the Church.* London: Burns & Oates Ltd., 1969.

Frisque, Jean. "Le décret 'presbyterorum ordinis': histoire et commentaire" *Unam sanctam 68: Vatican II — Les Prêtres.* Paris: Les Editions Du Cerf, 1968, pp. 123-186.

Galot, Jean, SJ. *La nature du caractère sacramentel: étude de théologie médiévale.* Paris-Louvain: Desclée de Bouwer, 1958.

Galot, Jean, SJ. "Le caractère sacerdotal selon le Concile de Trente," *Nouvelle revue théologique.* Vol. 93 (1971). Pp. 923-946.

Galot, Jean, SJ. *Theology of the Priesthood.* San Francisco: Ignatius Press, 1985.

Garrigues, J.-M, M.-J Le Guillou, and A. Riou. "Le caractère sacerdotal dans la tradition des pères grecs," *Nouvelle revue théologique*, Vol. 93 (1971). Pp. 801-820.

Ghéon, Henri. *The Secret of the Curé d'Ars*. London: Sheed & Ward, 1952.

Goldberg, Steven. *Male Dominance: The Inevitability of Patriarchy*. London: Abacus, 1979.

Greeley, Andrew, and Michael Hout. "The secularization myth," *London Tablet*, 10 June 1989, pp. 665-667.

Grollenberg, Lucas et al. *Minister? Pastor? Prophet?* London: SCM Press, 1980.

Hauke, Manfred. *Women in the Priesthood? A Systematic Analysis in the Light of the Order of Creation and Redemption*. San Francisco: Ignatius Press, 1988.

Hefele, Charles Joseph, and H. Leclerq, OSB. *Histoire des conciles*, Tome II. B.   Paris: Létousey et Ané, 1908.

Hickey, Raymond, OSA. "Priesthood and the Church of the Future: The case for an auxiliary married priesthood," *Clergy Review*, LXXI, No. 5. (May, 1986), pp. 158-164.

Hoge, Dean R. *Future of Catholic Leadership: Responses to the Priest Shortage*. Kansas City: Sheed & Ward, 1987.

Huck, Gabe. "Priestless Sundays: are we looking or leaping?" *Liturgy 80*. Office of Divine Worship, Chicago, October, 1987, pp. 4-5.

Hughes, Philip J. *The Australian Clergy: Report from the Combined Churches Survey for Faith and Mission*. Melbourne: Acorn Press, 1989.

Illich, Ivan. *Celebration of Awareness: A Call for Institutional Revolution*. Middlesex, UK: Penguin Books, 1984.

John Paul II, Pope. *Christifideles laici: on the vocation and the mission of the lay faithful in the church and in the world*. Homebush, NSW: St. Paul Publications, 1989.

Kasper, Walter. "The mission of the laity," *Theological Digest*, Vol. 35, No. 2 (Summer 1988), pp. 133-138.

Kennedy, Eugene. *The Now and Future Church: The Psychology of Being an American Catholic*. New York: Image Books, 1985.

Kenny, J.P., SJ. "Ministry: does priesthood command eucharist or eucharist priesthood?" *Compass*, Vol. 11 (No. 1, March, 1977), pp. 14-23.

Kenny, J.P., SJ. *The Sacramental Character*. Melbourne: ACTS, 1958.

Kilmartin, Edward J., SJ. "Office and charism: reflections on a new study of ministry," *Theological Studies*, 38 (1977), pp. 547-554.

Küng, Hans. *Why Priests?* London: Collins, 1972.

Lash, Nicholas and Joseph Rhymer. *The Christian Priesthood*. London: Darton, Longman & Todd, 1970.

Legrand, Hervé-Marie, OP. "The 'indelible' character and the theology of ministry." *Concilium* Vol. 4, No. 8 (April, 1972), pp. 54-62.

Legrand, Hervé-Marie, OP. "The presidency of the Eucharist according to the ancient tradition." *Worship*, 53 (1979), pp. 413-438.

Lemaire, André. *Ministry in the Church*. London: SPCK, 1977.

Le Sourd, H. "Un aggiornamento spirituel?" *Unam Sanctam 68: Vatican — Les Prêtres*. Paris: Les Editions Du Cerf, 1968, pp. 289-326.

Little, Joyce A. "The Church with a Human Face": Book Review, *The Thomist*, Vol. 52, No. 1 (January, 1988), pp. 158-165.

Martimort, Aimé Georges. *Deaconesses: An Historical Study*. San Francisco: Ignatius Press, 1986.

Martos, Joseph. *Doors to the Sacred: A Historical Introduction to Sacraments in the Christian Church*. London: SCM, 1981.

McBrien, Richard P. *Ministry: A Theological, Pastoral Handbook*. San Francisco: Harper & Row, 1987.

McMonigle, Donald William. *The Diaconate: Its History and Renewal in the Anglican Tradition*. Unpublished. Melbourne College of Divinity Thesis, 1988.

Messenger, Ernst C. *The Reformation, the Mass, and the Priesthood*. London: Longmans, Green & Co., 1936.

Messsori, Vittorio. *The Ratzinger Report*. San Francisco: Ignatius Press, 1985.

Murtagh, James G. *Australia: The Catholic Chapter.* New York: Sheed & Ward, 1946.

O'Brien, Bartholomew J. *Secrets of a Parish Priest: Biography of the Curé of Ars.* Chicago: J.S. Paluch Co., 1956.

O'Connell, Timothy E. "The Church in the 1990s." *Upturn: Association of Chicago Priests,* March-May, 1984, pp. 1-6.

O'Connell, Timothy E., ed. *Vatican II and its Documents: An American Reappraisal.* Wilmington, Delaware: Michael Glazier, Inc., 1986.

O'Malley, John W., SJ. "Priesthood, ministry, and religious life: some historical and historiographical considerations." *Theological Studies,* 49 (June, 1988), pp. 223-257.

O'Malley, William J., SJ. "Mass and teen-agers." *America,* Vol. 159, No. 9 (October 8, 1988), pp. 214-218.

O'Malley, William J., SJ. "Teenage spirituality." *America,* Vol. 160, No. 16 (April 29, 1989), pp. 390-394.

O'Meara, Thomas F., OP. *A Theology of Ministry.* New York: Paulist Press, 1983.

Osborne, Kenan B., OFM. *Priesthood: A History of the Ordained Ministry in the Roman Catholic Church.* New York: Paulist Press, 1988.

Percival, Henry R. *The Seven Ecumenical Councils of the Undivided Church: their Canons and Dogmatic Decrees,* Vol. I. New York: Gorham, 1901.

Pohier, Jacques, OP. *God in Fragments.* London: SCM Press, 1985.

Power, David N., OMI. *The Christian Priest: Elder and Prophet.* London: Sheed & Ward, 1973.

Power, David N., OMI. *The Sacrifice We Offer: The Tridentine Dogma and Its Reinterpretation.* Edinburgh: T. & T. Clark, 1987.

Rahner, Karl, SJ. "What is the theological starting-point for a definition of the priestly ministry?" *Concilium* Vol. 3, No. 5 (March, 1969), pp. 43-46.

Ramsey, Michael. *The Christian Priest Today.* London: SPCK, 1985.

Ratzinger, Joseph Cardinal. "Theology in the world of today: address to doctrinal commissions of national episcopal conferences of Latin America: Bogota, Colombia, 1984." *Christian Order,* Vol. 30, No. 4 (April, 1989), pp. 239-253.

Richards, Michael. "Priest or presbyter? The Pope at Ars, October, 1986." *The Clergy Review*, LXXII, No. 1 (January, 1987), pp. 30-43.

Rutler, George William. *The Curé d'Ars Today: St. John Vianney.* San Francisco: Ignatius Press, 1988.

Schepers, M.B. "Lutheranism." In *New Catholic Encyclopedia*. New York: McGraw Hill, 1967, Vol. VIII, pp. 1091-1098.

Schillebeeckx, Edward, OP. *Christ: the Christian Experience in the Modern World.* London: SCM Press, 1980.

Schillebeeckx, Edward, OP. *Christ the Sacrament.* London: Sheed & Ward, 1963.

Schillebeeckx, Edward, OP. *Ministry: Leadership in the Community of Jesus Christ.* New York: Crossroad, 1981.

Schillebeeckx, Edward, OP. *The Church with a Human Face: A New and Expanded Theology of Ministry.* New York: Crossroad, 1985.

Schotte, Jan P. *The Formation of Priests in Circumstances of the Present Day: Lineamenta for 1990 Synod of Bishops.* Vatican City, 1989.

Schroeder, H.J., OP, ed. *Canons and Decrees of the Council of Trent* London: B. Herder Book Co., 1941.

Sheed, Wilfred. *Frank and Maisie: A Memoir with Parents.* New York: Simon & Schuster, 1985.

Staniforth, Maxwell, ed. *Early Christian Writings: The Apostolic Fathers.* Middlesex: Penguin Books, 1968.

Taft, Robert. "The frequency of the Eucharist throughout history." *Concilium*, 152 (1982), pp. 13-24.

Thurian, Max. *Priesthood and Ministry: Ecumenical Research.* Oxford: Mowbray, 1983.

Towler, Robert and A.P.M. Coxon. *The Fate of the Anglican Clergy: A Sociological Study.* London: MacMillan, 1979.

Vanhoye, Albert, SJ. "Le Ministère dans l'Église: les données du nouveau testament," *Nouvelle revue théologique*, 104 (1982), pp. 722-738.

Vanhoye, Albert, SJ. *Our Priest is Christ: The Doctrine of the Epistle to the Hebrews.* Rome: P.I.B., 1977.

Vogel, Cyrille. "Laîca communione contentus: le retour du presbytre au rang des laîcs," *Revue des sciences réligieuses*, Vol.
47 (1973), pp. 56-122.

Vorgrimler, Hubert, ed. *Commentary on the Documents of Vatican II*
Vol. I, Vol. IV. London: Burns & Oates Ltd., 1967 & 1969.

Weers, André. "Les citations scripturaires de décret sur le
ministère et la vie des prêtres: 'Presbyterorum Ordinis.' "
Unam Sanctam 68: Vatican II — Les Prêtres. Paris: Les
Editions Du Cerf, 1968, pp. 327-344.

Williamson, Paul A., SM. *Contemporary Approaches to the Ordained
Priestly Ministry in Theology and the Magisterium*. Rome:
Typis Pontificiae Universitatis Gregorianae, 1983.

Winstanley, Michael T., SDB. "The shepherd image in the
scriptures: paradigm for Christian ministry." *Clergy Review*, Vol. LXXI, No. 6 (June, 1986), pp. 197-206.

World Council of Churches. *Baptism, Eucharist and Ministry*.
Geneva: WCC Publications, 1982.

World Council of Churches. *Churches Respond to B.E.M., Vol. VI:
Official Responses to the "Baptism, Eucharist and Ministry"
text*, ed. Max Thurian. Geneva: WCC Publications, 1988.

An Interesting Thought

The publication you have just finished reading is part of the apostolic efforts of the Society of St. Paul of the American Province. The Society of St. Paul is an international religious community located in 23 countries, whose particular call and ministry is to bring the message of Christ to all people through the communications media.

Following in the footsteps of their patron, St. Paul the Apostle, priests and brothers blend a life of prayer and technology as writers, editors, marketing directors, graphic designers, bookstore managers, pressmen, sound engineers, etc. in the various fields of the mass media, to announce the message of Jesus.

If you know a young man who might be interested in a religious vocation as a brother or priest and who shows talent and skill in the communications arts, ask him to consider our life and ministry. For more information at no cost or obligation write:

Vocation Office
2187 Victory Blvd.
Staten Island, NY 10314-6603
Telephone: (718) 698-3698